Britons and Romans:
advancing an archaeological agenda

In memory of Tim Potter

Britons and Romans:
advancing an archaeological agenda

edited by Simon James and Martin Millett

CBA Research Report 125
Council for British Archaeology
2001

Published 2001 by the Council for British Archaeology,
Bowes Morrell House, 111 Walmgate, York YO1 9WA

British Library Cataloguing in Publication Data

A catalogue card for this book is available from the British Library

ISSN 0589–9036
ISBN 1 902771 16 8

Typeset by Archetype Information Technology Ltd
Printed by Pennine Printing Services Ltd

The CBA acknowledges with gratitude a grant from English Heritage towards the publication of this volume

Front cover: A copper alloy 'eagle' mount from a baldric, found at Carlisle (courtesy Carlisle Museum & Art Gallery)
Back cover: Aerial photograph of the Flavian fort, annex and adjacent settlement at Hayton, East Yorkshire. To the left of the fort annex is an Iron Age type enclosure and round house apparently constructed after the fort. (Photo: Peter Halkon)

List of contents

List of illustrations

List of tables

List of contributors

Lindsay Allason-Jones, The Museum of Antiquities, University of Newcastle upon Tyne, Newcastle upon Tyne, NE1 7RU

Dr Barry C. Burnham, Department of Archaeology, University of Wales Lampeter, Lampeter, Ceredigion, SA48 7ED

Prof John Collis, Department of Archaeology and Prehistory, University of Sheffield, Northgate House, West Street, Sheffield, S1 4ET

Dr John Creighton, Department of Archaeology, Faculty of Letters & Social Sciences, The University of Reading, Whiteknights, PO Box 218, Reading, RG6 6AA

Dr Colin Dobinson, Consultant, Honeypot Cottage, Caldbergh, Leyburn, N. Yorks, DL1 4RW

Dr Keith Dobney, Department of Archaeology, University of Durham, South Road, Durham, DH1 3LE

Dr Jeremy Evans, Barbican Research Associates Ltd, 67, Dovey Road, Moseley, Birmingham, B13 9NT

Dr Simon Esmonde-Cleary, Department of Ancient History and Archaeology, The University of Birmingham, Birmingham, B15 2TT

Prof Colin Haselgrove, Department of Archaeology, University of Durham, South Road, Durham, DH1 3LE

Dr J.D. Hill, Department of Prehistoric and Early Europe, British Museum, London, WC1B 3DG

Dr Simon James, School of Archaeological Studies, University of Leicester, University Road, Leicester, LE1 7RH

Michael Jones, City of Lincoln Council/University of Nottingham, City Hall, Lincoln, LN1 1DF

Prof Martin Millett, Department of Archaeology, University of Southampton, Highfield, Southampton, SO17 1BJ

Dr Jeremy Taylor, School of Archaeological Studies, University of Leicester, University Road, Leicester, LE1 7RH

Summary

Arising from the English Heritage-sponsored session 'Romano-British Research Agendas' at the Roman Archaeology Conference, Durham 1999, this volume seeks to encourage those with an interest in the subject to think broadly, and to engage actively in shaping the future priorities of research into Roman Britain – it is not designed to dictate them.

The volume includes revised and expanded versions on the papers presented and discussed on: the Iron Age to Roman transition; Romanisation, gender and class; material culture and identity; material approaches to the identification of different Romano-British site types; the role of vertebrate zoo-archaeology; rural society; urbanism; soldiers and civilians; and the Roman to medieval transition, together with an additional contribution on urban research.

Within these themes, the contributions provide up-to-date syntheses of the masses of recently generated knowledge, and suggestions on what more we might want to know. They seek to break down the relative insularity of Romano-British studies, to open it up to new external perspectives, and to promote the value of its outstandingly rich archaeological evidence to archaeologists working in other fields, and on other territories.

In particular, it is hoped these papers will help to integrate academic research with the opportunities provided by the many archaeological interventions occurring every year in Britain, not least in developer-funded archaeology.

Résumé

Bilan de la séance 'Agendas de recherches romano-britanniques' parrainée par English Heritage lors de la Conférence sur l'Archéologie Romaine de Durham, en 1999, ce volume a pour but d'encourager ceux qui s'intéressent au sujet à élargir leur réflexion et à entreprendre concrètement la mise en forme des futures priorités de recherche sur la Grande-Bretagne romaine – ceci en dehors de toute contrainte.

Ce volume inclut des versions mises à jour et élargies des communications présentées et discutées, sur: la transition entre l'âge de fer et les Romains; romanisation, sexe et classe sociale; culture matérielle et identité; approches matérielles à l'identification de différents types de sites romano-britanniques; le rôle de la zoo-archéologie des vertébrés; la société rurale; l'urbanisme, les soldats et les civils; et la transition entre les Romains et le moyen-âge ainsi qu'une contribution supplémentaire à la recherche urbaine.

Dans le contexte de ces thèmes, les apports offrent des synthèses mises à jour sur la multitude de connaissances générée récemment ainsi que des suggestions sur ce que nour voudrions éventuellement savour de plus. Ils cherchent à détruire la relative insularité des études romano-britanniques, à les ouvrir à des nouvelles perspectives extérieures, et à promouvoir la valeur de ses documents archéologiques d'une exceptionnelle richesse auprès d'archéologues traveillant dans d'autres domaines et dans d'autres territoires.

En particulier, on peut espérer que ces communications contribueront à l'integration des recherches universitaires avec les opportunités offertes par les nombeuses interventions archéologiques ayant lieu tous les ans en Grande-Bretagne, entre autres dans l'archéologie financée par les promoteurs immobiliers

Zusammenfassung

Deiser Band soll diejenigen ermutigen, deren interesse dem folgenden gilt:

- dem 'Breitband-Denken' sowie dem
- aktiven Engagement am Mitgestalten zukünftiger Forschungsschwerpunkte von Römisch-Britannien.

(Es ist nicht als Diktat, sonder als Anregung angelegt.)

Er besteht aus überarbeiteten und erwelterten Unterlagen, die präsentiert und erörtert wurden während des 'Romano-British-Research Agendas' - Symposiums, das gefördert wurde durch die 'English Heritage' under stattgefunden hat während der 'Römisch-Archäologischen Konferenz' in Durham, 1999.

Enthalten sind u.a.

- die Zeirspanne Steinzeit bis zum Beginn der Römerzeit
- das Römertum: Geschlechter und gesellschaftliche Klassen
- materielle Kultur und Identität
- materielle Vorgehensweisen zur Differenzierung Römisch-Britannischer Stätten
- die Bedeutung der zoologischen Archäologie, Wirbeltiere
- (Vertebraten) betreffend
- Landbevölkerung
- Urbanisierung
- Soldaten und Zivilisten
- der Übergang vom Römerreich zum Mittelalter

Es gibt einen zusätzlichen Beltrag zur städtischen Forschung.

Innerhalb dieser Themenbereiche bleten die Beiträge aktualisierte Synthesen von jüngst generiertem Wissen dar, sowle Vorschläge weiterer Interessen-Gebiete.

Sie scheinen die relative Engstirnigkeit 'Römisch-Britannischer' Studien auszutauschen gegen neue, externe Perspektiven, die sich durch sie auften. Zudem fördern sie den Wert eines hervorrangenden, reichhaltig archäologischen Erfahrungsschatzes und tragen ihn weiter auch zu solchen Archäologen, die in anderen Bereichen forschen und arbeiten.

Insbesonder wünschen sich die Verfasser dieser Aufzeichnungen die Integration von akademischer Forschung und den vielfältigen Möglichkeiten, die sich alljährlich durch archäologische Interventionen in England auftun. Nicht zuletzt durch die Unterstützung privater Bauherren.

Introduction *by Simon James and Martin Millett*

My Lds. & Gent. the business of this Society whereof You are the founders, is to search for & illustrate the Roman Monuments in the Britannic Isles ... To save citys & citysens, Camps, temples, walls, Amphitheaters, monuments, roads, inscriptions, coyns, buildings & whatever has a Roman stamp on them, we are to redeem & illustrate whole nations & people, recover past ages, to cancel the obscuritys of the envious corrupter of valorous actions, & snatch from his rapacious jaws, the memorable transactions, the laws, religion & polity of our glorious predecessors, whatever concerns Romano-British Antiquitys. (William Stukeley, address to the Society of Roman Knights, 27 May 1723 (quoted in Ayres 1997, 94))

The papers in this volume arise out of a session held at the Roman Archaeology Conference in Durham in April 1999. Entitled 'Romano-British Research Agendas', it was designed as a response to the initiative by English Heritage to encourage archaeologists to develop academic frameworks for our understanding of England's past. Since 1990 the structure and organisation of archaeological activity in England has undergone a number of major changes marked in particular by the implementation of PPG-16 (*Department of the Environment Planning Policy Guidance Note 16: Archaeology and Planning*: Department of the Environment 1990) together with concomitant changes to the pattern of archaeological funding, and by English Heritage's statement of its research strategies as defined in *Exploring our Past* (1991). The publication of *Frameworks for our Past* (Olivier 1996) set the scene for widespread debate in the discipline concerning the development of national, regional, and local research frameworks. English Heritage's views on the development of research agendas had been presented in the draft *Exploring our Past 1998* (English Heritage 1998) and this formed the focus for our discussions at Durham. However, as the subject was Roman Britain, papers ranged beyond the borders of England.

We were encouraged to organise the session by Adrian Olivier at English Heritage who was also instrumental in both providing a grant to enable it to take place and in allowing this volume to be put forward for publication by the CBA with an English Heritage subvention. The conference funding provided by English Heritage included a subsidy to allow those responsible for archaeology in local authorities to participate in the session. This initiative was deliberately designed to help forge stronger links between academic archaeologists and those responsible for the day to day management of archaeology across the country. The format of the

day allowed the presentation of a series of papers followed in the evening by a debate on the issues raised, led by an invited panel of specialists. This volume includes all the papers presented that day together with an additional contribution, the report of a CBA working party, 'Themes for urban research, c 100 BC to AD 200' (Burnham *et al* this volume). This had previously been published as a leaflet by the CBA in 1997 but contains ideas which seemed to us to deserve a wider audience and a more permanent publication medium.

The conference session was well attended and debate ranged widely, with discussion on issues of professional and academic organisation as well as research directions. The day benefited greatly from the presence of a wide range of those interested in Roman Britain and the Empire as a whole. It was not confined to academics but drew in interested part-timers as well as a variety of those employed in field archaeology and heritage management in the UK, and a number of overseas visitors. We trust that their open discussion of the issues will be reflected in the use of this volume, which is designed not to specify any particular research agenda, but rather to encourage those with an interest in Roman Britain to think broadly about how future research might develop.

Background

To explain the organisation and content of this volume, it is important to understand a little of the background to the current state of archaeology in Britain, since the English Heritage initiative to encourage the development of research agendas is based on the perception of a twofold need.

Firstly, there is an awareness that for society to gain most understanding from archaeological and heritage management work it needs to address questions: we have long since realised that the kind of unstructured accumulation of data advocated in 1723 by William Stukeley in what must surely be the very first Romano-British research agenda (above) simply will not do. The past two decades have seen an enormous growth in developer-funded archaeology as well as individual research initiatives in fieldwork. These have produced a mass of new information which has not always been well-enough integrated into current syntheses. There is thus a need to pause, first to consider what potential this new information offers for enhancing our understanding of Roman Britain, and second to provide up-to-date reviews of what more we want to know. Such a process is intended to help inform those who have curatorial responsibility for designing and oversee-ing projects (in both local authorities and English Heritage). It should help to ensure that everyone is more aware of current thinking and this may facili-tate the development of projects which focus on *lacunae* in our evidence and understanding. In this way good development-led archaeology should be able to contribute more to the understanding of our common past.

Secondly, there is a need in the academic study of Roman Britain to take stock of new information and ideas. Roman Britain remains interesting and there is an enormous scope for new and interesting re-search. In 1982 Richard Reece wrote: 'Textbooks on Roman Britain to date make the subject appear like a nice sand-pit in which toddlers can safely be left to play. I am thankful that it is instead a wild over-grown garden in which anything might happen. And I shall continue to prove it' (Reece 1982). Since then, the study of Roman Britain has certainly become more varied and challenging, especially through the debates at the successive Theoretical Roman Ar-chaeology Conferences which have explored many of new and thought-provoking ideas that are being de-veloped. However, academic archaeologists have not been particularly good at either the synthesis of new information (eg results of the National Mapping Programme: Bewley 1998, 1999), or communicating new and interesting ideas to broader audiences, either the wider profession or the general public. There has also been a problem of unwillingness, if not an inability, to define which are most the impor-tant questions that we should be addressing. Academically, our post-modern pluralism may be a healthy state of affairs and exciting for insiders, but it does little to help a unit that wants to know how best to use limited resources in designing a particu-lar project.

It seems to us that this is a specific instance of a general problem afflicting contemporary archaeol-ogy: there is a growing, three-way divergence between the public and non-professional archaeolo-gists on one trajectory, the increasingly professionalised world of field archaeology on another, and the world of academic, largely univer-sity-based research on a third. (The last is increasingly taken up with profoundly important but too often arcane theoretical issues – for a highly rec-ommended and accessible introduction to contemporary archaeology theory, see Johnson 1999.) There is an urgent need to improve communi-cation across geographical, chronological, and not least professional and disciplinary boundaries. The benefits of addressing this became evident during the session, as is discussed below.

Scope of the session

The conference session was thus designed to explore a variety of directions for future research on Roman Britain. It is important that it should be seen in the context of other complementary initiatives both na-tionally and regionally. A proposed Iron Age agenda has been set out by one influential group of academ-ics (Armit *et al* 2000) whilst English Heritage itself organised and published a discussion on broad aspects of archaeological science (Bayley 1998). Sim-ilarly a series of regional discussions has taken place (eg in East Anglia, the East Midlands and the North-ern Counties); these discussions are in the process of being published.

In organising the session at the Roman Archaeol-ogy Conference we felt that it was important to try to avoid two pitfalls. Firstly, we did not want to produce anything that was prescriptive, even though some curators and contractors have said that they would like clearer guidance on selecting priorities. We con-sidered that any such statement would be both undesirable and unlikely to produce good results. We are especially keen that research is not seen as the preserve of a few academics but is instead the ulti-mate purpose of all archaeological endeavour. Secondly, we could not, and did not wish, to provide comprehensive coverage. In particular we started from the perspective that one can only really define a useful agenda for things that are in some sense pre-dictable. Thus we omit, for instance, the study of art: spectacular discoveries like the Cramond lion (Burnham *et al* 1998, 380) are not easy to foresee.

We therefore looked at the scope of the subject as laid out in *Exploring Our Past 1998* and drew out two sets of themes – 'Transitions and Identities' and 'Characterising Settlement and Society' – which seemed to unify several research directions. We used these themes as those around which the conference session was ordered.

The theme of 'Transitions and Identities' was based on the current debates in archaeology about how individual and social identities are created and how material culture is manipulated in their cre-ation. This enables us to consider the key phases of transition at the beginning and end of the Roman period, but it also raises key issues about how identi-ties within society were created and how we can better use the rich archaeological material from Roman Britain to address these interesting issues. We have both always been of the view that if you can debate these issues in interesting ways with evi-dence available from the Neolithic, we ought to be able to contribute considerably more with the rich evidence available from the Roman period.

Discussion of the theme 'Characterising Settle-ment and Society' also arose from a concern over the better use of our evidence. All too often Roman ar-chaeologists classify as an end in itself. Question like, 'is it a *civitas* capital?', still characterise much debate. We too often neglect the question of whether the categories used are adequate, and what more we could learn by attempting to understand what people were *doing* at a particular place. Finds analysts have been making progress in this sphere but much more could be done.

With these themes structuring the day, we asked

the contributors both to assess what is known and to make suggestions for the directions of future research. Reading the papers that they have produced we believe that they provide ample scope to stimulate debate and new research.

During the panel-led debate which followed the presentation of papers, several important points were made. We only wish to draw attention to a few that directly concern the future directions of research. Sue Alcock stressed that the best research is often done at the interfaces between traditional areas of interest or expertise. With this in mind she challenged us to define the edges of our knowledge. David Breeze laid emphasis on the importance of what we would call the empowerment of practitioners. John Barrett reminded us of the importance of always thinking about historical problems and the realities of people in the past. A further key point was the parochialism of current Romano-British studies, and the potential benefits of revitalising comparative studies with the rest of the family of provinces of which *Britannia* was a member. And of course such potential is bi-directional: the exceptional riches and intensity of exploration of Romano-British data could be of enormous value, not just to the study of the Roman empire as a whole, but also to wider fields of archaeology. Roman Britain could well provide ideal data-sets for addressing major contemporary questions in archaeological thinking which are more often discussed in the context of prehistoric archaeology. This emphasises again the profound need to break down barriers, and enhance communications, for our mutual benefit.

Finally, we must note with sadness that, as this volume approached completion, we heard of the premature death of Dr Tim Potter, Keeper of Prehistoric and Romano-British Antiquities at the British Museum. Both the editors enjoyed long and fruitful friendships with Tim. He was a scholar who was well-known for his support and encouragement of younger archaeologists. He combined the best of traditional approaches to Roman archaeology with pioneering work in survey and excavation in Britain, Italy, and North Africa, and showed an openness to, and sometimes amused indulgence of, the wilder flights of the 'TRAC generation'. He was a strong advocate of the importance of comparative approaches, of understanding Roman Britain by placing it firmly in the wider context of the Roman world, a view vindicated and re-emphasised at our conference session and in the subsequent debate, and supported in the present book. He also showed a strong commitment to spreading academic knowledge and ideas beyond the narrow confines of research institutions, as testified by his synthetic writings, and in the Weston Gallery of Roman Britain at the British Museum, created under his auspices. For these reasons, we would like to dedicate this book to his memory.

1   The Iron Age–Roman Transition   *by John Creighton*

Introduction

Archaeologists need to be engaged in storytelling about the past. Descriptions of the artefactual and settlement record alone will never gain the attention, win the interest or receive the support of the broader public. With the arrival of the Roman period, archaeology comes into contact with historical sources for the first time in Britain. This changes the way archaeologists tend to describe and explain their excavations. All too frequently the fragmentary archaeological record is linked to the equally fragmentary historical record in ways which create stories, but sometimes lack critical rigour. Once upon a time, when a 4th-century burnt deposit was found at a villa in Britain, it was often associated with the great 'barbarian conspiracy' of AD 367 (Ammianus 27.8.1), building this literary event into an archaeological reality of almost cataclysmic proportions. Contexts were associated with this event in the understandable desire to 'tell a story'; however, the variable reality of the dating evidence was unable to sustain this burden. The revolt of Boudicca is another example where the association of history and archaeology is always tempting. In the 1920s a shop stocking samian ware was excavated at Colchester. Unfortunately it had burnt to the ground just after the mid-1st century AD; inevitably this was associated with the destruction of the town by Boudicca in AD 60/1 (Hull 1958). However, more detailed analysis by Millett (1987) demonstrated this was not the case. The Samian assemblage was distinctive and earlier than that from other Boudiccan destruction deposits. A second example was the quest for Boudiccan destruction horizons at Gorhambury (Neal *et al* 1990; Creighton 1992). Sometimes the correlation of historic events and archaeological strata is too strong to resist, whatever the quality of the evidence.

Perhaps the one event we can feel confident about is the arrival in AD 43 of the Roman army. Unfortunately this, too, is not as straightforward as it seems. What I wish to show in this article is how the archaeological evidence from two well-known sites has been used to reinforce a particular interpretation of the historical sources, whilst alternative readings of what may have taken place in the mid-1st century AD are more than possible. The key objective here is to illustrate the subtlety with which associations between historical and archaeological evidence need to be made.

Friendly kings

In the early 1st century AD it is likely that much of south-eastern Britain was ruled by a series of dynasties who were in alliance with Rome. The Commian dynasty dominated the south, whilst the Tasciovanian dynasty ruled the east. Both displayed on their coinage imagery by which they associated themselves with the Roman revolution and the ideology of the emerging Principate. It is more than likely that these dynasts were 'friends and allies of Rome' (cf Stevens 1951; Braund 1984; 1996; Creighton 2000). However, the rule of kings in Britain did not stop with the Claudian annexation; Togidubnus continued to reign over dominions of an unknown extent in the south, Prasutagus ruled in East Anglia, and Cartimandua ruled in the north. The arrival of the legions may have marked a change of kingship, but it did not lead to the end of kingship in its entirety. What I wish to explore here is the relationship between these friendly kings and the Roman army, since this has a significant bearing on how we interpret archaeological evidence. To do this, the relationship between kings and their interplay with the late Republic and early Principate needs to be understood; this will involve a bit of history, after which we will return to the archaeology.

Throughout Rome's expansion, the Senate of the Republic formed alliances and friendships with territories around her. It was part of the natural strategy of defence in which many states engaged. Very occasionally members of royal dynasties would spend some time in Rome, or perhaps with the Roman legions. Jugurtha was one, spending time with legions in Spain in the late 2nd century BC. So impressed was his uncle, the king of Numidia, by reports of him, that when he returned home he became the king's heir. Indirectly, Rome had effected the succession of a friendly kingdom. In the late Republic this intrusion into the affairs of kingdoms became far more prevalent. So much so, that whereas under the Republic we find successors to kingdoms acceding and *then* asking for recognition from Rome, from Augustus onwards we find the *princeps* actually appointing the successor.

The vast majority of the kingdoms about which we have literary references were in the Hellenistic territories of the east. Many of the monarchs of these regions sent some of their children to Rome as *obsides* (the traditional translation of this as 'hostages' is less than adequate, so it is avoided here). Whilst in Rome they would be educated in Roman *mores* and develop important friendships which would assist them later in life when they became major players in the geopolitics of the Mediterranean world. Having a son many miles distant in Rome could also be advantageous to the monarch, relieving him of having a potential successor intriguing back at home in the royal court. This phenomenon, which particularly developed in the early Principate under Augustus, did not just enhance the relationship between centre and periphery; it also bonded together the territories around the edge of the Roman world as personal friendships were cemented with political marriages. Suetonius' description of this practice is so clear that it deserves repeating:

> Except in a few instances [Augustus] restored the kingdoms of which he gained possession by the right of conquest to those from whom he had taken them or joined them with other foreign nations. He also united the kings with whom he was in alliance by mutual ties, and was very ready to propose or favour intermarriages or friendships among them. He never failed to treat them all with consideration as integral parts of the empire, regularly appointing a guardian for such as were too young to rule or whose minds were affected, until they grew up or recovered; and he brought up the children of many of them and educated them with his own. (Suetonius, *Aug.* 48)

It is an unproductive argument to discuss whether friendly kingdoms were part of the empire or not. It is largely a matter of semantics. At times these kings could be viewed, in effect, as imperial administrators, a phenomenon which would be 'entirely in keeping with her general tendency to concede and encourage considerable local autonomy throughout her empire – most notably through cities – and thus pass to others the burden of day-to-day administration' (Braund 1984, 184). At other times they could be viewed as very much outside Roman dominion.

All too often the relationship with Rome is imagined as potentially oppressive, domineering. But that is to forget the authority and power which Roman support gave to the king. On Rome's side the Principate achieved a measure of control and stability around its provinces. It also achieved a military reserve which could be called upon at times of crisis. On the king's side, the relationship might involve receiving 'subsidies' from Rome to help him maintain his position. The relationship also conferred prestige upon the individual under many (though by no means all) circumstances. Finally, if the ruler's position at home became weakened, the relationship could also provide the ultimate sanctioning of force to back him up with help of Roman legions or *auxilia*.

Learning the use of force in the Roman army

Roman military matters, and use of force would have been relatively well understood in south-east Britain in the early 1st century AD. Part of this would have been historical, the simple memory of Caesar's conquest. Many Gauls also served in the Civil Wars, and military service continued afterwards in the Roman *auxilia*. If, after Caesar's Gallic wars, Gauls had gone on to fight around the Mediterranean, it is likely that Britons were similarly engaged. However, our interest here is the articulation of power by the ruling class in Britain, so it is the experience and mind set of the former *obsides* which we need to explore. We must recall the range of experiences which other sons of kings were exposed to, and then consider if the archaeological evidence in Britain offers any support for the notion that British 'royalty' were treated in the same way.

Obsides brought up with Roman *mores* were not just educated in Rome; sometimes they also spent time with the Roman army on campaign. This was a learning experience which some of them turned to their own advantage years later. One such was Jugurtha, the illegitimate nephew of Micipsa, King of Numidia. In his own kingdom the boy's talents overshadowed Micipsa's own two sons, so he was sent away. In this case he went, with a Numidian contingent, to assist the Roman general Scipio Aemilianus in his siege of Numantia in north-west Spain. Here he proved himself and won much admiration; he even learnt Latin (Sallust *BJ* 7). But more importantly he learnt the art of war. His abilities were so magnificent that Micipsa eventually appointed him as his heir. Upon finally becoming king he put this learning to good use when he eventually came into conflict with the Roman Republic itself. This is perhaps the fullest account we possess, as we learn of it through an entire volume on the Jugurthine War by Sallust; other knowledge we have comes from snippets and chance remarks which are rarely fundamental to the narratives in which they occur. For example, we find that Juba II, later made king of Mauretania, served in various campaigns of Octavian; however, this is only known to us from an aside in Dio telling us where all of Cleopatra's children ended up – Juba was married to one of Cleopatra's daughters as a reward from Augustus (Dio 51.15.6).

It was not just *obsides* from Hellenistic kingdoms who fought with the Roman armies. One of Rome's most implacable foes was Arminius of the Cherusci, author of the defeat of Varus' legions in the Teutoburgian Wood in AD 9 (Schlüter 1999). During the subsequent campaigns of Germanicus, undertaken to restore Roman dignity by recapturing the lost standards and burying the dead, the two armies came face to face at one point across the river Weser. This meeting gave the historian Tacitus the opportunity to provide one of his set piece verbal confrontations between Arminius on the one hand, and his brother Flavus, on the other. Flavus was fighting with Germanicus' army, and had gained earlier distinction, losing an eye, fighting under Tiberius. Whereas Flavus was made to speak of Rome's greatness and the emperor's wealth, Arminius dwells on patriotism and freedom. These are rhetorical themes which recur continuously in Tacitus. Nonetheless, it is interesting to learn that when the conversation descends into mutual insults 'Arminius was to be seen, shouting threats and challenges to fight – a good many of them in Latin, since he had formerly commanded a Cheruscan force in the Roman army' (Tacitus *Ann.* 2.10.3). Indeed there is other evidence to suggest that Arminius was not only a Roman citizen, but also of equestrian rank (Vell. Pat. 2.118.2).

The application of learning: adoption of Roman trappings

Gaining first hand knowledge of the Roman army in the field was one matter. Application at home was another. On a number of occasions we find foreign troops using Roman methods of fighting. However, occasionally native troops also adopted other Roman trappings. Antiochus IV Epiphanes of Syria spent twelve years in Rome in the late 2nd century BC. When he returned to rule his kingdom he paraded his troops equipped with Roman armour (Livy 41.20; Polybius 30.25.3; Braund 1984, 15).

But what of Britain? If a similar process occurred in Britain, we might expect to find traces of Roman armour in high status 'native' burials, or in imagery representing these individuals on media such as coinage. One coin of Cunobelin shows a military helmet (VA2091:E8), others allegedly show chain mail on horsemen, though in reality the details are unclear. However, the most obvious material to be found in burials with military associations is chain mail. This is known from only three burials and one other site in the south east: Lexden (Laver 1927, 248; Foster 1986, 82), Folly Lane (Niblett 1999, 159), a grave at Baldock (Burleigh 1982), and fragments from the Temple at Hayling Island (King and Soffe 1991). The cultural associations of chain mail are decidedly ambiguous. Whilst some classical authors associated it with 'the Celts' (Varro, *De Lingua Latina* 5.24.16), it was nonetheless worn on occasions by wealthy Romans (Polybius 6.23.15). Archaeologically it has been found from securely 'barbarian' contexts in 3rd-century BC Romania and Czechoslovakia, but also from the clearly 'Roman' contexts of the army siege works around Numantia (concluded 133 BC). So chain mail *per se* is not especially significant. Nonetheless, if the technical detail of its manufacture is examined, then we can say more. Recent reanalysis of the Folly Lane, Baldock and Lexden finds by Gilmour show all to have been made using the same method, with alternating rows of riveted and plain rings (Niblett 1999, 165). Fitzpatrick (1989, 337) noted the association of the mail in the Lexden tumulus with pieces of leather and types of buckle also found with military equipment, and concluded that it might come from Roman *lorica hamata*. Curiously enough, the only comparable pieces known from outside the Roman frontiers come from another grave of a potential friendly king, though this time from 2nd-century BC Numidia, and the 'Royal Tomb' of Es Soumâa in Algeria (Waurick 1979). This provides a very specific Roman link.

Direct use of Roman aid

The association between Roman force and a king's military display was not, however, always one of acquired knowledge and imitation. Rome could, and often did, play a direct role in the military affairs of friendly kingdoms. Their role was, after all, intimately related to the security of the borders of the Empire in many places.

In Mauretania a series of colonies had been established during the brief period between Bocchus's death in 33 BC and the kingdom being handed over to Juba II eight years later. From here on, the kingdom was 'independent' until the death of Ptolemy in AD 25. However, direct military intervention happened repeatedly because of unrest caused by nomads in the south of the territory. Intermittent fighting turned into larger scale revolt under the leadership of Tacfarinas: 'he had deserted from service as a Roman auxiliary. His first followers were vagabonds and marauders who came for loot. Then he organised them into army units and formations... Tacfarinas retained in camp an elite force equipped in Roman fashion, which he instructed in discipline and obedience.' (AD 17: Tacitus *Ann* 2.52). From this period down to AD 24, a series of Roman generals was called in via Africa Proconsularis to assist in quelling him (Dio 55.28.3; Tacitus *Ann* 3.20; 3.32; 3.73; 4.23).

Whilst some interventions simply involved Roman troops temporarily entering the friendly king's territory, they could also end up being garrisoned there more permanently. Sometimes kings need watching over (Braund 1984, 94). The highest profile case of this would be Egypt. First we find a garrison installed in Alexandria in 55 BC to protect Ptolemy XII Auletes, whom Gabinius had just restored to the throne (Dio 42.3.3). The military presence there remained until Pompey's arrival, closely followed by Caesar. When Caesar left, Egypt had two new rulers, Cleopatra VII and Ptolemy XIV; along with them he considerably left three or four legions (Suet. *DJ* 77). The functions of the legions were:

> to give support to the power of kings who could have neither the affection of their own people, because they had remained loyal supporters of Caesar, nor the authority of long usage, since they had been made rulers only a few days before. At the same time [Caesar] thought it important for the prestige of the empire and for the common good, if the rulers were to remain loyal, that they should have the protection of our forces, while if they proved ungrateful, these same forces could constrain them. (Caesar, *Bell. Alex.* 33)

Only a short time later, in 40 BC, Herod was granted the throne of Judea. When he finally arrived in Jerusalem in 37 BC, it was again with the support of a Roman legion (Josephus *Jewish Antiquities* 15.71–3).

Finally we have two examples from Claudius' reign. The first comes from the Bosporan Kingdom, where Claudius' nominee, Mithradates VIII was replaced by his brother Cotys I, aided by Roman forces led by Aulus Didius Gallus. After a while some of these were withdrawn, but a few battalions remained under the command of another Roman, Gaius Julius Aquila. As it happens, in AD 49 these troops proved vital when the ousted Mithradates tried to retake his throne by force. In the description of the conflict, we find, not surprisingly, the 'native' Bosporan contingents being described as 'armed in the Roman fashion' (Tac. *Ann* 12.15). Finally, a few years later, in AD 51, we also find a Roman garrison stationed in another friendly kingdom mixed up in a little local difficulty which threatened to escalate. This time the location was Armenia, where the Roman commander Caelius Pollio was running an auxiliary battalion (Tac. *Ann* 12.45). The details need not concern us; the importance is that Roman auxiliary units were by no means exceptionally, and legions very occasionally, deployed as garrisons in friendly kingdoms.

But what of Britain? Could there have been Roman *auxilia* or legionary troops in British friendly kingdoms before the Claudian annexation? Certainly the existence of kingdoms after this date proved no bar to Roman intervention in Britain. Cartimandua was maintained on her Brigantian throne with the use of Roman aid (Tac. *Hist*. 3.45). One thing we have to recall constantly is the patchy nature of the historical record. It is far from perfect. Not all military activity hit the headlines in Rome and made it into history; and even when history was composed, not all of it survived. There are two specific gaps which hinder the study of Britain. Firstly, the chapters of Tacitus' Annals are missing for all of Gaius' reign, and the first years of Claudius' reign. Not only that, but a section is also missing from Dio (59.25), just at the point in AD 39 where he was dealing with the forthcoming conquest of Mauretania, only to commence again with Gaius and his troops on the edge of the English channel picking up sea shells. Whatever he had to say about Britain was severely truncated. Nonetheless, there are some hints that Gaius had a real involvement with Britain.

Literary tradition is very hostile towards Gaius. Historical sources belittled his achievements in a retrospective justification of his assassination. Nonetheless he had raised legions for new conquests in Britain and Germany; triremes had been built (later forwarded to Rome for an allegedly mythical triumph). Suetonius (*Gaius* 46) adds that a tall lighthouse had been constructed to guide shipping across the channel. However history portrays Gaius, his preparations suggest a serious intent to develop a closer union between Britain and the continent. There is also an ambiguous phrase in Dio which almost suggests that some Roman soldiers did campaign in Britain:

> [AD39] ... [Gaius] set out for Gaul, ostensibly because the hostile Gauls were stirring up trouble ... When he reached his destination, he did no harm to any of the enemy – in fact, as soon as he had proceeded a short distance beyond the Rhine, he returned, and then set out as if to conduct a campaign against Britain, but turned back from the ocean's edge, showing no little vexation at his lieutenants who won some slight success – but upon the subject peoples, the allies, and the citizens he inflicted vast and innumerable ills. (Dio, *Roman History*, 59.21.2–3)

We fool ourselves when we believe we can precisely know what happened in antiquity. It was in Claudius' interests to play down any involvement Gaius had in Britain, and it was similarly in Flavian interests too. The young Vespasian had been part of Claudius' annexation of Britain; Claudius' invasion could be represented as a Flavian conquest – Gaius had no place in it, whatever the reality.

Reinterpreting the archaeological evidence

What has proceeded so far has been very historical, but it has stressed (a) the broader historical context of friendly kingdoms, and (b) the ambiguities of history. These are vital when we come to interpret archaeological evidence. Previous certainties have meant that alternative readings of the archaeological evidence have not just been dismissed, but never even been considered. We should be awakened to the possibility of alternative readings. There may have been soldiers of British kings who looked very much like Roman *auxilia*. There may even have been Roman *auxilia* in Britain, watching over and protecting friendly kings. There may even have been Roman military action in Britain under Gaius. None of these are certainties, but we should not dismiss the possibilities. As it happens there has been evidence around for decades which could fit such ideas. The aim of this is to show how this re-reading of history does not just alter the historical narrative, but it also potentially alters how we perceive some sites which are normally thought of as being well known and understood.

Example 1: Gosbecks

Very close to the enclosure traditionally described as 'Cunobelin's farmstead', a small fort was discovered by aerial photography. Certainly it looks like a Roman military camp, so the inevitable historical contexts for it were sought. Hawkes and Crummy (1995, 101) discussed various possibilities. They thought it strange that a fortlet should be contemporary with the legionary fortress a short distance away so they reviewed three other possibilities. Firstly, that the fort predated and overlapped the period of construction of the legionary fortress; in which case it dated precisely to AD 43 or very shortly thereafter. Secondly, the fort might be dated to after the conversion of the legionary fortress into a *colonia* (in AD 49). Finally, it perhaps dated to after the Boudiccan revolt (AD 60/1).

> Short of excavation, only the plan of the fort can offer any help with closer dating. The absence of a *porta decumana* is a distinctive feature shared by the three best known forts of this period, namely Valkenburg I, Hod Hill, and Great Casterton, all of which date from about the AD 40s . . . In other words, its plan favours a construction date of *c* 43 to *c* 48 but not as late as *c* 60/1. (Hawkes & Crummy 1995, 101)

So the date of AD 43 was preferred, and the discovery of a tombstone elsewhere in the town of Longinus Sdapeze, a First Thracian cavalry officer, was used as evidence to suggest the occupants of the fortlet.

However, other possibilities should be considered. Firstly, if Cunobelin had been trained in the Roman army, then like other friendly kings, he might have marshalled his forces along similar lines to the *auxilia*. Secondly, the fort may have been garrisoned with genuine Roman auxiliaries before Roman annexation. As we have seen there were such units in Armenia and the Bosporus, partly to protect, and partly to mind their kings. As noted above, Dio tells us that Gaius' generals did have some success in Britain.

This is not an academic point. Data are read and interpreted with a specific mind set, and we are prone to ignore evidence which does not fit, consciously or unconsciously. When Wilson (1977) published the air photograph and gave his first interpretation, the fort was represented as having

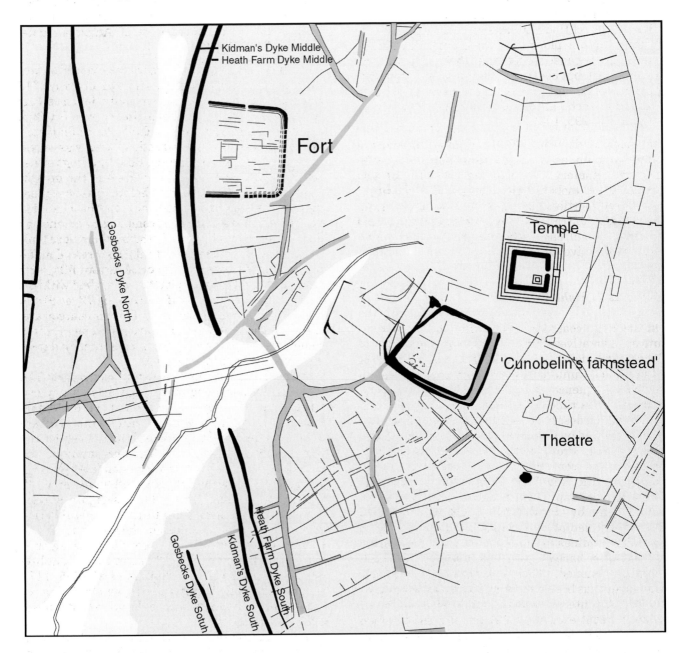

Figure 1   The Gosbecks region of Camulodunum, as revealed by aerial photography (after Hawkes and Crummy 1995)

rounded corners going under Heath Farm Dyke. The importance of this is clear, as it would suggest that the fort was earlier than that section of dyke (this is, of course, a heresy). Building rounded corners for an enclosure abutting a large dyke would be a very strange design. But if the fortlet was Claudian then it must be later than the dyke, so when Hawkes and Crummy redrew the fort (Fig 1) the junction was blurred. As they stated:

> In Dr Wilson's publication of the discovery, he stated that although he felt that the existing earthwork had been used to provide the western defences of the fort, the northern and southern military defences were nonetheless curved as if they had continued in an orthodox manner to form a west side. He shows just such a curve on the northwest angle in his plan (Wilson 1977, fig 2). Under the circumstances, such an arrangement would be surprising (cf Hod Hill) and no such angles are indicated in our plotting of the cropmarks. This is done, not because we feel that these do not necessarily exist, but because in our view the cropmarks are not quite clear enough in this part of the fort to support such an interpretation. (Hawkes & Crummy 1995, 100)

Nonetheless, it would be intriguing to imagine Camulodunum as a pre-existing burial site (the Lexden cemetery), remodelled by the clearly Romanised Cunobelin with massive dykes, with a Roman style fortlet right from the outset dominating the southern entrance to the complex and protecting his own special enclosure. No proof can be found without selective excavation.

Example 2: Fishbourne

On the south coast lies a site which has been built into our narratives of the Claudian invasion and the friendly kingdom of a client king, Tiberius Claudius Togidubnus. Cunliffe's excavations in the 1960s revealed a sequence of building which he believed started at the time of the Claudian conquest. The first phase he described as a supply base (Period 1a). It was followed by a timber building (Period 1b), and the Neronian 'Proto-palace' (Period 1c). All of this preceded the construction of a richly furnished palace in the Flavian period (Fig 2; Cunliffe 1971a,b). The supply base interpretation received reinforcement by Hind (1989) who provided an alternative reading of the historical accounts of the Claudian landings to suggest these might have been at Chichester harbour rather than in Kent, as traditionally assumed. This hypothesis was clearly argued and has been widely accepted as a strong possibility. The interpretation has also been reinforced by subsequent excavations at the site, all of which have retained the original phasing and interpretation (Cunliffe et al 1995; Cunliffe 1998).

Cunliffe's original interpretation was a natural one. 'Natural' here refers to something that is entirely consistent within the normative mind set of the late 1960s. Firstly, the solid gravel roads of Period 1a immediately evoked Roman precedents. Where else in Iron Age Britain did you have 0.07–0.30m thick metalled surfaces? Secondly the rectangular timber structures also immediately recalled parallels with Roman structures, especially military granaries. Timber Building 1 (Cunliffe 1971a, 39–41) comprised a series of six roughly parallel foundation trenches, each c 0.6m wide, in which upright timbers had stood.

> Such an arrangement is identical to that suggested for the buildings found at Richborough in an early military context, where the superstructures seem to have been granaries, the raised floor keeping the corn away from the damp ground and allowing the air to circulate freely beneath. A similar, though larger, structure was found at Rödgen, near Bad Nauheim, in a supply base of Augustan date. (Cunliffe 1971a, 40)

A second rectangular building was also raised on vertical timber posts, though this time in an array of 13 × 6 posts, each within its own individual posthole (Cunliffe 1971a, 41–2). Each timber was c 0.30m square and placed in a pit c 0.9–1.2m in diameter. Whilst different in construction, this was again thought to be a store building. Both buildings either rotted away at ground level or else had the upright posts sawn off at ground level before the subsequent buildings were constructed, also in the Claudian period (which is a somewhat compressed chronology for a building to rot). Since both buildings were built on relatively virgin land, virtually no residual material worked its way into the construction fills, with the exception of one post pit (D3), which had within it part of a 'native' jar (Cunliffe 1971b, fig 72, no 9) and a sherd of undiagnostic early Roman coarseware; and since the timbers might have rotted away, these could have been intrusive. Their construction date is therefore difficult to determine.

So far, the military interpretation seems clear. The buildings look as though they might be military granaries (though there are no other military-style buildings found in association with them). They are axial to well-made gravel roads, Roman in style; and Roman military equipment has been found on the site (though in different locations and later phases). The primacy of the military phase of the site in AD 43 made historical sense, and yet it was slightly at odds with some of the finds: analysis of the general Period 1a & 1b occupation material showed that, of the samian pottery recovered, a considerable amount dated from pre- and early Claudian times (Cunliffe 1971a, 41; 1971b, 260ff; Cunliffe et al 1995, 117). This was explained away as being an old dining set brought to the site from another location by its subsequent residents.

However, subsequent discoveries elsewhere mean that this reading can be contested. Firstly, the excavations at Silchester (Fulford 1993) clearly showed solid gravelled roads on an axial alignment in

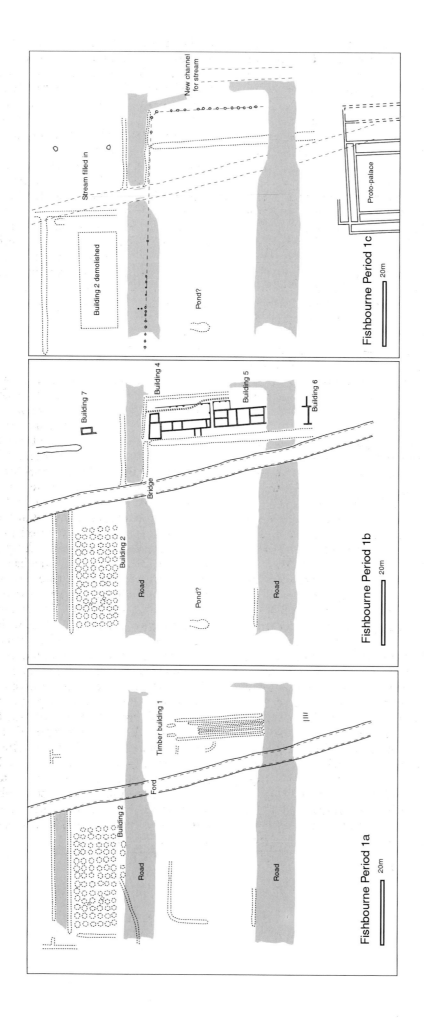

Figure 2   The early phases at Fishbourne (after Cunliffe 1971a)

Britain from around the 20s BC. The roads at Fishbourne therefore need not require a Claudian or later date. Secondly, the excavations at Gorhambury (part of the Verulamium 'oppidum' complex) revealed a granary construction technique very similar to Timber Building 1, though here again a pre-Claudian date was quite happily given to the building (Neal *et al* 1990: Building 10). Whereas the Fishbourne building was 6.7m × 30.5m, the Gorhambury example was described as 7m × 30m, almost identical in size, though here the trenches ran across rather than along the building. This structure was again interpreted as probably being a granary.

At Gorhambury, in the pre-Claudian phases, a wide variety of other buildings were constructed, many of which were described as probably having storage functions. One, early in the pre-Claudian structural sequence, was Building 5 (Neal *et al* 1990, 25–60). Like the second timber building at Fishbourne, this was made from massive 0.75m-wide load-bearing vertical timbers, presumably supporting a raised floor, and in Neal's interpretation a second storey. This 'granary' was, however, small at only 5 × 5m, in comparison with the second granary at Fishbourne of c 29 × 16m.

The discussion above means we should consider a number of alternative ways of interpreting Fishbourne. Neither the roads nor the granaries need point to a Claudian supply base, and the pottery and the otherwise compressed chronology would easily suit an earlier date for these features. But what could the site be if not a military supply base? One important aspect to realise is the small area of early deposits excavated; unfortunately the Flavian palace has not been removed and the earlier deposits elsewhere remain inaccessible. The granaries make up just one part of a presumably larger complex. The excavation at Gorhambury shows that the control of large storage facilities was important to the local dynasties, whether this was for supplying a retinue, or giving out political gifts/bribes to the population (as was happening in Rome). On the other hand, perhaps it was for locally raised troops organised like Roman *auxilia*, or even an actual Roman unit, protecting or watching over Verica, or whoever may have been in charge of the region at the time. A final alternative is to invoke the hand of an emperor, Gaius, responsible for so many of the harbour works which made Claudius' campaign a success. Perhaps his generals genuinely did achieve something in Britain, despite the hostile literary tradition to which he has been subjected. This achievement may have included improving the harbour works on this side

of the channel. Each of these possibilities is only a suggestion. On the present evidence I doubt if one could distinguish between any of them. But all potentially free the evidence from the straight-jacket of AD 43. It now means all the pre-Claudian pottery on the site has a potential context. It means that the granaries of Period 1a are not required to have been built, and to have rotted away, within a few years.

Fishbourne is fortunate. A further series of excavations is taking place there, conducted by John Manley, David Rudkin, and the Sussex Archaeological Society. New buildings are being found related to the early phases. However the test will be when it comes to interpretation, to see whether the new features are pressed into Cunliffe's original phasing, or whether the new evidence is interpreted in its own right, and perhaps leads to a re-evaluation of the results of the 1960s excavations.

Conclusion

In the context of a re-reading of the historical evidence, the archaeology can therefore appear in a rather different guise. This is not to say that the interpretations above are necessarily true. Let me be clear; I am not saying that Gosbecks fort and Fishbourne were occupied before AD 43. But what I do want to stress is that interpretations which automatically assumed they could not be, were based upon a naïve reading of history which failed to see Britain within its continental and Roman context; and that the continental context does not just mean what is happening across the English channel, but across the Roman world as a whole. Archaeologists must engage in constructing narratives about the past; but in doing so they have to be extremely self critical about any fusion of the partial archaeological record with the partial historical record. The present is complicated, and so was the past. Simple answers rarely exist, and for me they take away the mystery and interest from the past. Mystery can also be what engages people with the past, and archaeologists should be more prepared to embrace it. If archaeologists all too readily say they know what happened, then a large part of the rationale for further excavation at the public or developer's expense vanishes. My agenda for Romano-British archaeology would therefore be to encourage excavators and museum curators to think long and hard before repeating without question existing assumptions about the Claudian invasion, or indeed about any neat historical 'event'.

2 Romanisation, gender and class: recent approaches to identity in Britain and their possible consequences *by J D Hill*

Over the last decade Romanisation has attracted increasing attention from Romano-British archaeologists. The publication of *The Romanisation of Britain: an essay in archaeological interpretation* (Millett 1990a) provided a clear statement of a non-interventionist model for understanding the political and economic transformation of the province. This appears to have acted as a catalyst for a dynamic debate amongst a wide range of younger scholars which is leading to a transformation of how Roman Britain might be studied. At the heart of this transformation process is the annual Theoretical Roman Archaeology Conference, whose importance for making Roman archaeology a vibrant research area for graduate students needs far wider acknowledgement (eg Baker *et al* 1999; Cottam *et al* 1995; Forcey *et al* 1998; Meadows *et al* 1997; Rush 1995; Scott 1993). Although considered by many as 'alternative', it is hard to justify dismissing the debate about Romanisation, creolisation and ethnic identity in Romano-British archaeology expressed at these gatherings, which have constituted the main focus of discussion for the younger generations of Romano-British scholars over the last decade. The ideas of this debate may seem 'alternative' in 2001, but those involved in developing them are the future of Romano-British archaeology. The debate has seen the 'death' of Romanisation announced – probably prematurely – on several occasions. New concepts, such as creolisation, have been proposed to replace the 'R' word, while ideas of ideology, domination, and agency have all been raised. At the same time the ability of material culture, the pots and stones of Roman Britain, to tell us far more about all aspects of social life has been forcefully expressed. While the language of these debates is strange and alien to many of us, and their full working through is yet to come, at their heart they are all stressing the need to understand the social realities of different peoples' lives in Roman Britain. This new 'social archaeology' of Roman Britain, however, remains too obsessed with the 'R-word'. As I will suggest, there was probably more to life in Roman Britain than just Romanisation and areas of social life long neglected by study need greater attention in the future. These areas include regional and sectional differences, class, age, and gender.

Although identity may seem a new and foreign concept to be discussing in Romano-British archaeology, in many ways it can be argued that the study of Roman Britain has always been about identity. At the heart of the study of the province have long been the common distinctions between Roman and native,

military and civilian, Roman and Saxon etc. The fact that Romans conquered Britain has meant that interpretations of the period started from the assumption that the Romans were different from the Britons. Archaeologists and historians often sought to identify Romans, as opposed to native Britons. Or, more commonly in the last hundred years, they have sought to discover how thoroughly natives became Romans. These questions have at their heart how we identify both Roman and native in the present, which in turn is increasingly recognised as being related to how people in the past would have identified themselves. What is new about the current debates in Romano-British archaeology is not the subject matter, but that these issues are now being discussed in a far more sophisticated manner, drawing on recent developments from other human sciences. It is being increasingly realised that previous notions of 'Roman' and 'native' were too static, monolithic, and homogeneous: a single simple axis along which peoples and things were more – or less – Roman. Romanisation is increasingly seen as a discrepant and diverse experience; one in which people actively participated in different ways, often seeking to resist dominant political and cultural forms. At the same time, it is being emphasised that there was no one single Roman way of life to be adopted, transformed, or resisted (cf Woolf 1998).

While the new terminology can be off-putting, behind it are very simple points about how we now know humans work; that people's identities – who they think they are or want to be – are a fundamental part of our human nature. Just as importantly, people's identities are not fixed at birth: our identities can and do change – and can change through our own actions and intentions. The identities people have can also often be contradictory. Seeing identity in these ways questions the traditional distinction between 'Roman' and 'Native' and has obvious implications for the recent discussions of the process of the Romanisation of Britain. Indeed, John Barrett's critical discussion of the issue of Romanisation led him to argue that we can abandon the categories of 'Roman' and 'Native' as having nothing to tell us (Barrett 1997a, 60).

In like ways, the new concern with identity as an active creation and force within society has implications for the end of Roman Britain. Identifying the presence of Germans as opposed to Romano-Britons, or 'Celts' and Picts has been central to the study of 4th and 5th century Britain. This discussion has largely assumed that people's identities are simple, unchanging, and correspond to race and language. In other words, that identity is itself largely an unproblematic issue, unlike the more important task of identifying Germans or Britons through burial form, or, especially, types of object. However, this simple view of identity and its relationship to material culture has been the subject of intense discussion within early medieval studies. This debate offers many important pointers when considering different aspects of the Roman period. If the identification of major ethnic groups such as Romano-Britons and Germans in the 4th to 6th centuries is now recognised as problematic, then similar concerns need to be voiced in any discussion of the ethnic identity of soldiers, merchants, and other people from other parts of the Roman Empire who might have been present in Britannia.

New approaches to identity

Common to traditional approaches to identity in Roman Britain has been the greater emphasis on identifying people, rather than on understanding peoples' perceptions of their own identities. Identity is treated in a simple way; there are clearly defined groups of people of different race, tribe, or social role. Each has a distinct lifestyle and requisite forms of social practice and material culture unique to them. Hence, you just need to identify these to find the group of people concerned. The concept of Romanisation acknowledges that natives can become Roman, that they can change their lifestyles and, hence, social identity. However, this debate still polarises too often between native and Roman. People, even as late as the 3rd century AD, 200 years after the conquest, are still often described in terms of being more or less Roman(ised). The major issue in the Romanisation debate up to the early 1990s appears to have been encapsulated in the different possible interpretations of Tacitus' *Agricola* 21; whether Romanisation was enforced by coercion or more freely adopted by the natives. Compare Hanson's (1994; 1997) interventionist stance with Millett's non-interventionist model (1990). Yet, even in the most sophisticated discussions of the process of Romanisation, identity, culture, and agency are rarely problematised.

Up till the late 1980s then, the identities of people in Roman Britain were rarely considered as issues to be directly addressed by archaeology. While identifying groups and types of people was commonplace, how people constructed their individual or group identities was not considered a problem. This reflects the general treatment of culture and daily life within archaeology as a whole; more specifically it reflects how Romano-British archaeology has been successfully immunised against trends and debates in Anglo-American theoretical archaeology. For example, many mainstream issues such as the style debate, symbolic archaeology, or gender appear to have had little impact on Romano-British archaeology.

In Romano-British archaeology the impact of these new ideas has largely centred on discussing the beginning of the period. This is understandable given that the central leitmotif of the study of Roman Britain is the issue of Romanisation. However, similar debates are transforming the study of the end of Roman Britain, where early medieval scholars (but, as yet, fewer Romano-British scholars) have addressed the questions of identity in new and exciting ways that have much to offer the debate about Iron Age to Roman transition (eg Geary 1983; Harrison 1999; Lucy 1998; Pohl 1997). In the last 15 years the actual nature and processes of Romanisation have become an even more important part of Romano-British archaeology. Martin Millett has offered a detailed model to explain the process of Romanisation (1990, 1991). This essentially economic- and political-based approach has become the focus for a very active critique by a new generation of scholars. One unexpected aspect of this debate is how increasingly academic it appears to have become, even if this was not the intention of those involved. Of interest here is that there has been little attempt to 'test' Millett's model through detailed studies of archaeological data (Steven Willis' work on pottery in eastern England is a notable exception – Willis 1996). Yet Martin Millett's basic model provides a series of very straightforward expectations that can be assessed by studies of the evidence. Nor has there been much direct critique of the Millett model, which fails to address issues of ideology (although see Millett *et al* 1995), of individual agency, or of the active ways that the material culture of Romanisation – the actual archaeological evidence – was involved in these processes (but see Freeman 1993).

Rather, the debate has centred on a deconstruction of the intellectual basis of ideas about Romanisation in general. This deconstruction has used two main weapons. One is a theoretical consideration that draws on more recent advances in the social sciences than available for Martin Millett's model. Prime examples of this include papers by Grahame (1998), Barrett (1997a), and the extraordinary distillation of the complex debates over the nature of ethnicity offered by Sîan Jones (1997). The other arm has been a critical historiography of Romano-British studies that seek to uncover how the major ideas and debates within the study of Roman Britain have developed (eg Hingley 1993; 1995; 1996; 1997; Freeman 1996; 1997a). The most sophisticated current approaches build on both arms through drawing on post-colonial theory – a specific branch of anthropology, sociology, history, and literary theory – to offer a model of creolisation rather than Romanisation to explain the processes of change (Webster 1995a; 1996b; Webster and Cooper 1996). Several of these approaches stress how issues of power and dominion, largely absent in recent treatments of Romanisation, are essential to understand these processes (eg Barrett 1997a; Forcey 1997; Hingley 1997; Webster 1997; 1999). Many stress the active role of imperial ideology, while others recognise that relations of power have to be addressed in any discussion of large-scale social life, or the micro-scale of analysing household relations. This work shifts attention from ideology to hegemony. Webster's work on post-conquest British religion has particularly highlighted these issues (Webster 1995b; 1997; 1999). Discussion of power has led some to ask questions about domination and resistance – not the resistance in simple terms of revolt, but the ways in which subordinate groups in the province resisted the power and ideological projections of the Roman rulers in everyday practices using everyday things (eg Forcey 1998). This work stresses one very important central point. Roman things could be used in different ways and had different meanings to different people within the province. Romanisation in terms of the material culture and the practices that used these objects was not a stable, homogenous thing. To understand the discrepant ways Roman things were used means an ever increasing concern with studying and understanding the specific social context things were used in, and the archaeological contexts they are recovered from.

Major features of new debates

It is not my intention to outline these new approaches here. The introductions to Webster and Cooper 1996, and Mattingly 1997 give an overview. Papers in both volumes, in the proceedings of TRAC 97 and 98 (Forcey et al 1998; Baker et al 1999), along with Jones 1997, Freeman 1993 and Woolf 1992; 1997a; 1998 provide a good taste of the main themes and issues. Common to many is the recognition that the changes that took place in Roman Britain need to be understood as diverse, experienced and enacted differently by different people and in different places. The product of these changes was neither Roman nor native but a *new* dynamic creation of new identities, or a constellation of graded entities. This implies that acculturation is an inadequate term to describe these processes which, for Italy, Terrenato describes in terms of the metaphor of *bricolage*. 'This may be an appropriate term to describe a process in which new cultural items are obtained by means of attributing new functions to previously existing ones... (A process that) resembles a collage: that is a complex patchwork made of elements of various age and provenance: some of them are new, but many others are old objects, refunctionalised in new forms and made to serve new purposes within a new context' (Terrenato 1998, 23).

A central issue is that ethnicity and identity are situationally specific and are actively created. Identity is important because a key issue in the Romanisation debates is the ways in which people sought to adopt new forms of life and identities. The actual archaeological evidence for the Romanisation/creolisation debate is concrete, as opposed (too often) to the ideas discussed. It consists of the new public architecture that enabled and demonstrated the new political realities of life (basilicas, towns, forts, inscriptions, statues: eg Revell 1999; Aitchison 1999), the physical evidence for how religious practice and concepts changed, the small, forgotten things that show how domestic life altered, how people looked and walked differently, and so on. This physical evidence speaks of how people's identities were changing, often in a very active way seeking to identify with the new order, or to resist it. People's identities are not fixed givens; who and what people are and want to be are features of their lives. Identities are certainly open to change, even if they do not have to be actively made and remade in the light of changing circumstances. This making and remaking looks to things (buildings, costume, ways of eating) for reinforcement or challenges. This is a point recognised by Haverfield (1915), who probably devoted more attention to active roles of things and culture in these processes than does Millett's new version of his essay (Millett 1990).

These ideas, and the study of the evidence from the western Empire would suggest that there was/is no simple Roman or non-Roman identity, and that being Roman was itself differently understood and actively created at different periods. As such it is essential to attempt to understand why individuals and groups maintained or constructed their identities in terms of the specific social and political contexts in which they lived.

Of central importance for archaeology is that artefacts and ecofacts now matter in new ways. All aspects of material culture are no longer seen as simply the passive products of people's lives. Rather the objects and buildings are increasingly seen as playing an active part in sustaining existing social identities and creating new ones. People in Roman Britain can be assumed to understand the subtle ways that they and others read other peoples identities or asserted their own through a multitude of mundane activities and things. These include the types of houses people lived in; the types of foodstuffs they consumed, and their preparation; the details of how meals were staged; different forms of dress and physical appearance (eg Jundi and Hill 1998 for dress; Meadows 1995 and 1997 for foodways). The ways people used different things may not simply have been to show who and what they were to others. Identity is not simply about displaying your identity to others. Objects, from buildings through to foodstuffs and items of dress (van Driel-Murray 1999) can in different ways be seen as projections of how people perceived themselves. Identity has a deep psychological basis. It is about who you are, who you want to be, who you are happy *being* (Hill 1997). 'Being' is important. Becoming Roman leads to the understanding that Romanisation, a discrepant series of social processes, requires particular types of 'things' (pots, houses, clothes, monumental spaces, toilet probes etc). It is at heart an ontological process.

Whenever we hear the term 'Roman', we can now ask: how was it possible to recognise and embody that ideal, what did it mean at this time and in this place to make oneself Roman? This is not a mere question of legal status but one of bodily dispositions, movements, appearance, the occupation of places, relations of domination, and the submission of self to other authorities. (Barrett 1997a, 60)

These new understandings in the social sciences of material culture, identity, and daily life have one very solid conclusion for one of the longest running parts of the Romanisation debate: the 'veneer' model for the Romanisation of Britain is wrong. There has been a common assumption that the Roman impact on Britain was only skin deep; that Roman ways of life, social institutions, towns, etc were never fully adopted by the natives of Britain. As such, in some way the end of Roman Britain marks a return to 'authentic' native values, social institutions, tribal patterns, etc. This skin-deep model was captured in Simon James' famous picture for Richard Reece's *My Roman Britain* (Reece 1988, 3). From these new perspectives it is now impossible to see how the widespread changes in all aspects of daily life (not to mention social structure and political organisation) that occurred through out the British Isles from 1–400 AD, could not have brought about fundamental changes in all aspects of people's lives and understandings of their own selves. New manners and tastes are now seen as intimately tied up with deep psychological and ontological processes which are also tied closely to the ways that structures of power and domination are worked out in any society. These are not skin deep processes and suggest that Romanisation was not a veneer.

New identities to consider: where are class or gender in the archaeology of Roman Britain?

Is there too much Romanisation for Roman Britain's good? Romano-British archaeology has always been concerned with the study of identity, but only in one very narrow dimension. It is essentially just the study of Romanisation, of the differences and adoptions between Roman and native, or the de-Romanisation of Britain. The other identities that have been frequently discussed for Roman Britain are all closely related to this discourse (eg military *vs* civilian, the ethnic identity of troops and merchants, or German migrants/federates etc). Even the recent concern with regional differences and regional identities essentially comes out of the Romanisation debate (eg how the process of Romanisation differs from one part of the empire or province to another).

But Romanisation and ethnic identity were only one axis of identity that worked to structure the people of Roman Britain. The recent debate on Romanisation/creolisation and ethnic identity is necessary and has not gone far enough. But I want here to argue for greater concern with other identities that were as important in structuring Romano-British societies. Indeed, I wonder to what degree in certain periods (from the mid-2nd to the late-4th century?) and in certain places, these other identities

may have been of greater importance to the inhabitants of Britannia – more important than the extent of their Romanisation (whatever that may have meant). This is to suggest a need to consider other identities such as:

> regional,
> gender,
> age,
> sub-group (religious, craft, military),
> class.

Studies of contemporary and historical societies around the world stress that all these identities have a central role in structuring people's relationships with other individuals and in their perceptions of themselves. The voluminous literature on gender and feminism is proof of this, as is the now somewhat unfashionable concentration on class.

There has been almost no work on any of these areas in recent years, and what work there has been has tended to be often historical and epigraphic, rather than material-culture led. Gender is a very good example of this situation. Apart the pioneering work of Allason-Jones (1989), Richard Hingley (1990), Eleanor Scott (1995), and Carol van Driel-Murray (1995), there has not been much work on this topic. This appears odd, looking in from the outside of Romano-British archaeology. Gender and feminist archaeologies have been one of the most successful aspects of world archaeology since the early 1980s. Successful not only in terms of the number of publications but also in terms of the way in which gender has become an inescapable element of any archaeological investigation. If we were to stand back and ask where gender archaeology might most successfully take root in British archaeology, a strong case could be made to say that it would be in Romano-British archaeology. Here the quality of the data to address gender issues is considerably greater than for any prehistoric period, and as good, sometimes better, than much medieval evidence. The reasons for the lack of gender archaeology in Roman Britain are many. They relate to the structural gender biases in British academia and the traditions of studying Roman Britain (Scott 1998). But might they not also have much to do with the general lack of imagination that has typified approaches to Roman period data in this country compared with the study of other periods in this and other parts of the world? As the limited work by Allason-Jones (1989), Scott (1995), and Hingley (1990) show, there is considerable potential to explore gender issues in Roman Britain, but they should not be explored just because they are in fashion. One of the major realisations in the social sciences since the 1950s is the central place that gender and age have in structuring all human societies. It is impossible to fully appreciate a society or understand how it changes without considering gender and age. Viewed from these perspectives then, the traditional Romanisation debates could radically be opened up by considering issues of gender and age. The changes seen throughout the 1st century in the organisation of craft production, in the growth of towns, in domestic architecture, and in farming are grounded in changes in household relations at the time, in the division of labour. All these changes have significant implications in terms of gender relations, and might not necessarily all be seen as passively impacting on the lives of women. Why should men be seen as the main agents of change in 1st-century AD Britain? To what extent were the new social and economic opportunities provided by the conquest seized by women to change aspects of their lives and status? But again, why should the discussion of this central concern need Romanisation/creolisation as an 'excuse'? Cannot an engendered archaeology of Roman Britain stand on its own outside of this debate?

However, gender is just one of the identities to consider. Age, regional identity, and sectional identities are three others which could be rich seams to mine in the future. Simon James has shown how the identity of the Roman soldier as a soldier was an important cultural and social process that created and was sustained by particular types of material culture used in particular ways (James 1999).

Class is another obvious set of identities that have been little explored in the study of Roman Britain, even though it is indisputable that there were elites and commoners in the province. Elites have formed a natural focus in terms of the types of sites and finds on which archaeologists have concentrated. Through their role they were a medium for Roman rule and Romanisation. I am not here arguing that greater effort needs to be spent excavating the *plebes*. Rather, I am suggesting that those different class identities, and how they were created and sustained through buildings, activities and material objects could be another area for fruitful study. Something of the potential of studying elites (but only the elites) in later Roman Britain can be seen in the work on plans, access, and mosaics in villas (eg E Scott 1990, S Scott 1994). Again, class could provide another axis to refocus the Romanisation debate of the 1st century. This author has argued that the appearance in late Iron Age and early Roman times of the first class-based societies in British history is a process as significant as the conquest itself, which significantly enhanced the trend (Hill 1995). Again, this is not simply looking at the elites. An upper class identity presupposes the existence of other different class identities. Equally a missing aspect of many treatments of the Romanisation issue is an explanation of just why less powerful, non-elite groups in southeast England so readily adopted all things Roman. Is this too ready an adoption to be explained by the trickle-down model of Romanisation? What economic, if not political, opportunities did a newly Roman Britain offer to these groups? But, as with gender, to tie the archaeology of class in Roman Britain too closely to Romanisation is not necessary. Indeed, it might mask important changes in the nature and sources of power in 2nd- to 4th-century Britain that could be approached in terms of class analyses.

Identity, practice and the everyday

A concentration on identity can appear a highly abstract and intellectual aspect of archaeology. However, many studies show that people's identities – who they think they are, and who they want to be – are intimately bound up with, and expressed through, common things and everyday situations. The choice of wearing certain items of clothing, eating some things or living in particular types of houses and not in others are expressions of choices, often made by people who are extremely conscious (of some) of the alternatives and the reasons they have for rejecting them. As such, many of the finds recovered by field archaeology are direct evidence for how peoples' identities were expressed, created and reinforced through their choice and use of things. In today's world we can see how ethnicity, group/class, gender, age etc are expressed and played out through different aspects of daily life. The basic thesis adopted here is that similar issues were similarly played out in the daily life of Roman Britain. People shaped their aspirations by eating certain foods in certain ways with certain pots. Their dress contained important indicators to others about their class, status, and ethnic origins. The organisation of the houses reflected the simple and mundane ways in which the divisions of labour between the sexes, and between masters and servants, were played out and contested. If this is the case then, far from being removed from the concerns of the field archaeology of Roman Britain, these issues are at its heart. It is these processes that created the archaeological record of houses, farms, pots, and brooches which is so familiar to us all. The new approaches discussed here provide new questions and directly connect the archaeology of farm and field, hearth and home to the meta-questions of Romanisation, macro-economic change, and so on.

Unlike during large parts of British prehistory and early medieval archaeology, these questions can be addressed through a wealth of high-quality evidence. The very richness of the record can be regarded as a problem. There can appear to be simply too much. However, other data-rich archaeologies such as those of Mesoamerica or post-medieval North America and Britain provide examples of how data-rich, detailed studies on these issues can be written. Both these archaeologies could provide rich seams to mine for approaches to take to Roman Britain. Will we, should we, in the near future see a book called *In Small (Roman) Things Forgotten* (cf Deetz 1977)?

Consequences for field archaeology

It needs to be emphasised that these are not simply issues of academic interpretation of existing material. The basic link between the identities and aspirations of Romano-Britons and material culture and social practices has direct consequences for digging up Roman Britain. At a basic level the evaluation and excavation of Roman Britain could be seen as a project to monitor the process and progress of Romanisation/creolisation, especially through a concentration on key aspects of daily life:

The body – dress, physical appearance, the technologies of personal hygiene, medical treatment, the treatment of body in death.

Foodways – the cultural, social and political aspects of what is eaten, how it is prepared and by whom, how it is consumed, by whom and for what social purposes etc.

Settlement space – how the organisation of activities in the home and the surrounding settlement are organised in terms of gender/class/age, and how that organisation structures and is structured by the physical arrangement of spaces.

Consumption – how and why people felt they needed or required the wide range of goods and things that so typifies Roman as opposed to Iron Age or early Saxon Britain.

These themes may seem abstract, but they can provide ways to structure the findings of excavations – if not the excavation process itself – to address issues of age, gender, class and 'ethnicity'. However, it is important to stress that the consideration of all these issues is dependent on a greater concern with deposition on Roman period sites. How the archaeological record was formed is central to understanding all other aspects of that record and there have been few serious attempts to address these issues for Romano-British sites. Deposition is an essential component of studying finds in their full context. To address the themes of daily life and identity raised here requires far more than simple regional distributions of artefact types etc; it also requires closer examination of the specific social contexts in which things were used and of how they entered the archaeological record.

These new questions to ask of the data can lead to new ways of recording data in the field or marshalling it during post-excavation, as is happening with the Heathrow Terminal 5 excavations and with the Daventry International Rail Freight Terminal. But much can be done using existing excavation and post-excavation recording strategies, if the right questions are asked. However, the increasing concern with questions of the structures of daily life and the detailed nature of the contexts in which things were used and deposited, does raise the need for more detailed analysis in all publications. Studies of finds distributions across sites and within structures, attention to depositional processes, and addressing the issues listed above probably need to become far more common, even in the smallest of sites. If this is the case, then appropriate time and costings need to be put into excavation and post-excavation briefs. There is also a need for ensuring that all classes of ecofact and artefact are recorded to at least the minimum standards recommended by appropriate specialist groups. This is even more important than the recommended extra components of all site reports. Even if there is not the time or money for the excavators to address these issues – and I can fully appreciate why this might be – there is a vital need that site archives contain adequate standardised and contextualised data for others to pursue these issues in the future. Unfortunately, one of the greatest hindrances to carrying out this work to date is that surprisingly few, big published Roman sites have the level of detail required for all classes of finds in their archives.

This issue of the need for a high-level, detailed, standardised recording of all finds applies as much to evaluations as full excavations. The evaluation is the most important research tool in British Archaeology. Each year, thousands of small samples are taken across the archaeological landscape. Taken individually, evaluations usually provide relatively small numbers of finds and features. But over a given period – five years say – the numbers of evaluations across many parts of Britain will provide a great density of samples of all types of site and landscape feature. They provide snapshots, enabling us to consider the rate of change, local differences in the adoption of change, social differences, etc. Combined in this way and used imaginatively the results of evaluations offer considerable potential for answering the types of questions raised here. However, if this is to be the case, evaluations need to be conducted with these long-term aims in mind and not just as an opportunity to see what is there; and finds from evaluations need to be written up more fully than they can be at present.

Consequences for academic archaeology

The big problem is providing people with the time, the resources and the training to analyse material in these new ways. Possibly the two greatest weaknesses that face Romano-British archaeology are:

1. a lack of synthesis and analysis,
2. the growing shortage of key people with the specialist knowledge in all areas of material culture.

The lack of synthesis and analysis of the increasingly large number of excavations is a major problem. There are few recent detailed county or regional summaries of the results of recent archaeological work, and even fewer offer a detailed analysis and working through of the material. The same is true of simple catalogues and new studies of most categories of finds from Roman Britain. Nor, increasingly, is there the time or the money to provide detailed discussions of the results for most excavations. Here is an obvious area where directed masters and doctoral dissertations and other academic studies are needed. However, it is unfair to expect all of this work to be carried by state antiquities services or national museums. This is a major area where university archaeology departments will need to make their contribution.

The detailed study of many of the issues raised in this contribution depends on the new roles that objects and buildings are seen as playing in structuring people's lives. Detailed and subtle studies of different classes of material are one important way to discuss identity in Roman Britain, and such studies depend on the accurate identification and presentation of all classes of finds. However, there is growing concern that the number of people with this level of knowledge is steadily decreasing, at the same time as the quantity of excavations and metal detector finds increases. Few university courses now require students to learn their material culture – for very sound and proper archaeological and educational reasons. However, we will need to ensure an adequate and constant flow of finds specialists to simply replace the existing specialists over the next 10 to 20 years, let alone increase this number. This problem is recognised by many in the field, and bodies such as English Heritage are making important efforts to address the problem. Even so, the main responsibility must rest with university archaeology. The finds specialist shortage can be addressed by ensuring that a modest number of postgraduate students come through the universities on a regular basis over the coming years. This requires more of the ablest students to be encouraged to work with finds. The bodies who fund postgraduate students also need to be made more aware of the needs and priorities currently being identified for the British archaeological profession, so that they can take these into account when allocating their limited resources.

Conclusion: Where do you want to go tomorrow?

This short contribution has stressed the continued importance of issues of identity in Romano-British archaeology. It has reviewed the changing approaches to the question of Romanisation and highlighted the material implications these new approaches have for the study of all classes of archaeological data. This issue can be used to illuminate many different aspects of the period and can (only) be studied through diverse classes of material.

Clearly there is now a need for several studies that take a long-term perspective to consider how identities were constructed and change from the middle Iron Age through to the middle Saxon period. Much of the current debate has remained at a broadly theoretical level. There have been few thorough and detailed case studies using the large databases available for this period. Nor is there yet an equivalent to Millett (1990) or Haverfield (1915) expressed in these terms. Both types of study are probably necessary to demonstrate the worth and importance of these new approaches to a wide audience. However, I have been at pains to point out that there are many identities that need to be considered to provide a full understanding of the lives of people throughout Roman Britain. There is a case to be made to say that there is too much Romanisation/creolisation in the study of Roman Britain. Might a concentration on other issues such as age, gender, and class not simply counterbalance this emphasis, but throw up new perspectives on this, the main (some might say the only) theme in Romano-British archaeology?

An outsider has written this paper. I am not a Romano-British archaeologist. This may make it easier to ignore the issues I have raised here. However, it is sometimes easier for an outsider to recognise just how well off Romano-British archaeology is. Roman Britain has the potential to make contributions in a number of international debates within archaeology and the social sciences generally. At the heart of the exploration of human societies today are issues such as the construction of identities, the nature of material culture, how power and domination work at all levels of society, and the importance of the everyday. These debates are clearly beginning to influence the way we interpret and collect data from Roman Britain. But does this have to be a one-way process? Roman Britain has one of the best databases in the world to explore these issues. The high quality of excavation and recovery and the sheer density of research can be matched in few other periods and parts of the world. The potential for data-rich but theoretically informed discussions of these issues is immense. Roman Britain has great relevance for other archaeologies. Yet how often are studies of Romano-British topics discussed in general textbooks on household archaeology or identity, or included in edited volumes or the new flurry of archaeological readers on theory, gender, landscape, and power? Romano-British archaeology could have this international profile in the future. But does it want to?

3 Material culture and identity

by Lindsay Allason-Jones

When I was first asked to contribute to this session, by looking at those elements of English Heritage's draft, *Exploring Our Past* (English Heritage 1998) which were concerned with the study of material culture, I was somewhat reluctant because, at first glance, finds did not appear to figure largely in the document, either as one of the five primary goals or as one of the six priority groups. It was only on closer reading that references to objects began to emerge. This may be because finds work was seen as running through all the goals and priorities – it would be good to think this was so – but, realistically, it is more likely that the usefulness of objects to inform our understanding of our ancestors is still not fully appreciated.

For example, finds get an indirect mention under A2, which reads, 'encourage the creation of a national framework of research centres, to address issues of archaeological storage, curation and dissemination'. But this implies that objects are merely a storage and curation problem. As a museum director, of course, I might be tempted to agree; objects from excavations do take up a lot of space and some museums are presently being overwhelmed by the sheer volume of material which is arriving at their doors. Equally, museums accepting the material have to be able to find it again on request and provide educational and research facilities for 'all elements of the discipline and the public' (A2, para 1). Looking on the bright side, this section does seem to recognise that the finds from an excavation can provide a long-term research base, and the section continues by suggesting that 'there is much to be done integrating the results of past studies and collating national reference collections'. Honourable mention is made of the Roman National Fabric Collection at the British Museum and the Ceramic Thin-section Database at Lincoln (A2, para 4). Not all types of artefacts lend themselves to this type of database, however, and there is the further, very sensible, suggestion that we work on collating bibliographies of published and archived work (A2, para 4). Objects are often published in some very obscure places – the universities' Research Assessment Exercise may indeed, if inadvertently, be pushing academics towards publishing in foreign journals – and the publications, often PhD theses, which publish good lists of references are a boon.

The document's authors recognise that here 'there is considerable potential ... to build dynamic links with international, especially European, reference collections' (A2, para 4). This is extremely important because it is precisely in the field of artefact research

that the differences between the individual provinces can manifest themselves. Forts, towns, and villas in their ground plans can look very similar whether one is in Britain or Libya; it is the different materials used to build those forts and towns which make them appear different. Equally, whilst one can occasionally find precisely the same objects throughout the Roman Empire – openwork eagle mounts are a good example (Fig 3; Allason-Jones 1986) – there are also many items which will only appear in one particular province – certain types of brooches, for example. It is these differences which suggest tribal, ethnic or provincial identities. The British archaeologist can be as notorious as the British man in the street when it comes to ignoring foreign examples. This can often be because it can be difficult to get access to foreign publications and it is to be hoped that the use of the Internet will lead to greater communication between Roman scholars throughout the world. At the Museum of Antiquities, Newcastle upon Tyne, an interesting example of the Internet in action was recently revealed when the South Shields dodecahedron was featured as the Object of the Month on the Museum's web site and the staff found that they had inadvertently wandered into an international mine field – unbeknownst to them similar objects have recently been found in India and the world was full of dodecahedron fans, all eager to share their knowledge.

In Section A5 the Research Agenda goes on to suggest that synthetic studies should be commissioned and undertaken. As this is a document from English Heritage, one can only presume that the borders of these syntheses are likely to be limited. However, at the suggestion that 'a programme of commissioned artefact assessments should identify basic recording standards, guidelines for processing, shortcomings in regional and local sequences, and potential themes for future studies' (A5, para 2), one becomes a little worried that the approach to finds *reporting* could become bureaucratically obsessed with the logistics of finds *recording* with the result that we will fail to see the wood for the trees. There is a basic need for us to attempt to provide the same level of information for each site – the quality and quantity of data provided for each object can often depend on the number of artefacts found and the interest of the specialist in the individual artefacts – but we should not lose sight of why we are identifying and publishing these objects in the first place in our efforts to do so correctly and cost-effectively.

The late Professor George Jobey taught students that archaeology was the study of the people in the

Figure 3   A copper alloy 'eagle' mount from a baldric, found at Carlisle (courtesy Carlisle Museum & Art Gallery)

past, not just the buildings of the past. Stuart Piggot in *Approach to Archaeology* summed up the difficulties in approaching this study by saying:

> if we are going to study individuals, societies, communities or other groupings of people in the past, we have to use various techniques which will get round the fact that just because it is the past, the people we are studying are dead, and we cannot go and ask them questions or watch their daily life. (Piggot 1966)

Whether we want to study that daily life for our own interest or to provide exhibitions, reconstructions, television programmes, or books for the general public, we have to use all the tools available to build up the complete picture. Perhaps it is as well to remind ourselves occasionally of what makes up such a picture.

Straightforward excavation produces the ground plan of a building. But without finds how can one tell whether the building was a house, a factory, a temple, or a barn? What can one tell about even a house by the ground plan alone? How can one tell how many people lived in a house, what age groups were represented, what was their status? Can one tell if men, women, and children shared the accommodation or were there separate quarters for each group? Who were these people, where did they come from, and who did they think they were? All these questions rely on the finds for the answers.

It is a common misconception of the general public, and occasionally some of our colleagues, that we know a great deal about the past. The exponents of this theory are convinced that we know, for example, exactly what a Roman fort looked like; what Hadrian's Wall was for; what a particular copper alloy object was used for. Why then do we need to excavate more forts, do more research on Hadrian's Wall, or look at any more copper alloy objects? Would it not be better to concentrate on the periods, buildings, or objects which are not so well known? This is not an impressive theory – the more work that is done in archaeology, the more we discover how little we know and how often we are proved wrong in what we think we know. For archaeology to progress towards a convincing picture of the past it is essential for us to question continually all previously held ideas. Many so-called facts do not stand up to a second look. Every site excavated, whether for rescue or research reasons, can be used to test earlier theories. Every button-and-loop fastener found adds to the discussion of the dating, manufacture, and use of that particular type, whether the evidence is positive or negative. An informed view of button-and-loop fasteners can only be based on the sum of every fastener, and even if someone writes the definitive work on such fasteners, as John Peter Wild did in 1970, we cannot rest on our laurels, tick them off as 'done', but in the future every new button-and-loop fastener should be added to the debate and the hypotheses re-tested (Wild 1970). This is not only to add to our knowledge of fasteners but also to our understanding of the Roman Empire.

Studying mixed assemblages can also prove remarkably enlightening and the original plan for this paper was to provide an overview of recent work in this field. However, this was unlikely to be all-encompassing so instead a single case study is offered. In 1988 I attempted an experiment; quite a small experiment but with surprising results. I had been inspired by a comment published by Dorothy Charlesworth in 1973 when, in her discussion of John Clayton's excavation of Turret 29a on Hadrian's Wall, she referred to his finding: 'coins of Vespasian, Trajan, Hadrian, and Constantine the Great but no intervening emperors, fragments of millstone, coarse pottery, some samian, broken glass, animal bones, and horn'. 'In fact', she concluded, 'the normal range of finds from a turret' (Charlesworth 1973). But was this the normal range of finds from a turret? I did not have the knowledge to comment on her view of the coin assemblage or the pottery but her implication that no small finds might be expected didn't correspond with my own impression of the situation at all.

I decided to look at the small finds from all the turrets on Hadrian's Wall to test which view was the more accurate. This was not an unmanageably large piece of work as only 74 turrets have been excavated in full or in part, of which 47 appear to have produced no small finds at all; or, rather, no small finds are recorded or survive. Those that do survive are either housed at Tullie House Museum in Carlisle or in the Museum of Antiquities at Newcastle, so were reasonably accessible.

The results of this project are already published in the *Proceedings of the Fourth Military Equipment Conference*, edited by Jon Coulston, so the following remarks are merely a synopsis of the published report (Allason-Jones 1988).

Firstly, it became clear that small finds were present in the archaeological record of turrets in both quantity and quality. The turrets varied considerably in the quantity of finds produced, which may or may not reflect the efficiency and extent of the excavations, but it became clear that more finds had been recovered than had been generally believed. Charlesworth was correct in noting that quernstones were common finds in turrets as a high proportion had produced them. The implication that the soldiers were provided with basic provisions for several days and left to fend for themselves, however, is an interesting extension to our knowledge of daily life on Hadrian's Wall which goes beyond merely noting that turret excavations will produce querns. Equally, the number of gaming counters and gaming boards seem to indicate that the soldiers had a certain amount of leisure time between shifts.

The principle of the 'evidence of absence' also brought to light some curious points; there were no objects which could be unequivocally identified as belonging to women or children – this most people might expect, in view of the nature of the sites, but equally there was little weaponry: only a few spearheads and one arrowhead. The knives were of the domestic type rather than daggers. There was no harness equipment, no obviously religious objects, and no locks or keys: clearly there was no perceived need to lock the doors; one might presume the turrets were not left unmanned and in times of danger those inside would have barred the doors rather than locked them.

Having looked at the basic catalogue and commented on what was and was not there, I started to play with the evidence. I plotted the finds according to type and findspot and, most surprisingly, some of the objects appeared to group geographically. Shield bosses grouped between Turrets 18b and 29b; ballista balls were found only in the Areas 17 and 18. Iron nails tended to group in four distinct sections, irrespective of whether modern or ancient excavation techniques had been employed. They were, however, equally uncommon throughout and it was noticeable that they were as rare in the Turf Wall sector as in the Stone Wall sector. It should, of course, be remembered that the turrets were built of stone in both sectors but the lack of nails does seem to argue against the notion that the upper parts of the turrets were built of wood or had wooden parapets or roofs, whilst the strange grouping might indicate that there were some variations in turret design.

Other objects, such as belt plates, scabbard runners, chapes and the like also exhibited strange groupings and it was tempting to see this as evidence for the garrisoning of the turrets by particular units. By grouping the turrets by finds, and taking into consideration such factors as distance and the barriers formed by rivers, a hypothetical garrison list was produced: Turret 7b and its neighbours manned from Benwell, 10a to Area 17 manned from Rudchester, Area 17 onwards from Halton Chesters, 25b and 26a were assigned to Chesters. Area 29 could have been attached to Housesteads, as could turrets 34a and 35a on the knife evidence; 35a was already linked to Housesteads by a Taranis wheel motif. Other links between 33b, 34a, and 35a were spearheads, tools, enamelled brooches, and copper alloy vessels. Turret 45a may have been the responsibility of Carvoran, whilst the rest of the excavated turrets, with groupings of belt fittings, sheathings, studs, and pottery lids, may have come under the jurisdiction of Birdoswald. None of this evidence, of course, is conclusive or even provable, but it does provide food for thought and some interesting hypotheses for testing.

The finds were then considered purely on grounds of date. All the finds were of 2nd-century date with a very few late 1st-century examples. There was nothing which could be confidently assigned to the 3rd or 4th centuries. This was very satisfactory as the turrets are believed to have been built as part of the original plan of Hadrian's Wall in the 120s. When the decision was made to move the siting of the forts onto the Wall itself, instead of the Stanegate, some of the turrets were demolished if they lay directly in the path of the new forts but none of the others appear to have been given up. It was only when Hadrian's Wall was abandoned and the frontier moved north to the Antonine Wall that the turrets were emptied. The Antonine Wall was in its turn abandoned in the 160s and it appears that all the turrets so far investigated were put back into working order although the pottery evidence for 33b, 34a, and 35a suggests that some of this reoccupation was quite brief. Most, if not all, of the turrets were then abandoned during the modifications of the 180s with some having their doorways blocked and some being demolished totally. The evidence of the finds agrees that the turrets were occupied only from the 120s to the 140s and then from the 160s to the 180s. None show evidence of later squatter occupation or of the conversion to other purposes which can be seen in some of the milecastles (Haigh and Savage 1984).

This evidence that the turrets were only occupied for 40 years in two clear cut stages and only for military purposes led me to look again at the traditional division between 'military' and 'civilian' in the classification of small finds (Allason-Jones 1995). Take brooches as an example. These are invariably discussed in the civilian section of reports; yet the turret evidence indicates that soldiers not only wore brooches but also lost them with a great deal of unmilitary carelessness. Needles, nail-cleaners, and tweezers might also be seen as evidence for a civilian or even a female presence but civilian and military populations have similar needs: 2nd-century soldiers would have had to mend their clothes, clean their nails, and remove splinters whilst civilians could have needed arrows and knives for hunting, hobnails for their shoes, and chapes for their knife scabbards. The discovery at Vindolanda of a survival kit, known to modern soldiers as a 'housewife', shows that Roman soldiers were expected to mend their own clothes as well as look after the rest of their belongings. The evidence from the turrets suggests that the normal separation of finds into 'military' and 'civilian' by use alone – or rather, by what we presume was their use – has limited validity. As a consequence this also, of course, throws into doubt some of the recent debates which have worked on the presumption that it is possible to categorise finds into military and civilian, such as which areas around a fort were for the use of civilians. The project also threw doubt on the idea that it is possible to tell the difference between 'female artefacts' and 'male artefacts'. With the recent development of interest in gender issues in archaeology many researchers are being tempted to base their theories of space allocation, economy, role, or status on the evidence of the small finds. Much of this work seems to work on the principle that Roman Britain had the same gender values as Britain in the 1950s. Until we can get to grips with the question as to whether it is possible to identify objects used specifically by men, women, or children, attempts to assign areas of buildings or sites to male or female or child use are doomed to failure.

In what I said and concluded about finds from turrets in 1988 I made some wild generalisations about other types of sites. I said, for example, that more examples of spearheads, sheathing fragments, shield bosses, and scabbard fittings can be expected from the turrets and milecastles than from the forts on Hadrian's Wall. How can I say that without an equally detailed project on the milecastles and forts? Milecastles were not a great problem as few have been excavated to any great extent. Most of the excavations seem to have concentrated on checking the type of gateway a particular milecastle might have and gateways are not (traditionally) areas which produce many artefacts. It does not take long to check if a particular group of objects had been found in milecastles. Forts are a different matter.

As I have been involved in the cataloguing of a large proportion of the small finds from the Hadrian's Wall forts I have an image in mind – which might be better described as a folk memory – of what each fort has produced but it can take some time to check whether my folk memory is accurate. I also have a vague idea in my own mind of what a barrack block in a Hadrian's Wall fort might produce by way of finds, but again there should be doubts as to my accuracy and even less confidence shown in using that idea when claiming what a barrack block elsewhere might produce. But surely, in these days of feasibility studies, site assessments, cascade diagrams, and the like, isn't this the sort of information we should have at our finger tips? The precedent of my small project on turrets may suggest that not only would some quantitative work on finds assemblages aid our ability to calculate in advance the potential finds assemblage any site might be expected to produce if excavated – helping the forward planning of excavations enormously – but it could also pay unexpected dividends in our knowledge of the sites themselves and, more importantly, our knowledge of the people who occupied those sites.

The following are some suggestions as to areas in which qualitative and quantitative analysis could be worthwhile and which might highlight some gaps in our knowledge of the Roman world.

For example, are the finds from the forts on Hadrian's Wall typical of Roman forts of the same date elsewhere? Would it be reasonable to expect to find the same objects on a German *limes* fort as at Housesteads or Brough-on-Noe or Gelligaer? And what about inside forts? Do such buildings as barrack-blocks, headquarters buildings, hospitals, etc, have a typical assemblage? Would the assemblage from a barrack-block on Hadrian's Wall show differences or similarities to an assemblage from a barrack-block on a Welsh fort site or a barrack-block elsewhere in the Roman Empire? Does the assemblage from a barrack-block actually prove it is a barrack-block? If it does, is it reasonable to presume that if a similar assemblage emerges from another building then that too, irrespective of its ground plan, must be a barrack-block? As far as the Wall forts are concerned, the impression – so far unconfirmed – is that the bulk of the finds tend to come from the barrack-blocks and that the headquarters buildings, *praetoria* and hospitals were kept fairly tidy. This impression that the soldiers were living in cheerful squalor is based on the excavation of a few barrack-blocks at a couple of sites and as such may not stand up to much investigation, but it should be investigated.

There has been detailed debate as to whether *lorica segmentata* was worn only by legionaries (see, for example, Maxfield 1986), but looking at the wider picture, do we have a clear idea of how a legionary fort and an auxiliary fort might differ in their whole finds assemblage? This could be a tricky question as most forts started out with legionary garrisons which were later replaced by auxiliary units, but it might be possible. Equally, we are aware that the auxiliary units came from all over the Roman empire and we happily accept that many of these units retained their distinctive native weaponry or dress – the Syrian archers are an obvious example. But can we be certain as to what one might expect to find by way of finds at a fort which had been occupied by a cohort of Tungrians or Batavians? What about the Dacians? We know that the First Cohort of Dacians was present at Birdoswald at the beginning of the 3rd century because there is an inscription which makes this clear; it also depicts a Dacian falx, a distinctive curved sword (Coulston 1981), but the recent excavations at Birdoswald have not produced a single falx, or indeed anything else which might be hailed as being distinctively Dacian (Wilmott 1998). Is it possible to answer the question which I was asked some years ago, and which I singularly failed to answer: what might one expect to find on a site occupied by a numerus or even a cavalry unit?

Moving to the civilians: what is a typical villa assemblage? Most villa excavations have produced only small assemblages, possibly because the interiors would have been kept swept and tidy, and the exteriors, where the domestic rubbish would have been dumped, have not always been extensively excavated. But even when there is a statistically valid assemblage from a villa, how does it compare with the typical assemblage from a town house of similar proportions, pretensions or layout? How does the assemblage from a *vicus* dwelling compare with that from a town house? There are obvious difficulties in comparing villas and *vici* with towns as town sites tend to be damaged by later intrusions and a full assemblage may not be recoverable. Indeed, sites of any type may present problems in the possible level of artefact recovery and thus there are bound to be problems in comparisons, but some of the questions could and should be answered.

In dealing with apparently civilian sites, the problems of identifying artefacts as being 'male' or 'female', or 'civilian' or 'military', or 'native' or 'Roman', becomes more pressing as archaeologists struggle to identify by whom a site was occupied or how the different rooms or areas might have been used. An example of this might be seen at Shiptonthorpe, East Yorkshire (Millett forthcoming). The excavations of Shiptonthorpe revealed roadside structures whose finds assemblage bore a closer similarity to that from a fort and *vicus* site, such as Castlesteads (Cool and Philo 1998), than from a site which might currently be considered to be a civilian establishment, whether domestic, agricultural, or industrial. None of the artefacts recovered could be labelled indisputably military, but dagger or knife plates, button-and-loop fasteners, and bridle pieces could have been used by army personnel or civilians alike. The site also failed to produce objects which could be associated only with women, but it is unclear whether this can be taken as evidence that there were no women present – it may be that there were women on the site but none of their artefacts have survived, or, alternatively, that they did not use distinctive accessories. Equally, the range of objects included some, such as terrets, a bone toggle, vessel handle terminals, and button-and-loop fasteners whose forms strongly suggest a native element, whilst other objects, such as a lion knife handle, a spoon, a steelyard, a stylus, a sealbox, and a ligula, seem to indicate that the occupants, whether temporary or permanent, were comfortable with imported items from the Mediterranean. The artefact assemblage from Shiptonthorpe was substantial, so it is all the more frustrating that comparable assemblages are not available to confirm the nature of the site.

A number of temples have now been excavated: Uley, Bath, Coventina's Well, Harlow, to name just a few, and Lewis produced in 1966 a volume cataloguing the various types of temple architecture to be found in Roman Britain. Anyone asked to describe a typical temple assemblage might be tempted to do so in one word: 'big'. But is this true and can we do anything with this mass of data? Is there any relationship between the layout of a temple and the quantity or quality of the finds which are recovered? Why do some sites produce a large number of coins whilst others, such as *Mithraea*, produce none or just a few? Why do some altars have coins underneath them whilst others do not? The answers to all these questions might seem obvious in that the finds must relate to the ceremonial associated with the different deities but this apparently obvious answer has yet to be carried through to its conclusion with research on the finds to see if it is possible to identify a specific deity or the origins of particular groups of worshippers from the finds. Even if one looks at temples dedicated to the same deity, such as Jupiter, is it possible to detect regional variations in the number and type of finds and, if it is, are these variations due to economic factors or differences in belief due to the identities of the worshippers? One could go on.

In 1991 Robert Philpott published an extensive report on burial practices in Roman Britain. This is an invaluable work which catalogues all the evidence from the cemeteries excavated so far, and from the mass of data he produced some fascinating conclusions concerning the influence of immigrant groups, changes in rites, geographical variations in practice, economic trends, and fashions in jewellery and dress as well as pottery. Are the regional and chronological differences he pinpointed in the grave assemblages reflected in the corresponding settlement assemblages? The difference between the minimal assemblages of the military cemeteries of Petty Knowes and Lanchester and the material one might expect to find in an excavation of the barrack-blocks of their corresponding forts is marked. Is this related to the beliefs of the soldiers from particular geographical regions or was it, at the time, a widespread military custom? Too few military cemeteries have been excavated to answer this question but at least we know the question exists.

Increasingly, those of us who work with finds are confining ourselves to a limited range of objects. We regard ourselves, or are regarded by others, as specialists in brooches, or intaglios, or military equipment. This is, to some extent, forced upon us by the quantity of data and published sources currently available – it is difficult to keep on top of the new work for all finds and so much easier to keep abreast of the latest research on objects in a limited specialised group. This makes it more and more difficult for general patterns to emerge. When I questioned how a legionary fort and an auxiliary fort would differ in their finds assemblages those *au fait* with military equipment probably had an immediate picture of specific pieces of equipment which could be identified as legionary or auxiliary. But this is not the whole picture. A soldier's life does not consist solely of his uniform but involves his whole way of life: what he eats, how he eats it, what he believes in, how he spends his leisure time, as well as his specific job within his unit. All the finds used by that soldier need to be used to build this picture. The turret project, after all, showed that nailcleaners, tweezers and quernstones were used by soldiers in the 2nd century AD; this presents a somewhat different picture of a soldier's life than the *lorica segmentata* and scabbard runners. Perhaps it is time that we stepped back from our detailed typologies of strapends and looked at the wider issues about what the finds tell us – the 'us' in this context being the archaeological world, in which I include members of the interested public, and not just the finds specialists.

This brings me to my final point – who is going to do all this work? *Exploring Our Past 1998* refers in A6 to the idea that the establishment of inter-linked regional reference collections would restrict duplication of effort and enable resources to be engaged in more fruitful research. Whilst the suggestion that each generation of scholars should not have to start again from scratch but be able to build on the work of others who have gone before is to be applauded, there is concern that there are very few undergraduates or postgraduates wishing to work with finds. *Instrumentum*, the international Roman finds organisation, recently asked for a list of postgraduate theses currently in preparation within British universities which involved research into Roman finds; the final list was embarrassingly short. There has been a backlash against doing finds work in recent years, students often preferring to do their dissertations or theses on more theoretical topics. This is understandable in the short-term but regrettable in the longer term; after all, there are very few jobs in theoretical archaeology whilst finds research still offers a number of career paths through museum work, the new Portable Antiquities Recording Scheme, etc. It is also a policy that is likely to result in a skills shortage in future years. There is, at the moment, only one specialist in Britain working on Roman intaglios; without him who will identify intaglios? Romano-British studies include many other people who are ploughing a lonely furrow and who have a life-time's knowledge in a specialised sphere. These specialists need to be training the next generation because a working knowledge of objects cannot be learned just from published sources; even being let loose in a national reference collection is a less than satisfactory learning experience if someone is not present who understands the material and can tell you what to look at. Once again the woods-and-trees image springs to mind; to be able to build up a theoretical model of the activities which took place within a building, a fort, town, or even a province, one has to have the evidence identified – that is, to recognise a forest one has to be able to recognise a tree or at least have someone available who can tell you, 'those are lots of trees'. To be able to theorise as to why a wood changed from deciduous trees to conifers at a particular period you have to know that there is a difference between the types of trees and recognise what those differences are. Without this underpinning knowledge research into the 'Meaning of Change', or 'Chronological Periods', or the themes identified in *Exploring Our Past 1998* is going to be tricky if not impossible.

4 Material approaches to the identification of different Romano-British site types *by Jeremy Evans*

Introduction

The aim of this paper is to examine methods of differentiating between classes of Romano-British site from their finds assemblages. The author's research interests lie principally within Romano-British ceramics and it is mainly from research in this field that this paper is drawn. Methods of differentiating between types of site all rest in different ways upon the method of viewing *all* the ceramics from a site as an assemblage, to be recorded as such and compared with those from other sites. The presence or absence of individual types is of no use in demonstrating differences between types of site, whereas strikingly clear patterns emerge from the comparison of different aspects of quantified assemblages. Similar differences between rural and urban sites have been observed for a long time from Reece's (1989) work on coinage, again by examining coin lists as a quantified assemblage. Lindsay Allason-Jones has also done some pioneering work comparing small finds assemblages from Hadrian's Wall forts with those from turrets (1988; this volume). Hilary Cool (1995) has produced a fascinating study of spatial variations in small finds from the fortress at York, using correspondence analysis, and comparing them with a series of groups from other sites. This study was principally

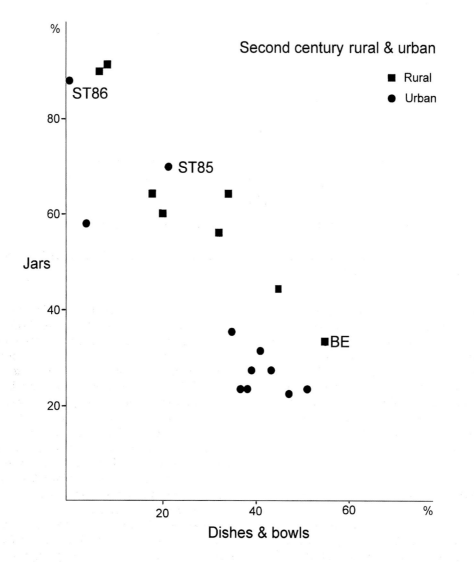

Figure 4 Proportions of jars and tablewares from 2nd-century northern sites. ST = Shiptonthorpe, BE = Bryn Eryr

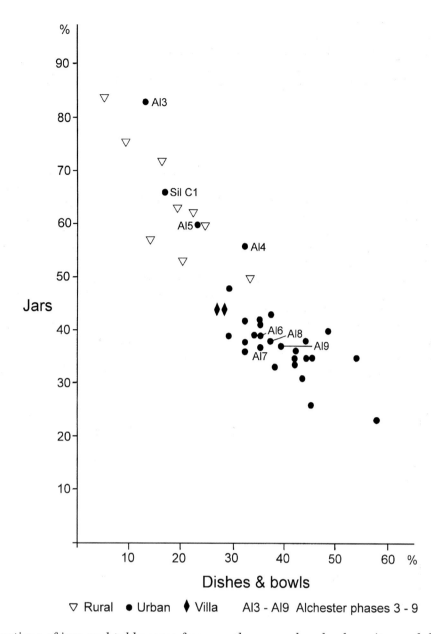

Figure 5 Proportions of jars and tablewares from southern rural and urban sites and data from the A421 Alchester sub-urban site phases 3–9. Sil = Silchester

concerned with establishing functional groupings, but the method could well be appropriate to comparing site types. Cool has also gone on recently (Cool and Baxter 1998) to examine variations in glass assemblages between different classes of site. King (1978; 1999b) has also suggested differences may be found in animal bone assemblages between different types of site, but there seems to have been little more modern work on this (although see now Dobney, this volume).

Functional analyses

The idea of functional analysis of pottery assemblages goes back to the 'New Archaeology' of the late 1960s, in particular the work of Longacre (1970). In Britain, Millett (1979) started off such work in the late 1970s with a study of the functional variations between different features within the Saxon Shore fort at Portchester and the presentation of function sequences through time from three southern town sites. He continued this work in his thesis examination of Boudiccan destruction deposits in the southeast (Millet 1983), and the present author has undertaken more general surveys of a range of sites in the north (Evans 1993) and the Midlands (Evans forthcoming (a); Evans forthcoming (b)). The method of functional analysis is to class vessels into general shape categories following a series of definitions mainly related to height–diameter ratios and to examine the proportions of these classes occurring at sites (Evans 1993, fig 1).

It is accepted that it is difficult to know how vessels were actually used in antiquity. However, evidence such as the disproportionately high level of sooting on heavily gritted jar fabrics does point to their predominant use as cooking pots (Evans 1993, fig 14).

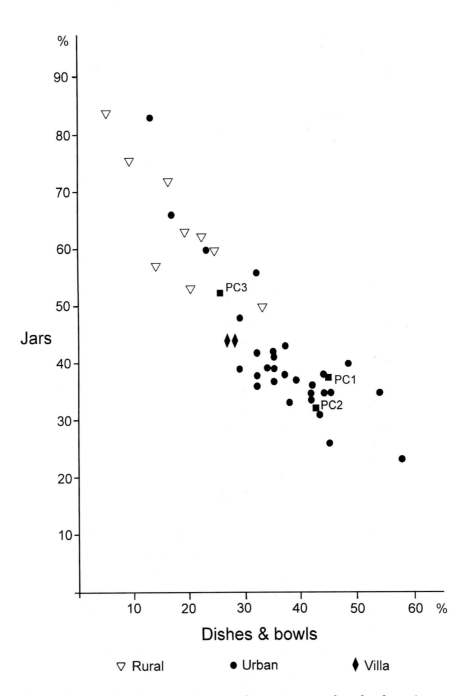

Figure 6   Proportions of jars and tablewares from south-western rural and urban sites compared with data from Plas Coch, Wrexham, phases 1–3 (PC1–PC3)

Similarly there can be no doubt about the primary use of *amphorae* and motto beakers, and it would be difficult to see what use could be made of flagons except as liquid containers.

The functional analyses of data from northern sites show both chronological trends in the composition of assemblages, as did Millett's (1979) southern towns, and consistent variations between, principally, forts and towns on the one hand and basic rural sites on the other, with villas tending to fall between the two (Evans 1993).

The functional composition of pottery from all sites (excepting *oppida* for the moment) tends to diversify from an Iron Age jar-dominated assemblage to more of a diverse one, with a higher proportion of tablewares (ie dishes and bowls) and other types. However,

this diversification takes place at different speeds, and to a greater or lesser extent on different types of site (cf Evans 1995a). Comparison of broadly contemporary data reveals consistent variations by site type.

Basic rural sites, like Iron Age ones, are usually much more jar dominated than urban or military ones. There is a clear differentiation between northern urban and rural sites of the 2nd and 3rd century on a simple plot of the percentages of jars against dishes and bowls from them (Evans 1993, fig 7). Similarly much the same pattern persists in the later 4th century (Evans 1993, fig 13), although absolute jar levels are higher on most of the sites.

As I noted earlier Allason-Jones (1988) has shown that small finds assemblages from Hadrian's Wall turrets differ markedly from those of forts,

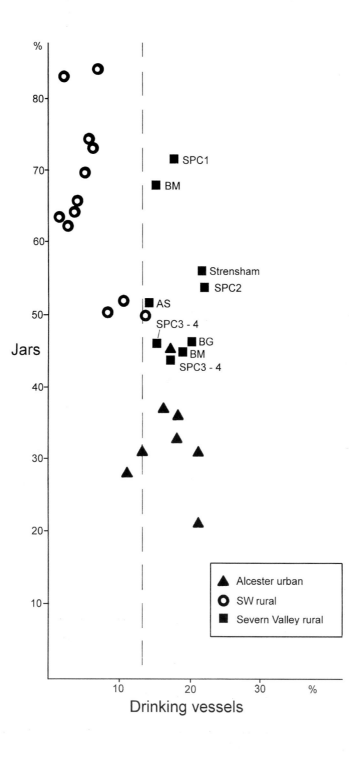

Figure 7 Proportions of jars and drinking vessels from Severn Valley rural sites, other south-western rural sites and the Alcester small town. AS = Abbots Salford, SP = Salford Priors, BM = Billesley Manor, BG = Bidford Grange

comprising only a subset of the material available, as might be expected given the much more limited functions likely to have been carried out on such sites. The function figures available from such sites show a similar contrast with military and urban sites; they look very like contemporaneous rural sites (Evans 1993, fig 6). This again probably reflects the limited range of ceramic uses employed there, ie basic food preparation and consumption.

It may well be said that we can distinguish between rural and urban sites, but so what? It seems obvious anyway; yet in fact it is not always the

case. It has, for instance, been argued that the linear settlement along the Roman road at Shiptonthorpe in East Yorkshire constituted a 'small town'. The site morphology is not so different from that of a number of sites regarded as small towns. However, a series of enclosures running alongside a Roman road is also seen along the length of the Woldgate in the Vale of Pickering, and it is difficult to argue that this is a small town stretching from Malton to Scarborough. The pottery assemblage from Shiptonthorpe is interesting, possibly suggesting its inhabitants were an intrusive group originating in Lincolnshire

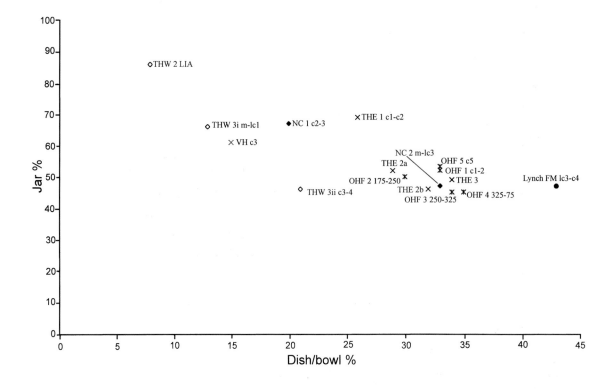

Figure 8   Proportions of jars and tablewares from various rural sites in northern Cambridgeshire. THW = Tort Hill West, VH = Vinegar Hill, NC = Normans Cross, THE = Tort Hill East, OHF = Orton Hall Farm, Lynch FM = Lynch Farm

(Evans forthcoming (c)). However, the function figures from the site clearly fall into the rural group, and the fineware and *amphorae* levels from the site, which I will discuss later, do likewise (Fig 4).

Turning to the Midlands, Figure 5 shows a fairly clear separation of urban and rural groups. There is some apparent overlap, but on more detailed examination all of the apparent exceptions can be fairly easily explained. The 1st-century Silchester group (Fulford 1984, 137) is from a peripheral site on the town defences which may have a rural nature. A similar phenomenon is seen on peripheral sites from the small town at Asthall, Oxfordshire, published by Booth (1997). The other main exceptions are the series of groups from Alchester, Oxfordshire (Fig 5; Evans forthcoming (a)). Here the A421 site is an extra-mural suburb and in Phases 3–5 really consists of a series of roadside enclosures. The site only acquires a morphology of more urban appearance in Phase 6, at exactly the point where the pottery achieves an urban-style functional composition.

An interesting assemblage in which analysis of functional patterns and finewares played a crucial role in the site's interpretation comes from Plas Coch, Wrexham. Here the small area of the site excavated was originally interpreted as a rural site of three phases (Burnham 1995a; Waite forthcoming). However, the presence of quite large quantities of ceramics on a rural site of this region appeared exceptional. The functional analysis suggested that the 1st- to 3rd-century Phases 1 and 2 from the site ought to be from an urban or military site (Fig 6), whilst the later 3rd- to early 4th-century Phase 3 group did seem to be heading towards a more rural pattern. The fineware levels from Plas Coch also suggested an urban or military site. Given the presence of a reasonably extensive coin list from the site and its vicinity the author asked Richard Reece what sort of a list he regarded it as being. Compared with his database of 140 sites Reece reported that it fitted very well into his group of strongly military sites, a pleasing confirmation of the ceramic evidence.

Although urban and basic rural sites can be distinguished in most cases through functional analyses, there are regional trends in the functional composition of assemblages, and sites should be compared with broadly contemporary ones from the same region. A notable regional identity can be observed amongst sites in the Severn Valley area where rural sites have very high levels of drinking vessels, usually tankards (Fig 7). This phenomenon does not seem to extend beyond this region, although copies of its tankards do occur in northern Warwickshire, Oxfordshire, and the north-west in small numbers. One area where the urban/rural divide may be obscured is in the Nene Valley (Fig 8). Here later 3rd- and 4th-century rural sites have very high tableware levels because the Nene Valley colour-coated ware industry, apparently uniquely in Roman Britain, produced large volumes of types previously manufactured in coarseware, eg

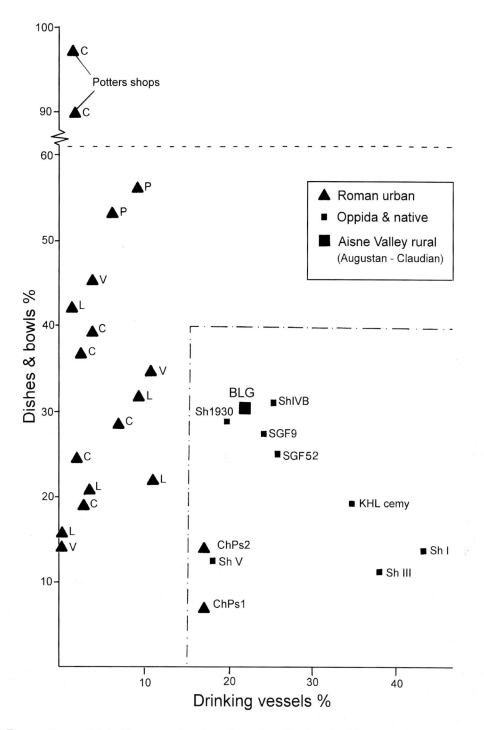

Figure 9 Proportions of drinking vessels plotted against levels of tablewares from oppida sites and Boudiccan urban deposits in the south-east. L = London, V = Verulamium, C = Colchester, Ch = Chichester, Sh = Sheepen, KHL = King Harry Lane, SG = Skeleton Green, BLG = Beaurieux les Grèves

beaded and flanged bowls. It appears to have done this at sufficiently low cost to saturate local markets and achieve very high fineware levels on rural sites (Hancocks *et al* 1996, wherein it should be noted that table 22 is erroneous). This is a complete contrast to the Oxfordshire industry, where its fineware types consistently remain a separate, and presumably higher-status, range (Evans forthcoming (a)). Unfortunately no urban data are available from the Nene Valley area to determine if urban sites produced yet higher tableware and fineware levels.

Finally, turning to *oppida*, a different pattern can be observed on a number of south-eastern sites from the jar-dominated assemblages which this author has suggested generally characterise the Iron Age. Figure 9 shows functional analyses for the King Harry Lane cemetery (Stead and Rigby 1989, table 42), several groups from Braughing (Partridge 1981) and the Sheepen excavations (Niblett 1985). It plots jars and drinking vessels alongside comparative data drawn from Martin Millett's doctoral thesis (Millett 1983), from Boudiccan groups from the

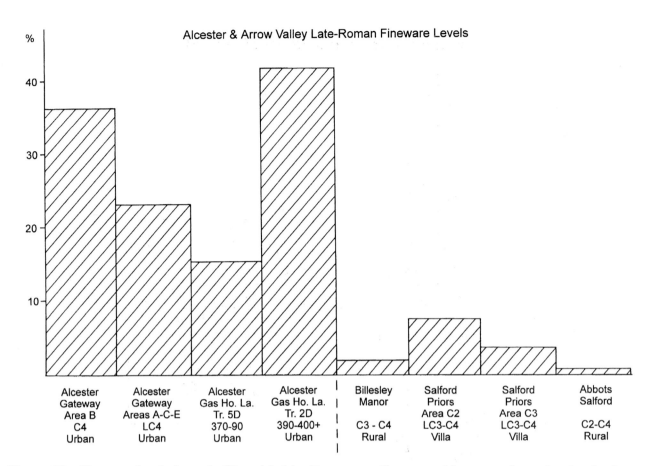

Figure 10 Fineware levels from the Warwickshire Roman small town at Alcester and nearby sites in the Arrow Valley

Roman towns at London, Verulamium and Colchester. For comparison a Gallic rural site at Beaurieux Les Gréves in the Aisne Valley is included (Willis forthcoming). As can easily be seen in terms of the levels of drinking vessels, the *oppidum* sites are much more 'Roman' than the early Romano-British urban centres, but their model of consumption, pre- and post-'conquest' is Gallo-Roman, rather than resembling the later Romano-British pattern. This is seen not just in the functional composition of the assemblages, but also in the use of Gallic imports, copies of Gallo-Roman forms, and in the use of Gallo-Roman *terra rubra* and *terra nigra* as dominant finewares, as in Gaul, rather than samian, as in Romano-British towns. Basically these south-eastern *oppida* assemblages seem to be strongly Gallo-Roman in character, something that fits in well with Creighton's re-interpretation of the deeply Romanised character of later Iron Age coinage in the Augustan and Tiberian eras (Creighton 1999; 2000; this volume).

Finewares

Turning to finewares, these are regarded for our purposes as samian ware and other colour-coated wares, plus mica-dusted wares, painted parchment wares, *terra nigra*, and very fine polished greywares such as Parisian ware. Figure 10 shows fineware levels from a series of sites in Warwickshire. Again there is a good separation between basic rural sites and urban ones, with villa sites appearing to fall between the two. Booth (1991) has also examined a series of West Midlands sites, including some in Figure 10, using a rather different formula, which includes not just samian and finewares, but also *amphorae, mortaria* and white-slipped and whiteware flagon fabrics. This again produced a very similar hierarchy of sites, from urban to rural.

The proportion of decorated samian ware also varies between urban or military and basic rural sites, as Dickinson has observed (pers comm), with urban and military sites generally having levels of over 20% of decorated ware, but basic rural sites often exhibiting much lower levels. This has been confirmed by Willis (1998) who has systematically examined a wide range of sites as part of the English Heritage samian project in the course of his assembling a quantified database of assemblages to AD 200.

There are, however, fairly frequent exceptions to this pattern in 1st-century South Gaulish samian ware. This was observed at Bryn Eryr in north Wales (Longley *et al* 1998) and at Rudston (Evans 1995a, 56) and a more general survey by Willis has shown it to be far from exceptional on rural sites (1997).

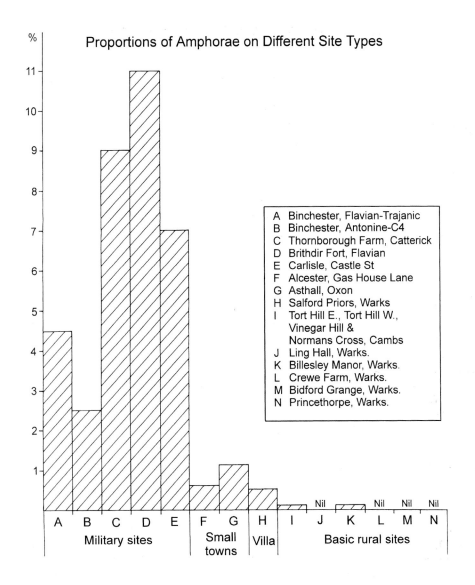

%

Proportions of Amphorae on Different Site Types

A	Binchester, Flavian-Trajanic
B	Binchester, Antonine-C4
C	Thornborough Farm, Catterick
D	Brithdir Fort, Flavian
E	Carlisle, Castle St
F	Alcester, Gas House Lane
G	Asthall, Oxon
H	Salford Priors, Warks
I	Tort Hill E., Tort Hill W., Vinegar Hill & Normans Cross, Cambs
J	Ling Hall, Warks.
K	Billesley Manor, Warks.
L	Crewe Farm, Warks.
M	Bidford Grange, Warks.
N	Princethorpe, Warks.

Military sites — Small towns — Villa — Basic rural sites

Figure 11   Proportions of amphorae (by count) from various site types

Amphorae

Levels of *amphorae* in assemblages are also very good indicators of site type, at least in the 1st to early 3rd centuries, when Dressel 20 oil *amphorae* were available in quantity. Carreras-Montfort, following Collingwood (Collingwood and Myres 1941, 242), has demonstrated that Dressel 20 stamps are commonest on military sites (Carreras-Montfort, 1994, fig 28) suggesting Dressel 20s were more frequently used there.

Quantified data from 1st- to early 3rd-century assemblages also indicates that military sites tend to have the highest levels of *amphorae* and may be distinguished from urban sites on this basis, whilst both military and urban sites can be distinguished from basic rural ones (Fig 11).

It is worth noting that these figures are all from sherd count data; weight data was not employed, because the bulk of the Dressel 20s would exaggerate the differences further, whilst rim equivalent data

would be of little use with most assemblages because of the rarity of Dressel 20 rimsherds and the 'chunkiness' problem (Orton and Tyers 1992).

Graffiti on ceramics

Over 10 years ago this author published a survey of graffiti in Roman Britain using the listings given in *Britannia*. The survey compared the number of graffiti with the number of excavations on each settlement site (Evans 1987). This indicated a hierarchy of sites in terms of the numbers of graffiti thus produced, with forts and *vici* at the top, followed by major towns, minor towns, villas, and basic rural sites.

Given the crude nature of the quantification in the 1987 paper, the author has also plotted the numbers of graffiti occurring against the assemblage size (Fig 12). These also reflect the very high incidence of

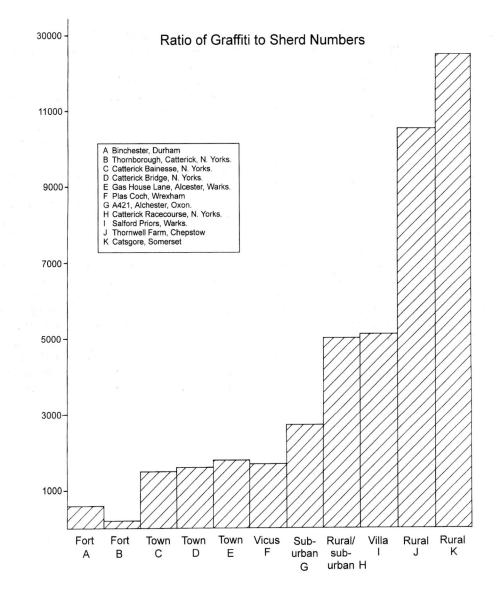

Figure 12   Numbers of sherds per graffito; data from various site types

graffiti on 1st- to 2nd-century military sites, reasonably high urban levels, and very low levels from basic rural sites.

Before concluding it should be noted that in some areas of Roman Britain some of the simplest data such as assemblage size, or even colour, can be extremely good indicators of site type. For example Flavian-Trajanic military associated assemblages in northern England and north Wales are predominantly oxidised, whereas non-military associated assemblages are predominantly grey or black. This difference is maintained at York, the major alien blot in the north, until the 3rd century, whilst the civilian greyware tradition flourished almost up to the city limits, as can be seen at Fulford, Stockton West Moor etc.

Similarly in the upper Pennines and the northwest or north Wales (and probably in much of Shropshire) sites producing more than 500 sherds are most unlikely to be of basic rural type, like Plas Coch, Wrexham.

The way forward

The author hopes to have succeeded in outlining a number of simple ceramic methods which, particularly if used together, can offer a powerful set of tools for characterising site type. In passing it might be noted that these indicators also have considerable potential in mapping variations in site type within major urban centres, such as London.

The methodological principle underlying all in this paper involves treating finds not as individual items of intrinsic interest, but as elements of an assemblage. The author believes there is still further potential in this method, in examining the patterns of co-occurrence of finds of different classes from different types of site. There are many difficulties in comparing entire finds assemblages from sites, the greatest being that they are rarely published. MAP2 (English Heritage 1991b) tends to discourage publication of classes of material deemed intrinsically uninteresting. Most publications fail to say if certain types of find were absent or merely not reported. An instructive exercise is to try and find from most Romano-British site reports how many iron nails were recovered, how much they weighed, and which phases they came from. Sometimes draft reports did include basic data but they have been expunged by over-assiduous editors before publication. Cool makes a similar point:

> It should never be forgotten that the specialist reports banished to the back of so many excavation reports, or even worse to the archive, are not so many optional extras. They are the very stuff of past lives and habits and should be treasured and used as such. (Cool 1998)

A further problem in developing assemblage-based approaches is the appallingly biased collection of sites excavated, particularly in some regions. It seems beyond much doubt that perhaps 90% of the Romano-British population lived on basic-level rural sites. As Hingley (1989, fig 2) and the author (1995b, table 3.1) have both noted basic rural sites are very poorly represented in the archaeological record. Only *c* 17% of the sites excavated between 1969 and 1988 were basic rural sites. To see if the situation had changed the author tabulated the sites explored section from *Britannia* 1995 to 1998. The results are encouraging: overall around 31% of the sites reported seem to be basic rural sites, although the results vary widely between regions. It is to be hoped that this trend will continue and that the sites will make their way into the published record and not simply be 'archived'.

A final obstacle to developing a study of finds assemblages is the abject failure to publish most urban excavations and to hide this behind the trend of producing urban synthetic volumes. Now, I have no objection to synthesis whatsoever, but most such work will age badly; it must if our discipline is moving forward because it is a statement mainly of current opinions. How many syntheses written around 1900 do we still regard as current today? We still, however, use late Victorian and Edwardian site reports – albeit regretting the lack of many data we would like. Indeed some of the data presented today are derived from reports published before 1914. Synthesis is a necessary supplement to the basic site data, but it is a poor substitute for them.

focus for the expression of social status throughout the Roman world.

Mid-Roman deposits from the General Accident Extension 83–4 site in York, also produced several bones of *Sparidae*, not as yet identified to species, but assumed to represent possible Mediterranean imports (O'Connor 1988). Similarly, the late Roman sieved fish assemblage from Thornbrough Farm, North Yorkshire (Stallibrass 1997) purportedly produced the bones of red mullet, also assumed to be of similar Mediterranean origin. These species would have been imported as cured/dried specimens or in sealed jars of oil. Even more remarkable was the identification of a Nile catfish bone (a species now extinct) from mid-Roman deposits at Dragonby, Humberside (Jones 1996), indicating long-distance links with the eastern Mediterranean. However, whether this represents a specimen which was imported and consumed at Dragonby by a high-status individual or a curio carried by travellers, is impossible to determine. Whatever its purpose, there is little doubt of its origin and its implications for long-distance trading contacts at Dragonby.

It would appear (from the somewhat limited evidence given above), therefore, that elements of higher social status were present at the *colonia* in York, the fort at South Shields, the civilian settlement at Thornbrough Farm, and the site of Dragonby.

Traditionally, discrete and concentrated deposits of small marine fish bones, whether found within the archaeological matrix or in a pottery vessel, have been interpreted as remains from the preparation of *garum*, a Roman fish sauce. *Garum*, as described by Aeschylus (525–456 BC), can be either a runny sauce or a thick paste and was manufactured from the viscera of large fishes (Cutting 1955). *Garum* was not the only type of fish sauce made and consumed during the Roman period; the classical authors described others. In point of fact, the likely sauce identified from these fish bones is *allec* (van Neer and Lentacker 1994), which contains the bones of fishes remaining when the *garum* (liquid) is removed.

Direct evidence for the importation of fish sauce into early Roman Britain is at present ambiguous. A possible example has been recovered from excavations at Winchester Palace, Southwark. Here, the remains of six heads of Spanish mackerel (a Mediterranean species) were found in a 1st-century *amphora* on which the inscription described the contents as '*liquamen*' – and the property of one Lucius Tettius Africanus from Antipolis (modern-day Antibes) (Yule 1989). However, the Spanish mackerel heads are more likely to be the remains of imported pickled/preserved fish present in a re-used container which originally contained '*liquamen*'.

Localised fishbone deposits excavated from the cities of London (Bateman and Locker 1982), York (Jones 1988), and Lincoln (Dobney *et al* 1996a) on the other hand suggest each may have been a local centre of *garum*/*allec* production during the later Roman period, since the species identified (namely clupeids and sandeels) are commonly available in the North Sea. This local production of fish sauce may have served to cater for a characteristically 'Roman' taste.

Until 1979, the black rat was generally accepted to have been a Norman introduction to England (Armitage *et al* 1984). Since that year, when Rackham published details of black rat remains from a Roman well at Skeldergate in York, pre-medieval finds of this species have proven its presence in both Roman and late Saxon England. At present in northern England, Roman deposits containing remains of black rat have been found at eight sites, the most tightly dated and reliable of these being from mid-2nd-century York (O'Connor 1988), the time when the main civilian *colonia* was established, 3rd- to 4th-century York (Carrott *et al* 1995), 3rd- to 4th-century Lincoln (Dobney *et al* 1996a) – where it appears with the remains of cockroach (another alien import) – and at the Roman fort in South Shields, Tyne and Wear (Younger 1994) where their remains are also from late Roman (late 4th-century) deposits. The presence of black rat bones indicates long-distance continental trade, the presence of 'urbanised' conditions, and also has implications for the living conditions and health of the urban population.

Although the examples outlined above are some of the most notable (and therefore rarest) examples of the accidental or deliberate importation of 'exotic' species from overseas, considerably more evidence for external contact networks in the zooarchaeological record is all too often overlooked.

Changes in height and general body conformation, inferred from measurements of archaeological bones, can provide a wealth of information regarding changing patterns of stockmanship through time. The presentation of such data can be used to address questions such as whether local improvements in husbandry practices were underway, or whether new varieties of domestic animals were introduced from further afield.

Changes in the size of cattle have been reported at a number of Roman sites in Britain and mainland Europe, mainly of late Roman date. For example, Albarella (1997) has reported distinctively large cattle from the late Roman villa of Great Holts Farm, Boreham, Essex. Dobney *et al* 1996a), have reported larger cattle in 3rd-century deposits from Lincoln (compared to 4th-century specimens from the city). From sites of Roman date located along the river system of eastern Holland, there appears to be a clear increase in the withers height of cattle from the 2nd century through to the 4th century, with taller individuals again apparent in the 3rd century (Lauwerier 1988, 169). The 4th-century individuals from Lincoln fall within the range of those reported at Nijmegen, but do not include those larger individuals some 200–300mm taller reported by Lauwerier, whereas a large proportion of those from the villa in Essex do. At these sites, and others, it has been suggested that an introduction of a larger, improved variety of livestock occurred in the 3rd century AD, and interbreeding between these larger individuals and the indigenous varieties may have resulted in a small size decrease by the 4th century.

A recent survey of the evidence from other sites in the north of England (Dobney forthcoming), show that there are a number which also show the possible presence of large individuals (Table 1). Unlike the pattern previously described, of a possible 3rd-century phenomenon largely restricted to the south of the country, these examples appear to occur during the early, mid- and late Roman periods, from the far north-west and the north-east, as well as the far south-east of the region.

However, one of the basic problems of interpretation is just what is being defined as 'large' in many of these reports. Some of the records of bones from the sites in question provide little or no details of measurement values or, when they do, provide only mean values for pooled datasets. Also, when considering relative size, descriptions of 'a few large individuals' may simply reflect the difference between larger robust bulls and smaller gracile castrates and cows of the same variety. Thus, the semi-subjective presentation of size change provides little in the way of useful comparative data between sites and cannot easily be used to explore the dynamics of stock development and introduction in the Roman period unless actual biometrical data is compared, ie values for individual measurements. Only then can we realistically confirm or reject theories regarding the importation of livestock and see if they are isolated to a few high status centres at particular periods with links abroad (as seems the case on the current evidence), or whether they are more regional or even national phenomena.

'Oiling the wheels of industry': evidence for the utilisation of animal fats

One particular characteristic of Roman vertebrate assemblages from many sites in England and northern Europe is evidence for the systematic butchery of cattle bones. There appears to be no distinctive pattern to its occurrence, being found in deposits of early through to late Roman date, and from both military and civilian settlements. This, however, may be too simplistic a conclusion since it is clearly difficult to separate military and civilian influences on these practices purely on the basis of the location of dumps of noxious waste. It may be that all these assemblages have their origins within the military machine (or may have been organised by it), and that rubbish deposits located within the confines of the civilian parts of the settlement (*vicus* or *colonia*) may be purely a matter of convenience of disposal. However, the general uniformity, scale, and systematic nature of carcass reduction found at many sites does provide much information regarding the nature, scale, and possible craft and industrial activities of the inhabitants at these sites.

It is clear that the practice is specifically a 'Roman' one and must have originated in the supply and provisioning of the military. Numerous early Roman examples have been identified, mostly associated with military and urban sites. An interesting early Roman example from a civilian *vicus* has been described from various excavations at The Lanes, Carlisle (Stallibrass 1993a; 1993b; 1996; Connell

Table 1   Sites in the north of England showing possible evidence for larger (non-native?) cattle varieties

Site	County	Type	Notes
1st–2nd century			
The Lanes 81–82 AML 96/93	Cumbria	Civilian	A few large individuals
Watercrook 74–5	Cumbria	Fort	A few large individuals
Blake St (9) 75 AML 196/87	N. Yorkshire	Fort	A few large individuals
Market Place Darlington DEAR 15/95	Durham	Urban	Mostly large individuals
2nd–3rd century			
Chesters Bridge DEAR 9/93	Northumberland	Barracks	A few long-horned individuals
General Accident Ext 83–4 (bones)	N Yorkshire	Colonia	A few large individuals
Watercrook 74–5	Cumbria	Fort	A few large individuals
Corstopitum (compared with Catcote)	Northumberland	Other military	Wide size variation
3rd–4th century			
Chesters Bridge DEAR 9/93	Northumberland	Barracks	A few long-horned individuals
Church Chare 90–1	Durham	Fort	A few large individuals
Church Chare 90–1	Durham	Fort	A few long-horned individuals
Spedding Head (Inglewood Forest)	Cumbria	Native	Mostly large individuals
1701Thornbrough Farm	N Yorkshire	Civilian	A few large individuals
Vindolanda 67–9	Northumberland	Fort	A few long-horned individuals

and Davis unpublished), although it cannot be proven that these remains do not represent waste disposed from the adjacent military fort.

At numerous sites (not all), butchery is characterised by systematic chopping of all major elements and the splitting of most long bones. Unfortunately, because of the variety of ways butchery has been recorded by various workers – some in detail, others merely in passing references – subtle differences which may exist between assemblages cannot, as yet, be detailed.

The fact that cattle and beef were obviously of paramount importance not only to the Roman military, but also to the residents of a great many of the emerging urban centres, has already been discussed. However, the exceptionally interesting question about the butchery occurring on many of their remains is: just why was it so extensive? A number of interpretations have been offered for this phenomenon. Traditionally it has been concluded that these remains represent a single activity, whereby meat was removed from the carcass, the remaining bones being smashed into smaller, more manageable pieces to be boiled in large cauldrons for the production of a number of bone by-products.

Van Mensch (1974, 163) has suggested that the heavily butchered assemblage from Zwammerdam, in the Netherlands, represents the waste from Roman 'soup kitchens'. Although there is little evidence to support this assumption, similar interpretations have been made for other assemblages from Britain. More recently, this interpretation has been re-evaluated in the light of further published evidence (Stokes 2000; Dobney et al 1996a; Stallibrass 1993a; 1993b; 1996). It is now thought that, after the reduction of the cattle carcass into smaller joints and the filleting of meat from the bones, systematic breakage of long bones was undertaken in order to extract marrow and marrow fat. This occurred on a large scale and was perhaps undertaken by tradespeople separate from the butchers, although the evidence for this is difficult to disentangle from large waste dumps, which can include the remains of a whole host of different activities. However, evidence from the late 4th-century Waterfront assemblage in Lincoln suggests that a range of different specialist activities is represented, mainly focused on the production of marrow-fat, undertaken possibly by separate craftsmen who were, in turn, responsible for a variety of animal products.

Recent evidence from several sites from the north of England has provided further tantalising evidence for the presence of more specialised trades linked with the production of animal fats. The systematic butchery outlined above has already highlighted the presence of a seemingly large-scale focus towards marrow-fat extraction from long bones, probably an everyday requirement of the inhabitants of settlements, both in the diet and for other less obvious uses. However, several assemblages have also produced cattle long-bones with evidence of both systematic burning and breakage. These burnt and broken areas are usually extremely localised on the bones and certainly do not appear to have a random distribution (Stallibrass 1991; Carrott et al 1994; Carrott et al 1995; Dobney et al 1996a). It may be the case that they have been present in other smaller assemblages, but have either not been recognised or not recorded since their significance has not been appreciated. It is perhaps more than a coincidence that all the examples of burnt mandibles have been noted by the present author.

It is difficult to determine what specific activity these burnt and broken mandibles and long-bones reflect. It is clear that the heating and burning of fresh bone renders it more brittle and easier to break, and the region of the diastema in the mandible, and the midshaft of long-bones is perhaps the weakest part of the element (P Stokes pers comm). But why was it necessary? The mandible corpus and shafts of major long-bones contain marrow, which is rendered liquid by heating the bone, and once the bone is broken, the liquid marrow can easily be poured out. In the case of mandibles, this would seem a substantial effort to recover what is after all a small quantity of marrow, when obviously larger quantities would have been available from the major limb bones. It is also interesting to note that at all these sites specific skeletal elements are affected to the exclusion of others.

All this evidence strongly implies that a separate specialist activity, involving a very specific product, is represented. Liquid mandibular marrow-fat may have been used to provide lamp oil, or as a base for cosmetics, soap or medicines, being produced and utilised by particular tradespeople or artisans. Alternatively, it may purely reflect a socio-economic difference within the marrow-fat extraction trade; for example, perhaps jaws were cheaper to obtain than the prime marrow-bones, and were all that could be afforded by poorer tradespeople for processing essentially the same final product. Whatever the reason, it is clear that utilisation of cattle products was undertaken on a large scale at many sites. It was highly organised, generally uniform and probably involved a whole range of economic activities.

'Off the bone': Evidence for the curing of meat

The presence of high proportions of cattle shoulder blades (scapulae) showing characteristic damage to the centre of the blade, and sometimes butchery around the joint region (glenoid cavity), also appears to be characteristic of numerous British and northern European Roman sites. These have been noted at a number of sites in the north of England (Table 2) and beyond (eg from other sites in southern and central England, as well as from the Low Countries and Switzerland). Once again there appears to be no particular pattern to their distribution, either in terms of period or site type. They show butchery which probably indicates curing (either by smoking

Table 2   Sites in the north of England where cattle scapulae showing 'hook damage' have been recovered

Site	Date	County	Type
The Lanes (2) 78–82	1st–2nd century	Cumbria	Civilian
The Lanes 81–82	1st–2nd century	Cumbria	Civilian
Hayton Fort 75	1st–2nd century	Humberside	Fort
Blake St (9) 75	1st–2nd century	N Yorkshire	Fort
Ribchester	1st–2nd century	Lancashire	Fort
Papcastle 84	1st–2nd century	Cumbria	Vicus
General Accident Ext 83–4	2nd–3rd century	N Yorkshire	Colonia
The Lanes 81–82	2nd–3rd century	Cumbria	Civilian
Blake St (9) 75	2nd–3rd century	N Yorkshire	Fort
The Lanes (2) 78–82	2nd–3rd century	Cumbria	Civilian
Birdoswald	3rd–4th century	Northumberland	Fort

and/or brining), and damage to the blade which is consistent with hanging the joints, possibly in a smoker and/or brine vat.

Detailed recording of 1st- and 4th-century butchery from *scapulae* recovered from the city of Lincoln showed diverse practices, consistent with different methods of curing. Those from the 1st century showed trimmed glenoid cavities and chopped *spinae*, probably representing 'brined' and cold-smoked joints, the trimming allowing access for the salt into the meat on the bone (this kind of curing, if carried out correctly, allows long-term preservation and storage of the meat). Some of the *scapulae* from the 1st-century levels showed the glenoid cavity to have been completely removed. This would seem a wasteful exercise, although if beef was plentiful there may not have been such a premium on its sale and consumption.

On the other hand, *scapulae* from the 4th-century waterfront dumps showed little or no evidence of trimming of the glenoid cavity or *spina*. This could suggest that the meat may have been utilised fresh, straight from the bone or, more likely, was hot-smoked without immersion in brine (this provides meat with a shorter 'shelf-life' than 'brining' and cold-smoking: Dobney *et al* 1996a). Small 'nicks' or 'shaving' marks are also often noticeable on the *margo thoracalis*, the shaving and 'nick' marks representing the slicing of the final stubborn, somewhat dried, pieces of meat (Lauwerier 1988, 156). This suggests that the cured meat was most certainly sold 'off the bone' from either specialist traders or butchers, and that whole *scapulae* can probably be interpreted as shop- or vendors'-waste, left when meat was cut from the bone (delicatessen-style).

'When the boat comes in': evidence for fisheries exploitation

From the available evidence, a tradition of fish eating and exploitation does not appear to have been part of the native Iron Age Celtic culture in Britain prior to the arrival of Romans and Roman culture. However, the place of fish in the Mediterranean Roman diet was far less limited in its extent. It is, therefore, surprising that assemblages of fish recovered from most Roman sites in Britain continue to show a somewhat limited number and range of species caught and eaten during this period.

Our understanding of the true picture is, unfortunately, limited by the small number of sieved Roman assemblages, and also biased by the fact that most are from large urban or military centres. Care is also needed before straightforward dietary assumptions are made regarding mere presence of species in an assemblage. For example, sieved samples from the late Roman Waterfront at Lincoln produced a number of the smaller freshwater species (particularly the cyprinids). These have been interpreted not as remains of human consumption and exploitation, but as natural death assemblages associated with periodic stranding due to flooding (Dobney *et al* 1996a).

In general, most of the Roman fishbone assemblages so far studied are more similar in nature to those from early and middle Saxon sites than to those of Iron Age date. In the case of Roman and Saxon sites, most species present are either freshwater ones, indicative of lowland, slow-moving and well oxygenated river systems, or estuarine/marine taxa which would have easily been caught inshore. Although a few gadid (cod family) species are also represented, these are present in very low numbers and were almost certainly caught near to shore rather than in deeper waters. Thus a limited, somewhat opportunistic and rather low-key, exploitation of the well-stocked and ostensibly clean rivers of the region appears to be the case, certainly for the 3rd and 4th centuries and probably before. A similar 'low-key' emphasis can be postulated for both estuarine and coastal fisheries.

Differences in the importance of fish between the

Iron Age and Roman periods could suggest that the Roman taste for fish may never have been completely fulfilled in northern Europe because of the absence of a fishing tradition amongst the native population. However, the lack of sieved early and mid-Roman assemblages means that more emphasis need be placed on discovering whether this was a normal pattern over 400 years of Roman rule, or whether even this level of exploitation developed/changed through time. Comparisons between sites, particularly outlying villas and urban centres, will provide further detail regarding possible socio-economic differences in fish exploitation. On the basis of the available evidence, there appears to be almost no clear 'Roman' influence on fish consumption in the north of England (or Britain for that matter), although at some sites it was clearly more important than in the preceding Iron Age.

'Let us pray': Zooarchaeological evidence for ritual and ceremony

The remains of domestic fowl (in addition to pig and some other birds) are not uncommon finds from graves dated to the Roman period, both from Britain and mainland Europe, and are usually thought to represent food offerings for the deceased (Lauwerier 1983; 1988; 1994; Philpott 1991). Often both the head and the meatless portions of the lower legs have been removed (some are even arranged in bowls or on platters), strengthening the assumption that they do indeed represent food offerings. Interestingly, however, only the lower legs and feet of a chicken were present in an example from Saltersford, North Lincolnshire, whilst the major meat-bearing elements, ie upper wings and legs, are wholly absent (Dobney and Jaques 1994). If this particular case represents a food offering to the dead, it may well be either a symbolic offering or all that remains of a ritual funerary meal carried out prior to burial.

Other food offerings, which have left no physical trace, may also have been originally placed in the grave. For example, Lauwerier (1994) points out that recipes using beef may have often involved filleted joints (unlike chicken where meat is usually left on the bone) and as a result would not have survived in the archaeological record.

Previous research on food offerings from Roman graves has attempted to show a correlation between certain categories of offering and the sex of the deceased. The results of this work apparently indicate that chickens are usually associated with female burials (Martin-Kilcher 1976; Wahl and Kokabi 1987; 1988). However, a more recent re-evaluation of the data on which these assumptions were based suggests that little or no real association exists between the sex of the individual and the category of food offering (Lauwerier 1994).

The common practice of placing what are interpreted as food offerings in the graves of the deceased is also a common feature of the Iron Age. Some notable examples from Iron Age cemeteries excavated in the north of England include sites such as Burton Fleming, Rudston, and Kirkburn in Humberside (Legge 1991), where all the material has been described as poorly preserved and severely eroded. Here, vertebrate remains interpreted as food offerings included joints and heads primarily of sheep and pigs, many of the latter showing signs of defleshing where the meat had already been removed from the head prior to deposition. Whether this means that the meat was offered separately in the grave (and has left no trace), that it was consumed during the funerary rites by the living, or that the presence of a defleshed skull is merely a symbolic representation of food for the afterworld, is impossible to establish.

Another well-known phenomenon from the Iron Age and Romano-British periods in England is the presence of articulated and semi-articulated domestic animal remains, usually recovered from pits. A number of researchers have discussed the possible significance of these remains to past societies, and the current consensus is that they represent forms of ritual/religious activity in the past. Grant (1984), in her detailed analysis of many such deposits from the Iron Age site of Danebury, discussed a tentative hierarchy of ritual activities on the basis of different species and different skeletal elements.

There are many other reasons why whole animals or articulated limbs may have been disposed of in such a way (eg spoilt joints of meat, or mortalities due to disease or accident) and it is frequently the case in archaeology that unexplained evidence is often given ritual explanation. There is a real danger therefore that skeletons and part-skeletons recovered from Iron Age and Roman deposits will always be primarily associated with ritual, whilst those from medieval deposits, for example, may be interpreted in a more functional way. The work of Grant (1984), however, indicated that ritualistic evidence can be gleaned from vertebrate remains and that the frequency and distribution of these so-called 'special deposits' paint a complex picture. For example, in the north of England, Iron Age and Roman pits at Garton Slack contained a large proportion of the skeletons of cattle (primarily calves), sheep, goat, and pig (Noddle 1979), whilst the disarticulated food remains were primarily recovered from ditches.

At Thorpe Thewles, it is interesting to note that 'special deposits' were only present in mid-Iron Age deposits and not in later Iron Age ones. These include the part-skeletons of several sheep and goats, as well as three horse skulls. Recent excavations at Garforth, West Yorkshire have uncovered further possible evidence of Romano-British ritual activities. Here, the species involved included a near-complete lap-dog (excluding the skull), a juvenile pig, a partial goat skeleton and a partial raven skeleton (Jaques 2000). From Romano-British deposits at Hayton, East Yorkshire, came a range of complete and semi-articulated animal remains, along with numerous infant human inhumations (Jaques pers comm).

At Creyke Beck, North Yorkshire, a complete cattle skull was recovered; the actual skull vault and horns had been removed. This may simply have been for access to the brain or, alternatively, may represent ritual activity (Gidney 1998). At Easingwold, North Yorkshire, although vertebrate remains were rare – a result of adverse soil chemistry – associated isolated horse teeth from single individuals were recovered from within roundhouse ditches. These could indicate the original presence of ritually positioned skulls within the buildings (Carrott *et al* 1993).

The presence of isolated skulls, particularly of horses, is also a phenomenon recorded at other Iron Age and Romano-British sites in England. For example, Dobney and Jaques (1996) described several horse skulls and associated post-cranial elements apparently deliberately placed outside a roundhouse at the Romano-British site of Wavendon Gate, Milton Keynes. At this site, skeletons of horse and sheep were present, as well as articulated limbs of various domestic species. Definitive evidence of ritual activity at this site came in the form of some quite unique evidence. In a waterlogged depression at the centre of the site, a unique wooden wheel-shaped object (the so-called solar or 'Taranis' wheel) was recovered. In an immediately adjacent posthole, the remains of a cockerel (the bones of which showed evidence of defleshing) were placed beneath an ovoid jar (Williams *et al* 1996, 68–9).

There is indeed a long-way to go before we can begin to understand complex ritual and symbolic behaviour as evidenced by the burial or placement of part and whole skeletons within pits, buildings, or ditches. Evidence for their significance, specifically in the Iron Age and Roman periods, is somewhat compelling and their presence in the north of England generally reflects the pattern for the rest of the country. Only by careful evaluation of all lines of evidence (including context type, associated finds, etc) can this question be more fully explored.

The apparent continuation of both these customs from the Iron Age into the Roman period appears to indicate that food offerings in graves, and the ritual inhumation of part or whole animals, are perhaps 'Celtic traditions', which survived the influence of 'Roman' acculturation and later become incorporated into the Roman 'ways of life and death'. It could be argued that the characteristic infant inhumations regularly encountered on numerous Roman occupation sites were a mere extension of, or were primarily influenced by, earlier Celtic rituals associated with animal burials described above.

'The end of an era': late Roman decline and fall

Views of the late Roman period in England have changed considerably in the past few years, with a tendency towards acceptance of a survival or resurgence of economic and political organisation despite earlier decline. Although traditional evidence provides some insights into the differential nature of these changes, the use of vertebrate remains as a tool in identifying economic, political, and social changes has long been ignored.

Archaeological research in recent years, indicates that in the early 3rd-century changing economic circumstances in the Roman empire caused a check in the growth of towns in Britain (Millett 1990a, 134–7) and a decline in manufacturing activity and interprovincial trade. After the early 3rd century, construction of public buildings declined and a reduction in the area settled, especially in London, is indicated by the accumulation of material, often referred to as 'dark earth', over earlier buildings (Ottaway 1993, 112–17; Yule 1990).

The currently accepted view is that the later 3rd century, and much of the 4th, was a time of prosperity in Roman Britain, but that the role of towns at this time is thought to have been primarily related to the administrative, political, and ceremonial functions of the Roman state. Towards the end of the 4th century, however, change in the urban order, traditionally linked to economic recession (Esmonde Cleary 1989, 130–4), supposedly manifested itself in declining populations and poorer standards of maintenance of public facilities.

Although there is now an element of consensus concerning the broad outlines of urban development in late Roman Britain, there are many aspects that are poorly understood. In particular, one might ask, did change in the early 3rd century affect the various components of the urban economy equally? Secondly, how quickly did the urban economy collapse in the late 4th century? Did the process begin in the mid-4th century or only in the last decade or so? In considering these problems, it is necessary to allow not only for differences between towns, but for a different picture to emerge from different categories of evidence, reflecting asynchronous decline in various economic activities and processes.

Moving away from the urban centres, similar questions can be asked. Are these possible patterns outlined above reflected in rural civilian and military sites? Does the army still remain in control or play a part in the provisioning of large urban and military centres?

The nature and conformation of the numerous vertebrate assemblages recovered from a range of settlement classes of late and sub-Roman date can be used to investigate a range of socio-economic processes which represent aspects of life not illuminated by structural and artefactual evidence. A number of the general characteristics of vertebrate assemblages, already outlined above, can be used to present new evidence for understanding economy and society in the late Roman period.

A variety of characteristics of the 4th-century Roman faunal (vertebrate and invertebrate) assemblages recovered from the Waterfront excavations in

Lincoln were outlined in a recent paper (Dobney *et al* 1998). In this paper, it is argued that large dumps mainly of cattle bones share many explicitly 'Roman' characteristics with numerous other Roman sites (of all ages) in Britain and mainland Europe (Lauwerier 1988; Levitan 1989; Maltby 1984; O'Connor 1988). The sheer scale of the dumps (and their apparent tight dating) is taken by the authors to imply that the population of Lincoln at this stage must have been of considerable size, and that a considerable degree of social organisation of at least some aspects of victualling, was in place.

This immediately leads one to address the problem of just how significant the 3rd-century changes in the urban economy really were. In common with Lincoln, the large 4th-century vertebrate assemblage from the fortress ditches at Piercebridge (Gidney and Rackham unpubl) were similar in general character to those from late 4th-century Lincoln. Similar patterns were also present at the northern forts of Birdoswald (Izard 1998), Housesteads (Grove 1988), and Vindolanda (Hodgson 1970; 1976; 1977), as well as at the civilian settlements of Carlisle (Rackham *et al* 1991) and Catterick (Meddens 1990). Most are indistinguishable in character from their early military and civilian counterparts.

In York, this picture is perhaps supported by evidence from the mid- to late Roman vertebrate assemblage from Tanner Row (O'Connor 1988), the 4th-century fill of the Skeldergate Roman well at York (Hall *et al* 1980), and a large group of as yet unstudied animal bone dated to after *c* 360 from the Wellington Row site situated within the *colonia* of York (Carrott *et al* 1995).

In a uniquely late Roman military context, bioarchaeological data from the signal station at Carr Naze, Filey, North Yorkshire (Dobney *et al* 1996b) has provided clear evidence of an efficient economic system at work at a site occupied in the last two decades of the 4th century. The signal station is one of a group of five situated along the east coast of Yorkshire. which are believed to have been constructed in an attempt to strengthen the coastal defences, possibly against invasions or raids from the sea. Bioarchaeological evidence from Carr Naze, Filey provided a detailed insight into the basic economic dynamics of the occupants, important information regarding the sequence of occupation and final abandonment, as well as some useful palaeoecological data concerning the environs of the site during the late Roman period.

There is no doubt that the vertebrate remains from Filey (ie the main domestic mammals – particularly pigs) provide indisputable evidence that the site received the vast bulk of its dietary provisions through organised victualling (this on the basis of the distribution of certain skeletal elements skewed in favour of meat bearing elements and away from primary butchers waste – in the form of heads and feet). Typically for the Roman period, there is little evidence to suggest any more than small-scale exploitation of wild resources, particularly wild

birds, fish, and edible shellfish. This phenomenon has great significance for this particular assemblage, given the immediate proximity of the site to the coast and what must have been readily available sources of all of these commodities. This observation not only lends strong credence to the provisioning hypothesis, but also indicates that many of the characteristic elements of a 'Roman' diet (see above) were present in this isolated East Yorkshire military outpost as late as the end of the 4th century.

Although several other late Roman signal stations existed along this particular coastline, the other excavated examples (Kitson-Clark 1935) were dug at a time when the recovery and study of bones and other bioarchaeological remains was not routinely undertaken. As a result, no comparative data exist. In terms of understanding the wider political, social, and economic significance of these late Roman coastal defences, the material from Filey, although standing in splendid isolation, can be used as a bench-mark for the others. It is reasonable to assume that contemporaneous sites, of ostensibly similar function and in such close proximity to one another, would all have been centrally controlled, administered and provisioned by a well-organised political body. The evidence from Filey indicates that this centralised administrative network still possessed much of the 'cultural baggage' of the Roman tradition as late as the very end of the 4th century.

Data from the signal station and elsewhere support the idea that, at least in some areas of the country, major Roman towns (such as Lincoln, York, Carlisle, and Catterick), and the hinterlands which they controlled, not only continued to flourish well into the late 4th century, but also maintained many of the economic, administrative, and political mechanisms of earlier Roman society. It is tantalising to suggest, on the basis of the vertebrate evidence from many Roman sites in the North of England, that the late 4th century was not, as traditionally thought, a time of gradual decline and decay of the 'Romanising' influence, but was instead a period in which society flourished prior to a rapid decline. The available evidence suggests that at least some aspects of the economic and social organisation of 'the Roman north' remained unaltered by the changes of the 3rd century and persisted until late into the 4th century (Dobney *et al* 1998). Whether a high level of organisation was the norm, or whether there was local variation between and even within towns is still very much open to debate.

How useful are Research Agendas?

Over the last two decades, the study of bioarchaeology has undoubtedly gone a long way in contributing to our wider understanding and interpretation of the Roman period in Britain. It is hoped that this paper has demonstrated that the breadth and depth of this contribution can be much wider than perhaps many have appreciated. This is particularly true when considerations turn towards the formulation of research frameworks for the period.

Over the past fifteen years, various attempts have been made in England to produce research agendas designed to provide academic goals for archaeological work. These have been produced by a diverse range of period, monument, and material 'interest groups', all of which have their specific biases. Successive framework documents and research agendas produced by English Heritage have sought to further the development of broad regional and national priorities for research. Although these have been constructive exercises, there are a number of obvious drawbacks to their implementation.

Firstly, within developer funded archaeology in England today, it is an unfortunate fact that realising the research potential of archaeological projects is very much a secondary consideration. Their main objective is simply to recover and record any remains to satisfy planning conditions. Any post-excavation analysis is usually limited to the basic and partial identification and presentation of data. Although this is designed to allow an assessment of the importance of remains, leading to further research-led analysis, in reality, financial constraints and pressure from developers often limits the opportunity to draw out the full research value from the generally small-scale archaeological intervention of the planning process.

Secondly, there are also problems inherent in the production of national research agendas in that a 'corporate' view is projected which may give the impression of universal acceptance of the priorities expressed. There are always bound to be academic differences of opinion with regard to the importance of specific research questions and how they are addressed, and also how they are integrated. Nevertheless, national archaeological research objectives provide a useful focus for debate.

Finally, recent years have also seen the emergence of assessments of the character and extent of archaeological work within the 'regions' of England, with a view to providing regional research priorities which can then feed in to the formulation of wider national research objectives for archaeology. Although this is certainly an important step forward, research agendas for certain periods and types of archaeological data are still under-represented. In the case of bioarchaeological remains, regional reviews of specific types of biological material have been (and are being) produced under the auspices of English Heritage (eg Huntley and Stallibrass 1996; Dobney in prep; Albarella in prep). However, both their individual and integrated research value to the wider archaeological world is still largely underestimated.

Conclusions

Although the study of bioarchaeology in the Roman period has undoubtedly gained its place at the table, it is still viewed by many as an entrée or merely an after dinner mint. We need to move beyond merely considering the disparate lines of archaeological evidence as separate ingredients or courses, and instead adopt a *cordon bleu* mentality, where all the different ingredients work together to form part of a richer and more highly flavoured dish.

6 Rural society in Roman Britain *by Jeremy Taylor*

I take as a starting point for this paper the intention to help characterise some key issues for study in the rural social history of Roman Britain. In the space available I do not wish to dwell in great detail on past perspectives but rather to look at how we can conceptualise the study of rural society in Roman Britain and suggest some areas in which we can put these ideas into practice.

The distinction made here between urban and rural is of course somewhat arbitrary (cf Woolf 1998, 143 for this point in Gaul). On reflection, however, it is worth separately emphasising rural or agrarian aspects of society during the Roman period for two reasons. Firstly, studies of change in Britain during the Roman period have long emphasised those spheres of social activity popular with students of the heart of the Classical world, in particular the economy, towns, the army, and to some extent religious belief, to the detriment of our understanding of agrarian communities. Long noted, this bias has frequently been commented upon (eg Jones and Miles 1979; Miles 1989; Hingley 1989; 1991; Reece 1988), but the response for many years seems largely to have been to focus on the collection of an impressive array of information within something of a conceptual vacuum. Where research aims have been made explicit they have tended to recapitulate a perspective of Roman Britain developed during the early 20th century and which has recently been the subject of much critical debate (eg Hingley 1991, 2000; Freeman 1993; Barrett 1997b; Grahame 1998).

Secondly, if we look at Britain as a whole, shortly before and during the conquest period there is little evidence that the varied communities of the island were anything other than predominantly or solely rurally based. Much recent discussion has surrounded our limited understanding of the significance and genesis of complex sites, predominantly in the south of England, often termed *oppida* (Woolf 1993; Hill 1995; 1999; Armit *et al* 2000 section F2.3), but there is little doubt that compared to many parts of the western empire, social life was orchestrated through rurally-based social networks, which expressed social relations through a range of material resources placed in a variety of important rural or religious contexts. For this reason alone it can be suggested that the study of rural society, and social practice in particular, is of especial significance to understanding the history of the province.

Before addressing this issue, however, it is useful first to provide some broader context to the discussion. The last fifteen years have seen a number of important shifts in position in the way archaeologists of Roman Britain view the complex series of interactions that were consequent upon the partial conquest of the island that we tend to discuss under the umbrella of Romanisation. It is not my intention here to rehearse those arguments, as there are numerous recent published accounts on the subject (Blagg and Millett 1990; Freeman 1993; 1997b; Mattingly 1997; Metzler *et al* 1995; Millett 1990a; Webster & Cooper 1996; Woolf 1992). For the purposes of this paper, however, it is important to distil from this debate several key points where issues relating to rural social development lie at the heart of broader debates about the Roman period.

At its core lies a concern for the nature of Roman society and the impact of Roman hegemony on the province of Britannia, as an understanding of what we mean by the term is the key to investigating relations between the peoples of the empire. This debate has lead to many publications on the subject that largely criticise the historiographical tradition of Romano-British archaeology and its attendant approaches to interpretation (eg Hingley 1991; Webster and Cooper 1996; Mattingly 1997). Approaches up to the early 1990s have sometimes been characterised as two sides of essentially a single debate in which Romanisation took place through either an 'interventionist' (eg Frere 1987) or 'non-interventionist' (eg Millett 1990a) stance on the part of Roman elites (Grahame 1998, 1–2).

A problematic issue with both sides of this debate is that in essence they leave out the question of what it was to be Roman, a point made by Freeman as long ago as 1991 (Freeman 1991, 104). Millett (1990) developed the debate significantly in recognising the variability of social conditions encountered by the Romans. In maintaining that Rome administered the province through native elites he provided the possibility for the creation of varied social histories under the empire. Unfortunately, the thesis then failed to develop further the possible implications of this by locating subsequent change largely in relation to acculturation and emulation of a set of Roman norms. This is perhaps best illustrated by considering table 4.3 in the *Romanization of Britain* (Millet 1990a, 100) in which models of Roman impact are seen to lead to success or failure to Romanise dependent on the nature of pre-Roman Iron Age society but without incorporating variability in subsequent Roman practice.

Earlier perspectives have been criticised for their normative approach to the complex social interactions that were attendant upon the incorporation of Britain within the Roman empire. It has been suggested that these developments, conventionally termed Romanisation, cannot be considered a purely acculturative process (Webster 1995b; 1996a) as this requires us to assume that to be Roman was to be part of a unified experiential whole, something which the recent literature on discrepant experiences both outside and inside archaeology seriously calls into question (Said 1993; Mattingly 1997). The tendency, as noted by Grahame (1998, 6) is that social relations in Roman Britain are 'conceived of as the articulation of Roman governmental institutions with native British social structure and not as the constitution of relations between people'. The danger is that this 'institution' is turned into an unchanging, unified, monolithic whole against which change or the lack of it is measured. To become Roman in this framework is to approximate to this single view of the world; not to do so is to resist, be conservative or 'native'.

Though archaeologists of the province have clearly had different visions of what constituted being Roman in Britain (cf Millett or Hingley in comparison with Salway, Potter or Frere), they have tended to centre implicitly on a loose amalgam of ideas based upon classical historical referents largely from the centre or the east of the empire. In doing so there is the potential to produce a somewhat ahistorical view of Roman identity and attitudes. Within such a framework it is frequently possible to explain particular social arrangements as being simply analogous to those better documented elsewhere, often without recourse to definition of why that should necessarily be the case. Furthermore, in Romano-British archaeology, this has lead to a tendency to read the presence of particular forms of material culture as a direct reflection of 'Roman-ness' or as a necessary corollary of certain social or economic institutions. This approach fails to address the ontological status of material culture in which recent reassessments have suggested that it is not an appendage of society but rather integral to it. Instead of looking for social processes (such as Romanisation) that created the material world, we study the ways in which it was inhabited.

This approach is based on structuration theory and maintains that society is constantly created and reproduced through the actions of human agents, who are themselves constrained by behaviours learnt and understood within that society. Thus, it is not an archaeology of material change based around a native-Roman dichotomy but rather one of ongoing social discourse that emphasises diversity and the continual reworking of social relations and identities through the material world. The material culture that constitutes our evidence is not undergoing change, rather the people who were using it. Thus, for a community to undergo social change under Roman influence, is not merely to have the appropriate material culture but to know how to act with it in an appropriate manner. If they do not then they are in effect engaging in a different social discourse. Different people were of course differently empowered and thus certain discourses were far more extensive and lasting, but these were always vulnerable and always changing. This viewpoint, neatly summarised by Ingold (1992; 1993; 1995) and Barrett (1994;

1997a; 1997b) and influenced by Giddens (1979; 1984) maintains that it is

> the extensive and long-term commitment to certain assumptions and their effective applicability to the conditions of the time, that gives social life its grand temporal and spatial scales of institutionalised form. The 'edges' of social institutions mark those places in time and space where those assumptions about the order of the world no longer held good, became ineffective, incomprehensible, or simply unliveable. (Barrett 1997a, 3)

Such issues are clearly very important as they lie at the heart of questions about how the Roman empire worked. Did, for example, the incorporation of a group lead to the development or dominance of particular social institutions, ideas and practices over large sections of society or areas of the province? Were new, different traditions adopted, or rejected as existing indigenous practices continued to hold sway? What, if any, complementary changes do we see in sectors of society or regions outside the incorporated communities, or in the traditions of the colonisers themselves? In a Roman context these issues have been partly addressed by Woolf (1998, 24–8) in relating the importance of the diversity of imperialisms experienced in both the ancient and modern worlds to the situation in provincial Gaul. In Romano-British archaeology, however, we have perhaps been slow to realise any such theorised agenda (cf Laurence 1999b).

How can we as archaeologists address these issues in our work? Though clearly a contentious issue, one of the advantages with the approach discussed above lies in the way it allows us to focus on how actions within particular areas of material life can be considered as part of a continuous making and remaking of society. One way forward therefore, might be to proceed through a comparative archaeology of past practice in different spheres of material life at a variety of spatial and temporal scales. Focusing on the routines of such practices through study of the details of their setting, frequency and the forms of material culture used may help us better understand the ways social relations were enacted and thus how particular discourses were maintained, changed, or invented.

Within the context of rural society we might suggest that detailed consideration of the role of material resources in agricultural practice, dietary tradition, attitudes to material consumption, and monetisation, household organisation, and the cultural and symbolic role of settlement architecture represent potentially fruitful areas for future research. Such an approach emphasises the significance of understanding the spatial extent of particular practices and the time over which they are maintained as a guide to the nature and extent of the different social discourses that were going on in any given context.

Such an approach opens up our understanding of how society changes from a debate around binary oppositions to more complex possibilities in the creation of new and changing identities that are neither 'native' nor Roman. It allows us to look at the dynamic and diverse nature of Roman identity through time and space and the varied imperialisms of the Roman world. In particular, we are no longer caught within the 'interventionist/non-interventionist' divide that has characterised much debate about the nature of Roman imperialism in Britain. Further, it requires us to focus on how people understood and manipulated material culture in various spheres of social interaction through time and across space within (and indeed outside) the province. Whilst, as Creighton points out in this volume, some powerful individuals were aware of, and sought to use, traditions of social display expressed at the core of the empire, it is likely when looking at the country as a whole that many did not, or developed social strategies with far more parochial considerations that had little to do with social conditions outside the province. This leads us to a series of important practical considerations relating to the way we do our archaeology of the period.

Firstly, it moves us away from a normative descriptive/classificatory approach to the material in which at times to classify was almost considered sufficient to explain (for example, that a certain type of building = a villa = Romanised). More important is how this inhabited material world was manipulated/used in social practice and the implications of this for social discourse. Potentially, therefore, the classification of buildings is not itself important; but why particular architectural forms were adopted, when and where they were, and critically, how their architectural space was used and understood (cf Revell 1999). An emphasis on spheres of life (areas of material resource used in social discourse) rather than the material record ensures we must take a contextual integrated approach to archaeological practice. We are less interested in pottery or buildings *per se* than how they were used and what their role was in the different areas of the social life of rural communities. This demands that projects take a more thematic approach to analysing archaeological information in which people with a specialised knowledge of a particular material resource work with others to look at improving our understanding of Romano-British social practice. Increasingly common practice amongst archaeologists, such approaches hold exciting possibilities for the role of artefactual, biological and structural evidence in, for example, agricultural practice, status display and diet.

Secondly, it pushes us to build up our understanding of the multifaceted and multilayered nature of Romano-British society by focusing our attention on the degree to which particular understandings of social practice extended over time and space. In one sense at least, the degree to which a particular discourse achieved hegemony within the bounds of a single community, a small region, the province, or across provincial boundaries provides us with a far fuller understanding of the way in which the empire worked. It allows us to consider the degree, for example, to which military conquest and subsequent occupation of an area related to the establishment, dominance, rejection, or adaptation of previously alien social practices. To put it more simply, and by way of an example, did the ideas, beliefs, and practices that the varied communities of the Roman army and its attendant civil agents brought with them significantly interact with indigenous attitudes to create new social networks? Do, as Clarke (1999) seems to have suggested in the context of Newstead, we seem to have two distinct almost unrelated social discourses living side by side in which little or no interaction took place?

Critically, a consideration of the spatial and temporal scales of particular social practices tends to lead us towards approaches that view archaeological evidence from the bottom up. It places a premium on local and regional syntheses using archaeological information that publication of earlier large-scale projects and the explosion of information from PPG16 have now put at our disposal. It is perhaps no accident that part of the reason many earlier syntheses focused on national overviews was due to the relatively thin spread of information available to authors for any specific area. It is now possible for us to look at particular traditions within spheres of daily life and the time and space over which they operated in some detail. The implications of this re-evaluation are many and varied but in the remainder of this paper I want to discuss how we might put the lessons learnt from this into practice for future research on rural society.

Themes in Roman rural studies

The concluding parts of this paper outline some themes that have the potential to provide valuable insights into studies of Roman rural society, illustrated with a few examples from recent work. They cannot be and are not intended as an exhaustive list, but help to show how we can invigorate the study of rural society in Roman Britain by the imaginative use of the extraordinary quality and quantity of information at our disposal within a conceptual framework that actively incorporates temporal and spatial diversity in social practice.

Rural societies: settlement and landscape

The study of Roman rural housing and settlement in Britain, has been characterised by an enormous body of empirical evidence summarised in many local or synthetic studies. The consideration of some theoretical applications, however, has not kept up with this body of empirical work. The reluctance to develop different explicitly defined theories is probably exemplified by looking at the lengthy list of regional and county-based studies incorporating sections on the countryside or rural settlement (eg Ramm 1978;

Branigan 1985). These works often display a limited range of different theoretical assumptions, which implicitly made, are not always immediately apparent. Often stated in varying forms, they have until recently been such an orthodoxy as to be largely unchallenged. It is difficult here to do justice to the history of this approach but two major lines of enquiry seem to typify much of it: typological studies and classicising socio-economic approaches.

Typological studies concentrating on the description and classification of settlements and house types, commonly according to their excavated plans, form one common strand of work. A well-developed tradition in Romano-British archaeology with a long history, this work has provided very valuable information on the chronological development and geographical range of particular traditions (eg Collingwood and Richmond 1969; Applebaum 1972; Hingley 1989). The problems with these approaches lie in the tendency to use implicit assumptions, such as acculturation or social emulation (in which innovation starts at the top of society and trickles down) that are rarely considered to be in need of explanation or justification. Particular innovations or novel practices are also deemed to be understandable in terms of practical advantages or in terms of the comforts of Romanisation. Furthermore, there is a tendency for the subject of study to become the object, in this case the building or settlement plan and details of its evolution overshadow the societies that created them.

Economic approaches to rural settlement in Roman Britain have also been of great value as they returned settlements and buildings to their historical context. In Britain this largely focused on examples in which they are considered in relation to changing economic conditions in the province (eg Todd 1978; Branigan and Miles 1989). The classic example is of course the economy of villas, and villa estates as indicators of wealth and status. Related studies of plant and animal remains and artefactual assemblages in particular, led to a revolution in our understanding of agricultural practice and craft production of material goods in rural contexts. The basic tenet of these approaches, however, has been that new developments in housing, settlement, agriculture, or craft production are considered to be largely due to new economic factors. In rural archaeology the classic example is probably the villa where the presence of villas is related to the development of Roman methods of wealth accumulation and status display linked to the establishment of taxation, significant landed estates, and urban markets. There are, however, problems with such an approach, not least of which is the tendency towards assumptions of a straightforward house–wealth relationship and that the absence of Roman forms of wealth accumulation and display can be taken to be indicators of poverty. In practice, however, whether any household or community chooses to invest in the construction and elaboration of particular building styles rather than, say, in livestock or portable material culture is a decision that is specific to each social context.

Recently, and particularly through the 1990s, there have been a number of attempts to analyse social organisation through the medium of rural settlement architecture in Britain. Hingley noted (1991) that the philosophy behind earlier studies had tended to inhibit work in this direction but some notable attempts had been made to build social models for the evidence (Stevens 1966; Smith 1978; 1987). Since then Hingley (1990), Smith (1997), and a number of others (eg E Scott 1990; Samson 1990a; Clarke 1990; 1998; 1999; S Scott 1995; 2000), have started to realise the potential of such approaches in revitalising our understanding of wider social or symbolic aspects of rural settlement. Much of this work has drawn on the experiences of research into the Iron Age in which it has become common to see the layout of settlements and housing as integral to the values and relationships of those who lived within them (Foster 1989; Oswald 1997; Hingley 1992; Sharples and Parker-Pearson 1997). In Roman Britain, Hingley (1989) and Clarke (1998) have raised the likely significance of settlement form in social discourse at a communal and inter-communal scale and it is to be hoped that such insights will be the subject of serious consideration in the future.

Much of this work has focused on the realisation that the form of buildings and settlements alone does not necessarily tell us much about the people who lived in them. To be understood we need to study how these architectural spaces were incorporated within the routines of relations between people and the use to which such spaces were put. There is an excellent tradition of similar work in classical contexts closer to the heart of the empire, especially in the study of Roman towns (eg Wallace-Hadrill 1994; Laurence 1994; Cornell & Lomas 1994; Revell 1999), while in a rural context Purcell (1994) and Scott (2000) have also ably demonstrated the ideological and symbolic significance of the villa to Roman society in Italy and Britain.

If we wish to study the roles played by housing and the wider built environment in the development of rural society in Britain, it is important that we do just that. Instead of giving primacy to certain predefined forms of building, which then usually become the exclusive focus of study, it is incumbent upon us to study all the buildings of a particular housing culture in their spatial and chronological context. To understand why certain architectural styles were adopted in particular places at particular times and whether they constituted a radical change in social organisation, for example, it is important to understand how architectural space was structured up to the point of change and whether such buildings were related to particular forms of social use. A short example may help to illustrate this point. In an earlier attempt to illustrate the significance of this issue Hingley (1989; 1990) briefly characterised certain trends in the organisation of Iron Age and Romano-British households. In it he argued for the division of many Iron Age houses into public and private areas and that the majority of Romano-

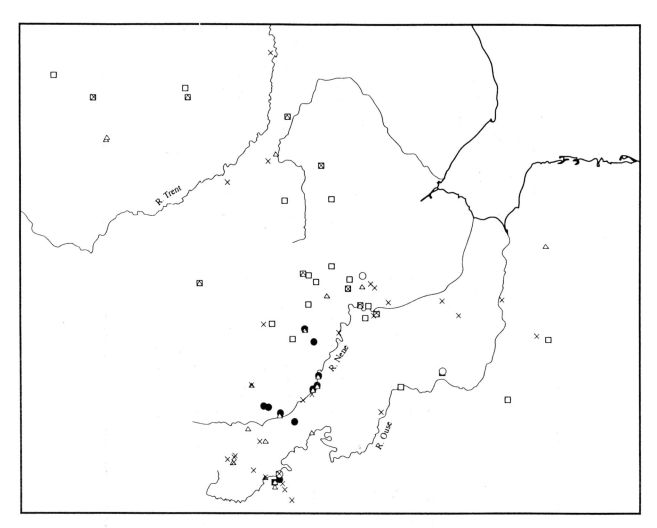

Figure 13   The distribution of common later Roman rural architectural traditions in the east Midlands (note that squares = aisled buildings, filled circles = stone built round houses, open circles = timber built round houses, triangles = row type stone buildings, crosses = other timber building forms)

British houses could be reduced to the same model and thus derived strong continuity from indigenous traditions of architecture.

Such studies have rarely been followed through in any detail but provide an opportunity for far more nuanced understandings of how housing and settlement architecture were involved in the social relations of rural communities. The marked regional and temporal diversity of housing traditions in Roman Britain provides a good subject for study and by way of illustration the following is a short example from the East Midlands. The housing culture of the Roman period in this area shows significant differentiation in the adoption and use of particular house forms between the south and west, and the northeast. Figure 13 shows how this dichotomy is most apparent in the adoption of aisled buildings or the continued use and adaptation of round houses on rural settlements across the region, alongside the more widespread adoption of other forms commonly considered under Smith's (1997) categories of row-type villas. A consideration of the function and possible status of such buildings, however, suggests that straightforward equations of form and function or status clearly do not work. Some act as shrines or barns/workshops, but common to both areas is their use as multipurpose domestic/agricultural/craft buildings. In essence, therefore, the forms alone do not help take us far, but by taking a closer look at the individual contexts of their use on each settlement it is possible to draw out some major differences between the housing traditions of the two areas that are otherwise not immediately apparent. By looking at evolving methods of construction and the arrangement and use of spaces created and recreated through time it is possible to suggest that key changes took place in the role of rural domestic architecture, and that these differed significantly between communities in the south and west of the region and those in the north and east (Taylor in prep (a)).

Analysis of the location of architectural features, finds groups, and deposits from a number of excavated examples suggests that the central–communal, peripheral–domestic rule of the spatial organisation of activities within round houses suggested by Hingley was generally followed within this area. Although few in number, the well-preserved examples that it was possible to study (Fig 14a)

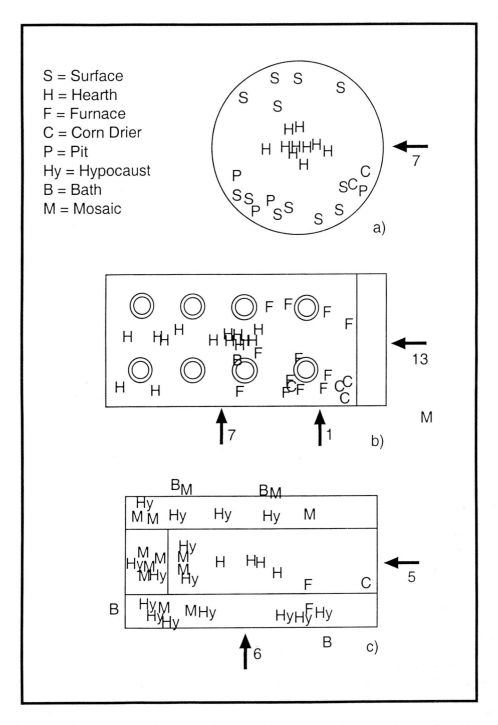

Figure 14 Schematic diagram of the location of key architectural features within, a) late Iron Age to early Roman round houses, b) 2nd- to 3rd-century aisled buildings, and c) 3rd- to 4th-century 'developed' aisled buildings

indicate that particular activities were restricted to certain locations within houses. Roman-period round houses continued this pattern of usage but increasingly seemed to occupy marginal locations or ancillary agricultural or craft activity roles on larger rural settlements.

In the south-western part, these developments are accompanied by the early adoption within some communities of new forms of architecture in which domestic space was separated from other craft and agricultural activities and segregated by the construction of ranges of rooms. This ongoing shift in discourse towards the spatial segregation of domestic and productive activities, was achieved in the south-west through the adoption of new architectural forms from the Flavian period and the establishment of a notable dichotomy between these and round houses. Other architectural traditions were available but were rarely used. Aisled buildings are notably rare and where present occur early, on especially large and seemingly prosperous rural settlements (eg Stanwick, Bancroft, and Stanton Low) and, interestingly, are soon demolished and replaced by row-type buildings. Round houses, by contrast,

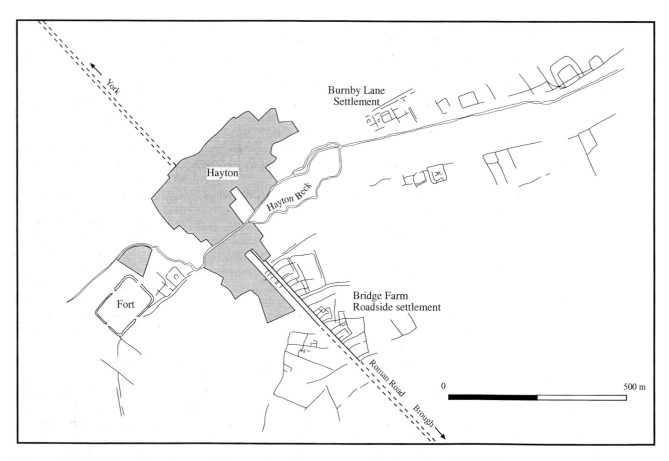

Figure 15 The later Iron Age and Roman landscape around Hayton, East Yorkshire

information about settlement and social change across entire landscapes (eg Meheux 1996; Fincham forthcoming b; Taylor forthcoming b). Such approaches can be time-consuming but are inexpensive compared to the initiation of new projects to address such themes, and they can produce extensive rewards.

Agricultural and dietary practice

Inevitably, given that the aim of this paper was to discuss rural society in Roman Britain, studies of agricultural and dietary practice are key concerns. At the beginning of this decade our view of those aspects of rural society dedicated to the production, preparation and consumption of food in Roman Britain focused very heavily on the agricultural economy and its perceived development under Roman rule (eg Millett 1990a; Jones 1989). At that time developments were already underway which placed innovations in agricultural strategy, consumption patterns, or butchery practice in a social context (eg King 1984; van der Veen 1989; 1992; Grant 1989) but since then, much of this work has really started to bear results. In a recent important review, van der Veen and O'Connor (1998) highlighted some particularly visible characteristics of agricultural practice during the late Iron Age and Roman period in Britain. In it they noted the particular significance

to this period of the rise of settlements (ie communities) not primarily involved in agricultural production, and a parallel expansion in agriculture. Of especial importance within these broad developments they noted how the adoption or rejection of new agricultural strategies and the particular choice used, represents a key aspect of much of the regional diversity in societies we see across the country during this period. Critically, van der Veen and O'Connor see the study of this development as a key area for future research.

Whilst agreeing wholeheartedly with this sentiment, van der Veen and O'Connor subsequently focus their discussion of the social context for the varied developments in strategy they define, in largely normative economic terms. Thus, though they recognise that farmers in subsistence societies have different priorities from those in market economies (van der Veen and O'Connor 1998, 128), they largely focus on economic explanations for these developments though, as has been alluded to earlier, we need to remain aware that a far wider range of social and symbolic considerations may have been important.

Foods and the production of food surpluses represent a powerful material resource in the social relations of agricultural communities. In the context of Roman Britain, we have tended to look for the explanation of innovations or developments in relation to generalised models of idealised villa economies, in the supply of military or urban communities, or in Romanisation. Thanks largely to the enormous amount of empirical evidence that is available to us, it is now possible to ask searching questions about the degree to which this was necessarily true and question the changing roles of agricultural practice and food consumption further. What is required is a more holistic approach that encourages us to dispose of the tendency to compartmentalise botanical and zoological reports. One possibility is to focus on a form of rural social archaeology, or what has recently been termed an 'agrarian sociology', for the period (Armit *et al* 2000 C2.2) that focuses on understanding the routines and development of farming life and the spatial and temporal extent of particular traditions.

In relation to dietary practice and cuisine for example, recent work by King (1999b) has demonstrated that, for meat consumption at least, Gaul and the Germanies appear to have established their own dietary traditions that display little Mediterranean Roman influence. This pattern then appears to have been influential on subsequent developments in Britain. Pre-conquest patterns in Britain appear different to continental ones with the probable exception of some neighbouring regions within Belgic Gaul. Subsequently it is, as King notes, possible to suggest that the more common Gallic/German traditions, probably already established as the military dietary pattern, became the models for dietary change in the new province (King 1999b, 178). King does not comment, however, that this only really seems to be true of legionary sites in Britain with many auxiliary sites adopting dietary supply patterns closer to indigenous British practice than to auxiliary or legionary traditions on the continent (King 1999b, figs 9 and 12). This may simply relate to different strategies of supply but is worthy of closer inspection in relation to how indigenous dietary traditions may have themselves influenced the practices of communities new to the province. King's work has provided a very useful overview but there is still great scope to address issues of food production and consumption practices at regional and local scales and in particular to assess the extent to which gross trends relate to regional patterns of agricultural production (higher numbers of cattle may, after all, relate to a shift towards the production of cereals) and supply, or specific social traditions of culinary preparation and consumption.

At one level King's review suggests that these new patterns of dietary balance became prevalent during the later Roman period (King 1984), and Robinson's work in the Upper Thames valley suggests that even low-status settlements had adopted the consumption of spicy, oily foods by the 3rd century (Robinson 1992, 58) but there are good reasons to suspect that these developments were highly regionalised and not necessarily always status related. Certainly, culinary exotica seem to have been adopted at a fairly restricted range of places (cf van der Veen and O'Connor 1998, 137) and increasingly detailed work is now possible on how food habits changed. Faunal studies of butchery practice, skeletal element representation, and context of deposition, linked to palaeobotanical and artefact analysis should help us to better determine shifting cultural attitudes towards food production, preparation, and consumption and how and why they occurred (eg Meadows 1995; 1996; Hawkes 1999; Hamshaw-Thomas 2000).

Jones (1981) long ago noted how many aspects of agricultural innovation and change in Britain occurred during the late Iron Age and later Roman periods but it may again be worth reconsidering the possible social implications of some of the changes that do seem to have followed the initial conquest of the province. The introduction of novel foods and agricultural regimes such as market gardening may have been limited to small sections of society but their differential distribution may have had considerable impact on local circumstances. The discovery of several probable vineyards in the Nene valley (Meadows 1996) or the concentration of the growth of particular cash crops around emerging urban centres, seem likely to have been accompanied by important changes in local rural life and land use that deserve greater attention. Likewise, many areas of southern and eastern Britain in particular see the adoption and construction of larger-scale mills, corn dryers, and granaries or large barns that imply changes in the scale of agricultural processing and storage on some rural settlements or an emphasis on its overt display.

Whilst it is quite likely that the conquest and subsequent incorporation of many rural communities did not see the adoption of many novel agricultural strategies we need to consider the local and regional implications of the evidence we do have for the centralisation of production on larger rural settlements, the large-scale processing and storage of agricultural produce on some settlements, extensive attempts at water management on floodplains and in wetlands (eg Macaulay and Reynolds 1993; 1994; Rippon 1997) and the evidence for a switch from predominantly pastoral to arable land management strategies in some areas (Rackham pers comm). Similarly, and perhaps even more pressing a concern, we need to support recent efforts to establish even a basic understanding of rural society in areas where our information is still very poor (such as parts of north-west England, cf Newman 1996) or where past emphasis on the military has lead to important issues being ignored. It is especially important if we wish to seriously consider evidence for change in areas where conventional explanations of resistance, or economic supply to the military or towns are based on only one side of the equation (eg Huntley and Stallibrass 1996).

The articulation of economic relations

In thinking about the development of rural society in Britain in the aftermath of the conquest due consideration deserves to be given to the relationship of monetisation to taxation and material consumption in rural contexts. To date we have tended to model such ideas at a provincial scale and focused on larger, commonly urban settlements (eg Reece 1991; 1995), but the sheer number of excavated rural sites with coin reports now allow us to look at this process more closely. Preliminary results from a recent re-evaluation of coin usage on rural settlements in eastern England (Taylor in prep (b)) suggests that common categorisations of the status and role of settlements based on structural evidence may not necessarily reflect their role in monetary aspects of the economy. Although still at an early stage, the results of this work suggest, for example, that some of the larger villa settlements have coin patterns very similar to those of small towns but that many villas are essentially no different to other farmsteads. Some non-villa settlements are surprisingly 'rich' in comparison to contemporary villas and it is evident that regional trends existed in the level of coin usage, with higher levels in parts of the south-east and east Midlands than on similar settlements in the Fenland and west Norfolk (also noted by Davies and Gregory 1991), where figures are commonly similar to those found on rural settlements in Devon and Cornwall.

Such studies have much to say in regard to our perceptions of monetisation, status definition, and material wealth in rural society in Roman Britain. In the past we have seen much discussion of the concept of towns and villas as socio-economic institutions but little offered by way of alternatives in the many areas of the province where villas of any form are rare or totally absent. If we have situations in which non-monetary taxation or exchange was prevalent or even the norm, do we have corresponding non-landed or non-classicising forms of social display such as ritual feasting, livestock control or, as appears to be the case in parts of the Fens and East Anglia (eg Fincham forthcoming a), the hoarding of precious metalwork? This raises the serious issue of how we treat material culture consumption in social terms. Ferris (1995) and Matthews (1997) are right to point out the tendency amongst many Roman archaeologists to assume poverty when they do not find large amounts of the types of consumer goods or architectural forms they value highly. We still tend to be hung up on the idea that durable material goods equal wealth, which they obviously do not outside specific social contexts. A pressing priority in Roman rural archaeology must, therefore, be to address this issue, especially as it may help us to understand better the social traditions of rural communities over much of the province, such as the north-west (Matthews 1997), Welsh Marches (White and van Leusen 1997), Wales (Fasham et al 1998; Longley et al 1998) and the far south-west (eg Quinnell 1993; Ashbee 1996) where social discourses may have been embedded in different spheres of material life to those that are commonly considered.

The central position of the perception and power of land ownership to Roman society (and seen in the centrality of land in surveying, taxation, and patterns in property holding, or rather utilisation) have often been highlighted by students of the period. Clearly this is a difficult area to attempt to address from an archaeological standpoint in Britain, given that we are highly unlikely to be able to access important tenurial and proprietorial issues that lie at the heart of such concerns, an issue which hampered so many earlier narratives on the presence of villa and imperial estates in Britain (Taylor 2000). At one level, however, it should be possible to study the dynamics of changing patterns of settlement location, land division and land use as a guide to changing rural social organisation even if we cannot access tenurial and political relationships directly. Archaeological strategies that deliberately focus on the role, extent, form, and chronology of field systems utilising prospection, geoarchaeological, and palaeoenvironmental techniques hold out exciting possibilities for extending our understanding of the complex patchwork of land use strategies suggested by some important extant surveys (eg Whimster 1989; Bewley 1998a; Fenner not dated) Many areas of the country already have good basic surveys of field systems, or where these are not apparent, palaeoenvironmental sequences (eg Cowell & Innes 1994; Leah et al 1998; van de Noort and Ellis 1997) upon which to base new programmes of research.

Rural societies and conceptions of urbanism

A final theme I wish briefly to cover may at first seem to lie outside the subject of this particular paper. Traditionally, one of the great characterising features of the Roman empire in the West has been the evidence for and significance of towns as the core of social life. Many issues covering this subject are better considered elsewhere in this volume (Millett) but to artificially isolate the two areas, as was noted at the beginning, could lead us to ignore an extremely important field of future research in Roman Britain, namely the origins, development, and social role of nucleated non-agricultural settlements during the Roman period. In this respect Britain bears comparison with Gaul where the levels of urbanism identified in the Roman period are also low and where many nucleated settlements 'displayed a markedly rural character' (Woolf 1998, 143).

One of the lessons of recent academic work is that urbanism is a way of life and a way of organising social relations by locating them in a particular kind of place. Towns, whatever the specifics of their method of organisation, are social institutions that require constant maintenance. Thus, superficial similarities in architectural form and layout can be shown to have been involved in a variety of complex social discourses (eg Parkins 1997; Grahame 1997).

Studies in regions where various forms of urbanism existed before conquest are showing how new and changing social relations were mediated through them, creating a range of subtly different

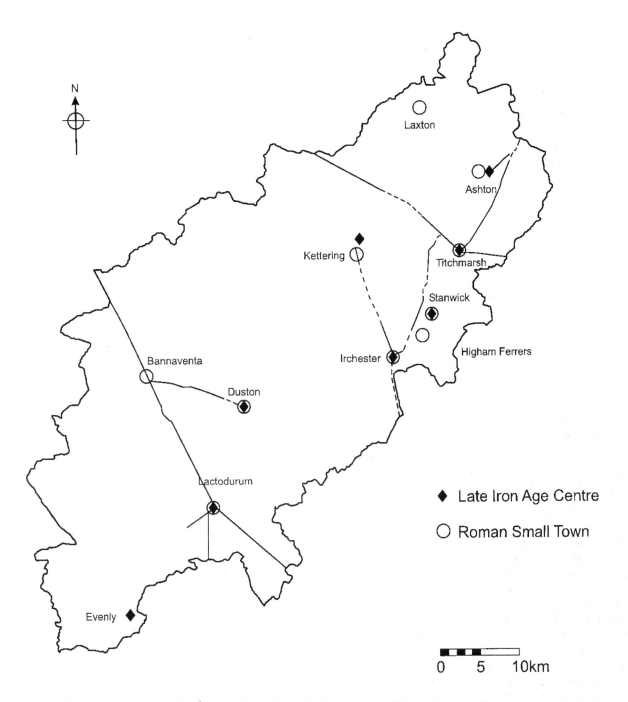

Figure 16   The location of significant late Iron Age religious and political foci and Roman nucleated settlements and roads in Northamptonshire

social institutions. Much of Britain, alongside for example the Low Countries and parts of north-western Iberia, provides a fascinating counterpoint to these kinds of analyses as it gives an opportunity to address how forms of social discourse traditionally based upon a variety of conceptions of urban life confronted a social milieu in which these traditions were partly or largely alien. We know that, to a greater or lesser extent nucleated settlements developed during the Roman period over much of Roman Britain, but we still have little understanding of whether such places were similar or very different social foci to those in Gaul or the heart of the empire. In part this may stem from a tendency to focus on

classification rather than trying to understand their roles as emerging social institutions (cf Millett 1995). In practice, this has had the effect of isolating the study of towns from their social, temporal and spatial context. These nucleated settlements cannot be understood on their own but rather in relation to the changing social landscape in which they developed. Here is not the place to elucidate a detailed agenda but the close study of the developing social landscape in which towns subsequently develop should be a key part of future studies. There is already a good tradition of this in relation to some of the major late Iron Age centres such as Silchester (Fulford and Timby 2000), St Albans (Hunn 1992;

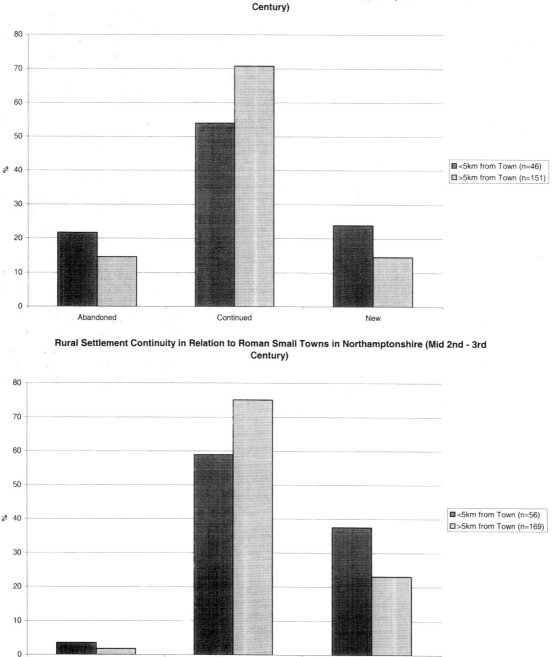

Figure 17   Rural settlement continuity in relation to Roman small towns in Northamptonshire. a) From late 1st to mid-2nd century and b) from mid-2nd to 3rd century

Haselgrove and Millett 1997) and Colchester (Hawkes and Crummy 1995) but much work needs to be done in relation to small towns and other roadside settlements across the country.

Close study of the rationale for and effect of the construction of new networks of communication and supply, the analysis of material flows, and the reorganisation of local agrarian practice should show how key changes occurring in rural social relations may have played one important role in the establishment of such places. Recent evaluation of a group of small towns in the East Midlands, suggests that a

number were relatively small but nevertheless key religious/political foci during the late Iron Age, whose significance to the new administrative geography of the province was fixed by their incorporation within the network of main roads subsequently constructed (Fig 16). The landscapes in the immediate vicinity of these places then became the primary foci for agricultural reorganisation (Fig 17), possibly linked to the perceived benefits of the creation of greater agricultural surpluses, which may also have had the effect of creating socially marginalised, former agricultural communities that moved to larger rural settlements or the roadside centres (Taylor forthcoming).

Taking such an approach is only one suggested answer, but by focusing on the existing social landscape of an area and questioning why urbanised forms of settlement should necessarily exist where they had not before, helps us to start thinking about why areas such as Cornwall and much of Wales did not appear to need such places. Furthermore, it also helps us to consider military *vici* as a particular social phenomenon not dissimilar to small towns but related to the social requirements of military communities and alien and seemingly isolated from neighbouring indigenous society (cf Clarke 1999; James this volume).

Concluding remarks

There are, of course, a number of other themes in rural social change that deserve to be addressed in future, some of which are covered in other contributions to this volume. Examples of other lines of enquiry that fit well within the broader theoretical framework outlined above include the creation and reproduction of differing social identities through dress and bodily adornment (Hill, Allason-Jones, and James this volume), and the range of exciting developments currently underway in our understanding of the roles of burial and other depositional practice in rural social contexts (Pearce 1999b; Pearce *et al* forthcoming). Webster's work on religion (Webster 1995b; 1997), and Bowman's (1991) and Evans's (1987) insights into the evidence for literacy show how far we have still to go.

In all, these examples help to show how it is possible to build up an understanding of the degree to which particular social traditions may or may not have become established over large parts of society in Roman Britain. The extraordinary quantity and diversity of information we have available to us allows us to envisage the complex and multivocal nature of rural society in Roman Britain. If only we are willing to take up the challenge, we should be better able to consider the degree to which particular dominant readings of the world understood at the core of the empire, established hegemony in Britain, and the degree to which these show similarities to the evidence from other regions or provinces. This may ultimately provide a way into understanding better the degree to which Roman Britain was ever part of a 'common culture' in the terms noted by Barrett (1997b, 6–7) and of the ways in which it came to an end.

7 Approaches to urban societies *by Martin Millett*

Introduction

A considerable amount of work has been done on Romano-British towns. Indeed, it is probably true to say that towns in Britain have been more extensively explored than those of any other Roman province. The early stages of research on towns in Britain were concerned largely with the recovery of topographic information, the understanding of which was set firmly within the context of assumed Greco-Roman norms (eg Haverfield 1913). Although knowledge was often limited by the piecemeal and uneven availability of information and superimposition of later settlements, a considerable body of data was accumulated, especially as a result of the excavation of modern towns damaged by World War II bombs or post-war redevelopment (Wacher 1966; Rodwell and Rowley 1975). This volume of information permitted the preparation of two valuable syntheses. The first presented the evidence from the major towns (Wacher 1975; 1995), whilst the second drew together the more diverse evidence about the better known of the so-called small towns (Burnham and Wacher 1990). These books are important landmarks in our understanding of Romano-British urbanism, and although it will become clear that I dissent from some of their conclusions, their enduring influence should be firmly acknowledged.

More recent studies have added to our knowledge of particular aspects of urbanism in Roman Britain, looking at groups of related sites and themes (eg Dobinson 1993; Brown 1995; Hurst 1999). Equally, considerable progress has been made in understanding certain individual sites. We now have especially good knowledge of certain major towns (eg Colchester and London) and a much improved understanding of a wide range of others (eg Canterbury, Silchester, Heybridge, and Gloucester). However, we may note in passing that most sites remain known only on the basis of relatively small excavated samples. This raises key issues of broader significance about the extent to which we can legitimately generalise, firstly about whole sites from excavated samples, and secondly about all towns on the basis of those we know best. There is a definite need for fundamental research into the first question whilst the second raises wider issues about the diversity of Roman urbanism.

It is certainly time to take stock of the evidence now available from Roman towns in Britain, evaluate it and propose appropriate new questions which might be addressed. A thoughtful and well-presented attempt at doing this for the period down to AD 200 has already been produced by a CBA working party, and deserves to be much more widely read and acted upon; consequently, the editors have invited the working party to include it in the present volume, which they have done (Burnham *et al* this volume). Since I support most of the conclusions drawn in that study, the current paper instead provides a more personal perspective which I trust complements it.

Underlying issues

We can begin with two general, underlying issues which I believe are fundamental to current work on Romano-British towns. Firstly, whilst acknowledging the importance of Wacher's (1975) synthesis, I find it depressing that there remains an almost unquestioning consensus on what is interesting about towns. In this context we might note that Wacher's second edition of *The Towns of Roman Britain*, published 20 years after the original, did not feel it appropriate to alter its approach. The key themes which recur in the discussions of towns are: origins, military influence, status, public buildings, morphology, town walls, and the process of decline and fall. The collation of information about such basic concerns is certainly important, but not in its own right; only as a means to an end. The broader aims are too often lost sight of in debates and syntheses. At the beginning of a new millennium surely we can do something more interesting and worthwhile than simply collate information relating to these now rather ageing themes? In particular, it seems important to do something that reintegrates the study of Romano-British towns with the study of urbanism on a broader scale. After all, as I have already noted, we do have a lot of rather good information.

Secondly, there is a strong, implicit – but I believe unrealistic – belief in the uniformity of Roman urbanism. On the basis of Wacher's synthesis, the view that we are looking at an 'urban programme' which was 'applied to Britain' is still often present. Information from other parts of the empire suggests a much less even patterning in the process of urbanisation (cf Woolf 1997b; 1998, 106–41). I would see the Roman world as having an as-yet poorly understood patchwork of urban centres with varying functions and forms. My doubts even extend to whether clear categories of sites (eg *coloniae*) share real similarities across space and time (cf Millett 1999). We certainly cannot simply assume that the character of towns was geographically and temporally uniform. Equally, the idea of an urban programme which underlies Wacher's synthesis does not seem credible as it is absent in earlier stages in Rome's dealings with her overseas territories. We are at an exciting stage of uncertainty and should recognise the potential the study of Roman Britain has to contribute to more general debates.

Current opportunities

If we turn to consider the current state of archaeology in England specifically, there have recently been two sets of changes (beyond purely research-led frameworks) which potentially provide key opportunities for developing our understanding of Romano-British towns. Firstly, a planned programme of syntheses of major urban sites has been initiated by English Heritage through the project announced in *Managing the Urban Archaeological Resource* in 1992. The first results of this programme are beginning to come to fruition and we should soon see a series of volumes which review the archaeology of a

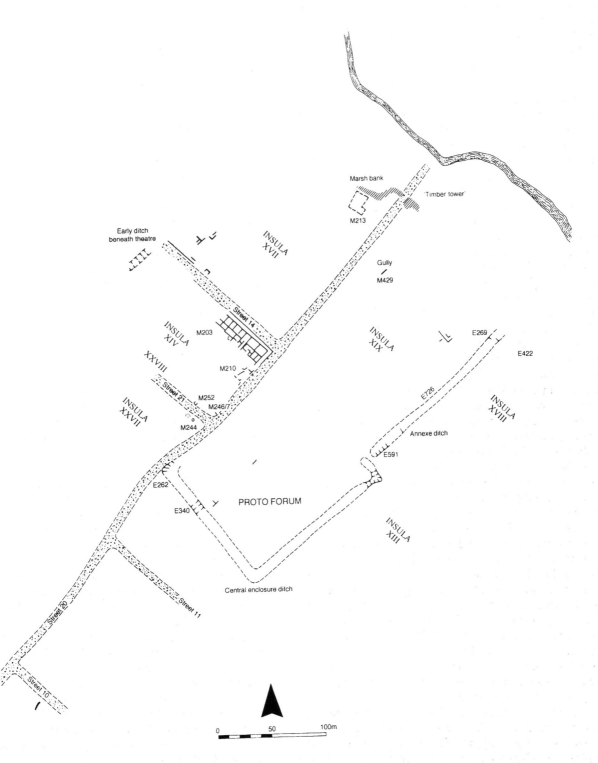

Figure 18   New plan of Verulamium prior to its destruction in the Boudiccan revolt of AD 60/1 based on the thorough reassessment of previous work undertaken for the English Heritage funded urban assessment of St Albans (Niblett and Thompson forthcoming). Reproduced by courtesy of English Heritage and Ros Niblett

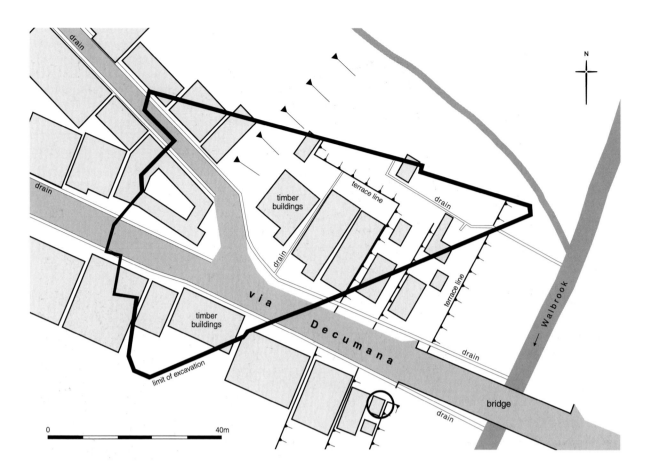

Figure 19 Excavations at No 1 Poultry and adjacent sites in the City of London have shown that the area had undergone extensive development by the time of the town's destruction in the Boudiccan revolt of AD 60/1. The site lay along London's main east–west road, just to the west of the Walbrook stream. General terracing, road layout and drainage work was followed by the construction of timber buildings on the roadside plots. The drawing includes some conjecture based on the excavated evidence. Reproduced by courtesy of the Museum of London Archaeological Service and Peter Rowsome

series of towns. These studies will be founded on the GIS databases, resource assessments, and strategy documents which are being created for 30 or so major towns, and are complemented by less intensive regional surveys of smaller nucleations. The programme is primarily designed to help local authority planners manage development in relation to the archaeology of modern urban centres, but as the work is based on the systematic synthesis of existing information, it is forcing a fundamental reconsideration of all the archaeological and historical evidence from each town examined. The drafts of some of the reports that I have seen suggest that they will be of fundamental importance for academic understanding as well as future planning policy. For instance, the report prepared by Ros Niblet and Isobel Thompson on St Albans/Verulamium provides a fundamental re-evaluation of the site, questioning many preconceptions and providing new insights into the available evidence (Fig 18; Niblett and Thompson forthcoming). The first of the new database projects (after the pilot studies at Durham, Cirencester, and York) are nearing completion at important Roman centres like London, Lincoln,

Winchester, St Albans, and Cambridge. Furthermore, less detailed, extensive surveys covering sites including 'small towns' are finished or nearing completion in a number of counties including Gloucestershire, Hampshire, Essex, and Somerset. The publication of the syntheses and the accessibility of the GIS data promise to provide a key new resource for urban studies allowing much more imaginative analysis than has hitherto been possible (analysis of visibility, viewsheds, structural density, etc). Whilst we should acknowledge the enormous potential of this information for enhancing our understanding of many Roman towns, the selection of the sites has been based on contemporary planning criteria. This will leave a sequence of Roman sites unprovided for in the planned programme. Whilst comparable information is already being generated by research work at selected sites, for instance through the geophysical survey of Wroxeter <http://www.bufau.bham.ac.uk/> and continuing work at Silchester (Fulford and Clarke 1999), there is clearly a need for a series of detailed systematic studies of the other important greenfield sites. This should include not only the major towns like Caistor by

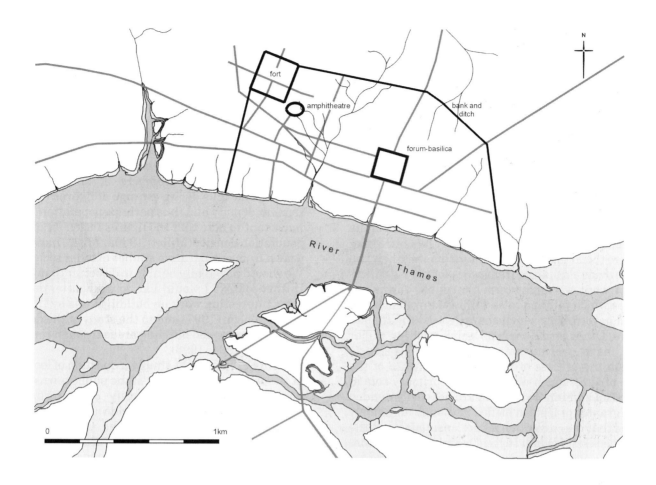

Figure 20 Summary plan of Roman London, including Southwark, in the 2nd century showing the principal roads, streets, and public buildings in relation to the reconstructed physical geography. The plan has been drawn using the Museum of London Archaeology Service's GIS system which is being developed to incorporate results from all their excavations. Reproduced courtesy of the Museum of London Archaeology Service and Helen Jones

Norwich or Water Newton, but also a variety of the lesser nucleated centres about which we remain remarkably ignorant. The current programme of survey work by English Heritage at Owmby, Lincs, provides a potential model for such work (Olivier 1997).

Second, changes in the organisation and management of archaeology in response to development (ie the introduction of PPG 16 and MAP2) have had two positive effects on the evidence available to us. First we have much new information being collected, although pre-development assessment work often provides very low grade data. However, we do need some more thought to be given to the problem of how data of this type can best be used to good effect. For instance, in the urban context it might be worth thinking about the use of residual dated finds, like pottery, for mapping the extent and density of earlier phases of settlement (cf Lowther *et al* 1993, figs 41–4). It is also well worth noting that the new system is generating a number of major projects which are very well executed and satisfactorily resourced. It is especially important to note that publication work is now much more carefully planned, with academic input, than used to be the

case. This is providing important scope for the investigation of major research themes within the new regime of public archaeology. As major excavation projects come to fruition, like No 1 Poultry in London (Fig 19) or the small town cut by the Scole–Dickleburgh by-pass on the Norfolk–Suffolk border, we will have a major new source of extremely high quality research. Within similar frameworks, we are also seeing some sustained attempts to publish backlog excavations imaginatively. For instance, the books that will result from the current Museum of London Archaeology Service programme are more synthetic than conventional reports and have used GIS to obtain a clearer understanding of overall patterns within the town than could have been provided in reports on individual excavations (Fig 20).

Rethinking some questions

If we are really to move forward in the study of the Romano-British towns we do need to begin to rethink some of the questions which are to be addressed. I would like to offer two lines of thought, both of wider

There is a particular problem which is important in the context of regional variation in Roman Britain. There are some grounds for believing that we can distinguish 'typical' public towns within the south and east of the province, and we perhaps have a fair idea of how such sites functioned within society. However, I am certain that we do not even begin to understand the equivalent major centres in the frontier zone (eg York, Carlisle, Malton, Catterick, Piercebridge, and Corbridge). Our understanding has not been helped by past approaches to the archaeology that have been almost wholly dominated by military questions. Equally, Corbridge (Bishop and Dore 1988) and Malton (Wenham and Heywood 1997) have suffered more than they deserve through excavations of inadequate quality. Current and forthcoming publications of Carlisle (McCarthy 1990, 1991, 1999) and Catterick (Fig 21; Wilson 1999; Wilson forthcoming) may help improve our understanding. In the meantime, it does seem clear that these are key sites on an imperial scale since they represent comparatively rare examples of nucleated settlements established late in the process of imperial expansion in areas of permanent military occupation. Thus, whilst we have a clear historical perspective on the more widely spread phenomenon of *civitas* capitals in the civilian areas of the south and east, based on the evolution of the category in Gallia, we have fewer comparable sites to help us understand the nucleated settlements near the frontiers. This makes these sites especially important.

Burnham's (1986) careful study of the origins of 'small towns' provides a model of approach and produced very useful insights into regional patterning. However, others have not moved beyond it to consider the patterning in other types of site. Equally, there has been little discussion of the meanings of regional or provincial patterns and the extent to which variation resulted from the varying dynamics of Roman imperialism at different periods of conquest or contact.

Concluding thoughts

In summary, I would argue that we need to rethink Romano-British urbanism from fundamentals and use evidence from archaeology to attempt to distinguish the various roles of particular sites. I would propose three complementary approaches, working from the finds, architectural evidence, and cemetery data.

Key in this enterprise are the approaches developed by other contributors to this volume which use objects and food residues to try to characterise site assemblages. Some important studies have already been published (eg Dobney *et al* 1998). In the study of

finds we should work from the type of approach defined by Reece (eg 1993; 1995) for coins. Thus, we should not assume that there is such a thing as an assemblage characteristic of a particular type of site, for instance a *colonia* or fort, until there is evidence to show that 'sites called *coloniae* or forts' have demonstrably different types of assemblages from those found at other places. In other words, in the primary work we need to set aside current site typologies and use approaches to explore the data about finds assemblages themselves. We cannot even yet assume that an assemblage from a nucleated site will be different from one found on a rural settlement (although Evans 1987 has shown certain distinctions). Only once we have explored the settlement evidence itself using the finds will we be able to use them to more adequately address economic issues. Approaches to issues like production, consumption, and the degree of integration with hinterlands can surely only proceed once we understand better the nature of the nucleated centres.

In characterising nucleated settlements, architecture and planning also have key roles to play. Through them progress has already been made in addressing conventional issues like public and private space, and settlement organisation. However, they also offer considerable potential for examining the organisation of social power through architectural symbolism, landscape dominance, and the control of communications. We are as yet at a very early stage in even conceptualising these issues (Revell 1999).

Finally, I think we need to stress the importance of nucleated sites as centres of human population. We can, for instance, envisage that the establishment of nucleated centres involved the disruption of existing social networks as those from a variety of different social groups came together in the new settlement. This may have allowed the development of socially disembedded groups who were able to act in ways that were not constrained by existing social norms. As such, there may have emerged new social groups who were more open to innovation. I have argued elsewhere that this process can be seen in the late Iron Age to early Roman cemetery evidence from King Harry Lane at Verulamium (Millett 1993). This is only an example of the type of approach that might enable cemetery data to be brought to bear on major issues of social interest. We are now beginning to see a variety of attempts to use this evidence more imaginatively (eg Pearce 1999a), but the considerable potential of these data has hardly yet been realised.

I hope it is clear that I do not want to decry the work that has already been done on the archaeology of towns in Roman Britain. However, I believe there remains great potential that can only be fully realised through the application of innovative approaches to the integration of various aspects of the archaeological data.

8 Themes for urban research, *c* 100 BC to AD 200

by Barry C Burnham, John Collis, Colin Dobinson, Colin Haselgrove, and Michael Jones

The following text was originally prepared as the report of a CBA working party, consisting of Barry Burnham (chair), John Collis, Colin Dobinson, Colin Haselgrove, and Michael Jones; it was originally published electronically by the CBA in September 1997, at <http://www.britarch.ac.uk/research/urban1.html>

Introduction

This report is the product of one of several working parties, set up by the CBA, to review themes for urban research in Britain. It covers one of three separate chronological blocks, each designed to cut across traditional period specialisations, in this case that of the later Iron Age and early Roman period, *c* 100 BC to AD 200. From the outset, the working party was conscious that many familiar explanations of this period are currently under discussion, such that the opportunity to review broader research themes seemed timely.

The group was also conscious that their brief placed the emphasis on defining themes for 'urban' research. This inevitably raised the thorny problem of urban definition at a time when there is increasingly less agreement on such issues, not just in terms of the *oppida*, but also with respect to some of the lesser settlements of Roman Britain. Taking the view that too much time has been wasted on such debates, the working party decided not to involve itself in any prolonged discussion, preferring instead to concentrate on defining themes of relevance to the broader question of the changing settlement hierarchy during the period from *c* 100 BC to AD 200.

Although there are considerable advantages to be gained from cutting across traditional period specialisations, any study of the period must avoid creating equally arbitrary boundaries at either end. This is particularly critical for the transition to the late Roman period, where there is a danger of reinforcing postulated differences between early and late towns rather than encouraging a more detailed assessment of their implications and the reasons which lay behind them. It is also clear that there are divergent opinions on the relative importance of the changes in the later Iron Age, with some arguing that they represent a sudden break with the past, consequent on increasing Roman influence, and others viewing them as an acceleration of longer-term processes rooted in the middle Iron Age. For this reason, no analysis can afford to ignore the role of a series of changes which occurred well before 100 BC, most notably population increase, settlement expansion and the colonisation of new land, agricultural innovation and intensification, and changes in the nature of production. More broadly still, no review of the period can afford to ignore continental research, or current debates among classicists and ancient historians.

One of the fundamental prerequisites for any study of this period is the need for a more precise chronological framework, as the basis both for analysing change and for assessing how and why it happened. On the continent, the absolute dating of the later Iron Age has been significantly revised in recent years, with the implication that existing chronologies are too late by as much as 50 years. Many British archaeologists have been slow to absorb the implications of these revisions, which effectively demonstrate that the changes traditionally associated with the later Iron Age were already underway at a time when southern Britain remained untouched by direct contact with the Roman world. These refinements have important implications for our traditional explanations of change and for the relative importance of internal and external factors.

Chronological precision is equally critical for the study of the immediate late Iron Age/Roman transition. Much has been learnt recently from the later occupation phases at Braughing-Puckeridge and Silchester, while the realisation that the *oppidum* complex at Bagendon-North Cerney probably came to prominence after AD 43, rather than before, must raise questions about currently-accepted interpretations of the interplay between it and the military site at Cirencester. Advances such as these demonstrate that clarity can only come from the identification and excavation of sites where the transition is well represented, from continued refinement of dating among imported products (especially finewares), and from a re-assessment of local pottery and coin assemblages in the light of this. Considerable importance also attaches to the rapid dissemination of new material and fresh interpretations from excavation, field survey, and aerial photography, and to securing the publication of outstanding material.

In what follows, our suggested themes for research have been arranged under a series of broad headings, variously concerned with the general character of the settlement/urban network, the question of urban functions, or specific themes bearing on the internal character of the sites themselves.

The changing character of the settlement hierarchy

The period from *c* 100 BC to AD 200 is traditionally associated with several shifts in the character of the settlement network, with respect to the latest stages of hillfort evolution, the emergence of the *oppida* and other large settlements, and the development of early Roman towns, both large and small. The literature abounds with a range of explanations to account for these individual shifts, couched either in terms of continuity or change, or a combination of both, against a backcloth of various internal and external agencies. Few studies, however, have been directed at a wider analysis of the settlement networks right across the period, nor at the range of factors responsible for determining settlement location, continuity and change. This omission opens up an important avenue of research, both in relation to individual site complexes and the overall network.

Recent publications reveal divergent opinions about many aspects of settlement in the later Iron Age. Questions have been raised about the character and function of those hillforts which survived into the 1st century BC, following the excavations at Maiden Castle. Similarly, spatial and temporal variations in the character of the *oppida* have been re-examined, both on the continent and in Britain, prompting alternative ideas about the extent to which the visible changes in the settlement network represent a significant break with the past. All this has a bearing on wider questions in the early Roman period, where the relative importance of the Iron Age contribution to urban development has been the subject of much debate, alongside familiar arguments about military origins and Roman administrative requirements. Any assessment of the wider settlement/urban network, therefore, demands a re-evaluation of the situation in the later Iron Age as an essential prerequisite.

A particularly pressing requirement is a re-evaluation of the British *oppida* and related settlements. These sites have generally been linked with processes of urban development, political centralisation, and incipient state formation in the later Iron Age, as well as being seen as the urban precursors of Roman towns, both large and small. Whilst this model may be sustainable in some cases, there is a growing feeling that our perception of the character and relative importance of the pre-existing sites has been coloured by the fact of their continuity or otherwise as Roman administrative centres. Closer examination of the evidence suggests that the better-known sites extant on the eve of the conquest may be simply the most conspicuous in a continuum of broadly similar settlements, with or without linear dykes, all of which are associated with the upper echelons of society. In fact, focal sites may be commoner in the later Iron Age settlement network than either our evidence, or our perceptions, currently suggest, a possibility raising wider implications for the question of continuity and change into the early Roman period. Worthwhile advances could be made by further targeted research at different classes of site, on the model of work at Silchester, Bagendon-North Cerney, Stanwick, Baldock, and Heybridge.

A re-evaluation of *oppida* and related settlements should also embrace the factors which determined how and why such sites emerged in the landscape, not least the relative importance of internal processes and external contacts. Traditional explanations often emphasise intensified trade with the continent and the expansion of Roman territory as major factors in promoting significant socio-political change, usually within a core–periphery framework. Recently, however, such models have come under scrutiny from those who would doubt just how fundamental the changes actually were, citing instead the suggestion that their apparent significance is more a function of the increased visibility of the later Iron Age as a consequence of highly-visible foreign imports, inscribed coinages, and the availability of textual sources. As the introduction has emphasised, the resolution of these issues will require not just a refinement of the chronological framework within which the changes occurred, but also an examination of several factors rooted ultimately in the middle Iron Age.

A clearer understanding of the settlement network in the later Iron Age also provides an essential reference point for the early Roman period. Here too, recent publications have revealed a variety of opinions about the nature of urban development. Questions have been raised over the degree to which Roman urbanism was a disruptive process or a comparatively smooth evolution from pre-conquest forms, and about the relative importance of pre-existing centres, the native elites and the military in the origins and early development of towns. Alternative views have emerged about the mechanisms by which the sites for the new administrative centres came to be selected, whether by a process of self-selection, negotiation, or imposition. Such issues clearly affect the large and small towns in different measure, even if in the early stages of their development the distinction between the two may be somewhat blurred.

At the level of individual sites, much has been learnt in recent years about those where a military to civil transition is manifest, not least the *coloniae* and those *civitas* centres which emerged from fortresses or forts. Much the same is true of London, even if the initial stimulus remains open to debate. The situation is much less clear, however, for the large class of sites displaying an Iron Age to civilian transition, with or without intervening military occupation. Verulamium, perhaps, is the best known site in this group, in contrast with the position at Canterbury, Leicester, and Silchester, among others. The picture is hardly better for the small towns in either category, though recent advances have been made at Baldock and to some extent at Heybridge. Interest necessarily focuses not just on site location, but also on the processes of physical transformation, not least the transitional developments preceding any decision to create a more regular street system. Much can also be learnt from a study of those sites like Bagendon North Cerney/Cirencester, where the transition involved a shift of site. Equally interesting are those sites which failed to achieve *civitas* status despite their apparent importance in the Iron Age, among them Badbury Rings, Braughing, and Old Sleaford.

At a macro level, the factors shaping the character and development of the urban network during the early Roman period offer considerable scope for further research. The potential of this wider approach is exemplified by the publication of recent research in east-central France, most notably in the areas of Franche Comté and the Côte-d'Or, where attempts have been made to investigate the Roman urban hierarchy in some detail, assessing its regional evolution within the context of the relief geography, the development of the communications network (road and riverine), and its Iron Age antecedents. Interesting trends have emerged, contrasting the patterns of movement and exchange in the late Iron Age with the increasing complexity of the Gallo-Roman period, consequent upon the development of inter-regional and local communications networks. The potential of similar approaches in Britain is amply demonstrated by recent work in the east Midlands, though a far wider range of environmental and cultural factors may need to be included. Analysis of the changing settlement network, both urban and rural, will be further enabled by the adoption of GIS packages.

Although much has been learnt about the process of urban development in southern Britain, the situation in Wales and the North presents obvious contrasts. With few exceptions, Mediterranean urbanism failed to gain a hold in these areas, and what towns there were reveal a closer relationship with the military network. This has often been explained by the absence of a developed system of pre-existing centres, but recent work has begun to focus on the role of the army itself in promoting or retarding the urbanising process. This clearly requires closer attention, not least because it is a theme which carries over into the later Roman period.

Urban functions

In their attempts to define urbanisation archaeologists have regularly used criteria which directly or indirectly relate to function, including size, nucleation of population, hierarchy of settlement types, variety of building types, evidence of corporate activity, industrial production and specialisation, concentration of cultural activities, zoning of social and other activity areas, and concentrations of wealth and status. While such features are obviously not exclusive to urban sites, it is widely represented that all of them gradually came together over the period from *c* 100 BC to AD 200, culminating in the appearance of the well-known pattern of Roman *civitas* capitals, themselves part of a competitive hierarchy of large and small urban sites. This process is commonly enshrined within simple models emphasising the following trends:

- mid-Iron Age (2nd century BC): some concentrations of population (in hillforts) and settlement (Thames Valley, Wessex); communal constructions (linear dykes in Yorkshire, hillforts); dispersed industrial production; little evidence for marked social hierarchy.
- mid- to late Iron Age (c 120 to 80 BC): appearance of specialist sites for external trade (Hengistbury), production (Glastonbury, Droitwich), or religion (Hayling Island).
- late Iron Age (1st century BC): increasing social differentiation (burials, inscribed coinage); appearance of rural sites as political(?) centres of high social status (Braughing, Silchester) or lesser centres of wealth and status (Baldock, Gussage), characterised by concentrations of population, high-status goods and burials, coinage, and small, non-defensive dyke systems.
- latest Iron Age (AD 1 to 50): appearance of *oppida* or royal centres, characterised by loose agglomerations of settlement incorporating religious centres, high-status burials, and massive dyke systems.
- earliest Roman (AD 47 to 70): imposition of nucleations of population (military sites and vici, retired soldiers, administrators); reinforcement of importance among some native sites (Verulamium, Bagendon); elite rural investment (Fishbourne, Eccles).
- Flavian to Hadrianic (AD 70 to 120): advance of army to the north and west; establishment of *civitas* capitals and emergence of small towns, often as a development of military *vici* or the *cursus publicus*; growth of a competitive hierarchy of sites; elite investment in urban public buildings and town houses.

However satisfying such simplified models are, much still remains uncertain about the underlying functional aspects of urban development. Questions have been raised about the character and function of late Iron Age settlements and about the assumption that each stage in the process necessarily started in the south-east, before diffusing north and west. It has also become increasingly clear that the situation was not homogeneous across the south and east, such that even if we assume that the Roman urban system was conceived in an idealised form, once imposed it would have been reacting with different native systems. Even within the post-conquest period, much still needs to be learnt about the date at which the archetypal Roman system appeared, whether it possessed all the functions claimed for it (especially in terms of production and marketing), and the extent to which we can identify a hierarchy of sites and the competition between them in the way that is assumed in much central-place theory. Such issues are also cut across by the on-going debates in ancient history over the role of Roman towns as consumer cities or as centres of innovation and production.

At the regional and provincial level the functional dimension necessarily overlaps with wider issues, already discussed, concerning the changing character of the settlement network, since function is but one of several factors influencing continuity and change in the landscape. Critical to any advance in this area is a re-assessment of the functions of late Iron Age sites, the extent to which these dictated subsequent developments, and the degree to which new Roman-inspired functions influenced the survival or failure of existing settlements, or themselves contributed to the emergence of new centres. In this context, modern opinion has tended to emphasise the role of the native elites and the importance of economic factors in shaping the character of the Roman urban network; but a recent restatement of the thesis that many roadside settlements were deliberate creations, developed as part of the *cursus publicus* and the wider infrastructure for governing the province, should remind us that much still remains uncertain about the critical phase of overlap between the latest Iron Age and the early stages of Roman development.

Much more critical to the functional dimension of urban development is the study of production, distribution, and consumption, because so much of this obviously underlies the model of an increasingly hierarchical pattern of urban sites in the Roman period and the debate over the role of early towns as consumer cities or centres of production and innovation. Despite recent advances in our understanding of how production was organised in the period c 100 BC to AD 200, few comparative studies have been undertaken of the character, extent, and chronology of specialised activities at different classes of site, both urban and rural. Particularly critical is a comparison of production between late Iron Age and early Roman military and civilian phases as a way of identifying periods of change: sites like Colchester and Verulamium offer obvious opportunities, though they may not always be typical of wider trends. This needs to be paralleled by a study of shops in early Roman towns, in order to establish their character, the scale of production and, if possible, the destination of the finished product. Current models emphasise the extent and diversity of commercial activity in the cities (influenced by Verulamium), but questions need to be asked about how typical this is, not just of Verulamium itself, but also of early levels at other sites and of the emerging small towns in the later 1st and 2nd centuries. Only then will we be in a position to assess the quantitative aspects of early urban development and provide a firm foundation for studying the changes seen in the later Roman period.

Beyond the sites themselves, research should focus on the impact of settlement (urban) development on local agricultural and industrial production and on its market role (or otherwise). Critical to this is an increased awareness of the potential of both environmental and artefactual evidence (discussed further below). Important advances have certainly been made in studying the patterns of agricultural consumption in later Iron Age centres and early Roman towns (using animal bone assemblages and plant remains), but the time is now ripe for an extended programme of sampling across as wide a range of urban and rural sites as possible, capable of providing valuable comparative data across the province. Much has also been learnt from studies of artefact distributions (especially about early pottery production) and from analyses of site assemblages (most notably pottery supply at Chelmsford), but despite the potential of this material few answers have emerged about the extent to which late Iron Age centres and early Roman towns acted as markets. Even less is known about the economic implications of actually creating the urban fabric, in terms of trying to estimate the amounts of material involved, the sources of supply, and the mechanics of procurement.

Research into the extent of any symbiosis between town and country must also incorporate a regional dimension, as a way of assessing the important problem of rural change in the vicinity of late Iron Age centres and early Roman towns. Interest must necessarily focus on three aspects: firstly on the landscape itself, in terms of changes in land boundaries, field systems, and patterns of land-use; secondly on the regional settlement pattern, in terms of changing densities of sites, internal structural changes, and the development of the villa; and thirdly on the inter-relationship between any identifiable changes and the socio-economic stimulus provided by new markets and nearby centres. An obvious starting point would be an assessment of the impact of the *coloniae* on their immediate hinterlands, as a way of comparing and contrasting the position at the *civitas* capitals and the small towns. In this context, the example of the Wroxeter Hinterland Project, with its pioneering use of GIS techniques in conjunction with large-scale geophysical surveys of the city itself, represents a major advance and offers a valuable working model for adoption elsewhere. Equally important is an investigation of the function of military *vici*, not least their relationship (or otherwise) with the local hinterland. Recent debates have tended to minimise the extent of any symbiosis, but much still remains uncertain.

Beyond the economic dimension, the socio-political and religious roles of late Iron Age centres and Roman towns have often been neglected. In the socio-political sphere, considerable interest attaches to the function of earthworks, whether designed for defence, symbolic or legal definition, status, control of population movement (eg for toll collection), or protection of official features. This last is particularly relevant for the earliest defended circuits around Romano-British towns (especially the *coloniae*) and for the phase of earthwork defences traditionally assigned to the later 2nd century. The separation of different functions in much research has often had the effect of isolating religious aspects from the wider debate over settlement (urban) development. Recent work on ritual deposition at Iron Age sites has done much to redress the balance, however, while there are encouraging signs of similar shifts in Romano-British studies. Lessons could also be learnt from the self-evident importance of religious rural sanctuaries in certain parts of Gaul, where the dividing line between religious and urban centres is seemingly so blurred as to suggest they are different manifestations of the same broad phenomenon in the rural landscape.

Demographics and social identity

Current research has little to say about demographics or the social identity of the inhabitants of Britain's urban centres in the century or so following the conquest. Suggested population levels are often achronic, and seldom closely argued. A quick survey of current views in print shows that estimates of urban population density, seen in heads per hectare, vary by a factor of ten. Beyond the familiar ideas that veterans settled in *coloniae*, that London (in particular) supported a community of traders, and that the public towns formed the power-base for the cantonal elite in Roman guise, the question of identity – who these people were – is almost dormant. To some extent both omissions might be explained by a recent preoccupation with the later town, where the focus of research has not forced these issues into the open. Equally, however, the shortage of searching enquiry in this area might be explained by the continuing acceptance of models which, despite looking tired, at least have the virtues of familiarity and convenience. Archaeologically, the points of contact with demography and identity are few, and tenuous, but studies encompassing a sufficient range of comparative material – particularly from Rome's core provinces – may show where progress is to be made, and help to frame realistic questions. In turn, more explicit linking of these questions to data, and recovery methods, seems a vital prerequisite to informed discussion.

How many people lived in the towns of Roman Britain in the century after the conquest? Who were they, and how did they differ from the populations of pre-existing nucleated centres which, in many cases, share the same sites and the same agricultural hinterlands? The social implications of these questions are large, and the possibilities diverse. Among the *civitas* capitals, we have generally accepted a model of continuity between elites in the decades spanning the conquest, with the new towns acquiring modest populations, chiefly of indigenous origin. Yet the evidence, so far as it has been examined, precludes neither alternative explanations, nor even direct opposites, involving large scale in-migration,

disruption of the existing hierarchy, and resulting social tension. Clearly, the question of numbers, demands, and needs raises some fundamental issues for the economic base of the early towns, their impact upon the agricultural economy, and potential transformations of pre-conquest relationships.

The study of population begins from a core group of questions, rather than a particular category of material, and demands an integrated approach, with the evidence, direct and comparative, eclectically derived. Working towards absolute numbers at any point is naturally beset with difficulties. At present, the emerging picture of Roman housing is, perhaps, the most straightforward body of evidence for early urban demography. It is becoming clear that the early shape of urban housing stock implies a need to accommodate large numbers of people in small spaces, using building styles whose structural affinities are Italianate, and whose life, within Britain, appears to be contained within a narrow timespan of around half a century following the conquest. Although further comparative work is required, the use of house and shop complexes of types familiar from Trajanic Ostia or the later phases at Pompeii and Herculaneum testify to density of population, and carry implications – if more debatably – for the nature of landholding, property tenure, and the mix of occupations. This evidence stands in sharp contrast with the message from housing two centuries on, when the general pattern is one of big houses standing in a townscape of dark earth.

The reasonably unambiguous evidence for relative change in housing stock and density suggests that we should broaden the scope of the enquiry to embrace a wider range of material, searching for parallel variations in measurable things: the rate of consumption among manufactures, for example, or the deposition of food remains – particularly in relation to social variations in dietary practices – or the more general question of how refuse was managed over time in terms of the provision of cess pits, sewers, and infrastructure services. Studies on the demography of the ancient Mediterranean town, again particularly via the prism of building stock, offer comparative figures which can and should be set against the emerging archaeological picture from Britain. At present, the largest urban population density figure proposed for Romano-British towns is somewhat higher than any which have yet been suggested for the densest urban centres of the Mediterranean. Is this to be believed? If not, then why, and what are the alternatives? Could we, for instance, look at the density of similar types of buildings, rather than estimates of population, to obtain figures from different cultural areas?

Measuring internal variety among populations, although equally complex, has an extensive body of material with which to work, and our questions in this area might again benefit from the application of more comparative and circumstantial evidence. Given what we appear to know about 1st-century life expectancy, for example, what biological constraints operate upon the ability of a social group to reproduce itself over many generations, and what might this say about the possibilities of continuity between the pre-Roman and early Romano-British tribal elites? Even ethnicity can be obliquely glimpsed. The pan-imperial evidence of epitaphs shows that the composition of the legions in the 1st century was still largely Italian and Mediterranean. The legions, we believe, were the donors for our early colonial populations, so in Colchester, for example, we might envisage a situation in which the new urban population was distinct from the indigenous group not simply in its military affiliations and relationship with the new power base, but in its mixed ethnic origins. We can point to the decade between the founding of the *colonia* and the Boudiccan fire as one in which the origins of the male population can be defined, at least with as much confidence as will ever be possible in the absence of biological evidence. Might it be useful to extend the enquiry into other areas? Is there anything distinct about the material culture deposited by this group when compared to, say, London and Verulamium in the same period? This might be seen as an area in which all answers are equally interesting.

In the ground, it is clear that the domestic archaeology of the early Roman town is rich in variety. A more general aim might be to work towards the archaeological characterisation of households, or at least the sets of material associated with buildings of particular types. Two decades ago it would have been difficult to assemble a body of published evidence of sufficient size and quality to do this, but London, Colchester, and Verulamium already furnish good data (some of which has already benefited from studies of this kind) and other towns are following. Much might also be learnt about identity and the processes of transition from a review of early cemetery evidence, as the valuable work on the King Harry Lane material at Verulamium emphasises, though to date its potential has hardly been realised. The barriers here are partly ones of tradition and approach. The compartmentalisation of specialisms in Romano-British studies limits our ability to see the relationships between categories of material, and their behaviour over time.

The dynamics of internal morphology and land-use

The study of internal morphology, land-use and buildings provides an essential foundation for many of the issues raised in this report. It is unfortunate, therefore, that so few sites are well enough known to allow detailed spatial analyses to be undertaken, despite some significant advances in our understanding. Aerial photography, for instance, continues to reveal much new information at sites like Silchester, Water Newton, and Kenchester, while the potential of large-scale geophysical surveys has become increasingly apparent from the

work at Baldock and, more recently, at Wroxeter. All too often, however, such surveys emphasise the later, rather than the earlier patterns, hence the importance of those rescue and research-related excavations which have investigated the early levels at sites like Colchester, London, and Caerwent. Although every chance needs to be taken to enhance the available data base, the time must now be ripe for a more co-ordinated research approach, particularly at those greenfield sites which afford the opportunity of combining cost-effective, non-invasive surveys with judicious excavations in key areas to elucidate the early plan. The current Wroxeter project and the ongoing work at Silchester and Aldborough offer a useful working model for other sites like Kenchester or Caistor by Norwich. Excavators should also seek to target sites where the earliest levels are known to be waterlogged, as for example at York and Carlisle, since these afford significant opportunities lacking elsewhere – better preservation of organic materials and environmental data, details of early construction techniques, and samples for precise dendrochronological dating.

Morphological questions among the Iron Age centres focus on the extent to which the emergence of *oppida* and related settlements was accompanied by increasing internal complexity as a consequence of growing centralisation. Much has been learnt in this area from recent research at Camulodunum, Verulamium, and Silchester, where the evidence ranges from dispersed activity across a wide area to examples of rectilinear organisation. The situation at lesser settlements has been clarified by work at sites like Baldock and Dragonby. The resulting picture, both here and on the continent, seems to be one of significant diversity in internal layout. Nonetheless, the picture still needs much clarification, partly because it bears upon the differing roles performed by individual sites over time, and partly because it provides the framework at key settlements for assessing the transformations wrought by the Roman presence. No opportunity should be lost for investigating this diversity across the whole range of sites, as part of the wider re-evaluation advocated elsewhere in this survey, irrespective of their adoption as Roman towns.

Considerable importance attaches to charting the earliest stages of Roman urban development, particularly at those sites which saw the provision of a formalised street grid and a range of public buildings and amenities. At those towns which succeeded earlier legionary fortresses – among them Colchester, Gloucester, and Exeter – much has been learnt about the critical transition between military and civilian phases, showing that the military street grid provided the basis for the town, being variously adapted, modified, and re-aligned to meet local needs. This has raised interesting questions about the units of measurement involved, which cannot simply be ignored either at the global site level or in the case of individual *insulae*, despite the many acknowledged problems. In the future, precise measurements of individual buildings and properties will be essential, making use of the latest technology.

The situation is much less clear, however, for the large class of sites where the Roman town seems to have superseded a pre-existing native settlement, with or without a military horizon. The exception is obviously Verulamium, but at other key sites, such as Canterbury, Leicester, Silchester, and Winchester, the generally later dates now being assigned both to street grids and the earliest public buildings are increasingly revealing a morphologically opaque period from the mid- to late 1st century. This must be an urgent priority for investigation. In such cases, the decision to add a formal street system was a critical step; hence the very real importance of establishing its original extent and date, and the mechanics of its creation.

It is becoming increasingly clear that the rate of urban development at the major towns varied from site to site, depending upon the level of commitment and economic resources of each community, irrespective of any state encouragement. In addition, while it remains true that the Flavian period saw considerable urban expansion, recent analysis of the evidence at many sites has tended to shift the emphasis forward into the Trajanic era and succeeding decades. From a morphological perspective, this clearly emphasises the need for several inter-related lines of inquiry, if we are to draw useful inter-site comparisons. These include:

(a) refining our dating of the key elements in the townscape;
(b) establishing the character and extent of the early street grids;
(c) examining the character and location of the public buildings and amenities; and
(d) defining the character, range, and location of the domestic and workshop units.

Useful information about early town boundaries might also be gleaned from a study of cemetery location, and from the inter-relationship of intra- and extra-mural settlement where defences are known to have been constructed. In particular, those areas which were abandoned or became marginal in the process, might well provide valuable evidence on the earlier history of a site.

Information gained in recent years about the nature of early street layouts increasingly emphasises a diversity of practice and date. Some towns clearly inherited elements of their street system from pre-existing forts, and took the opportunity to add a drainage system (as at Lincoln). Others suggest dynamic development beyond a planned core (as at London), whilst at Canterbury and elsewhere there is a surprising level of variety in road alignments and *insula* size, clearly indicating that earlier presuppositions of the presence of a rigid grid cannot be taken for granted. Elsewhere the grid is clearly not a primary feature, raising questions about how it came to be imposed (as at Caerwent). Such diversity demands further clarification, since the extent to which sites were 'planned' lies at the heart of much traditional thinking about urbanisation in the western provinces.

The rate of provision of public buildings and amenities in the major towns has also been clarified in recent years, despite the difficulties of establishing precise dates for structures which may well have taken years to complete. Improved excavation techniques have also shown that stone buildings can have timber antecedents. This and the self-evident variations in overall plan and size raise questions about the source of architectural inspiration for public monuments and their degree of dependence upon Gallic expertise and design, or military prototypes. The prevailing view favours continental influences, especially in the architectural detail, even though some plans still bear a resemblance to contemporary military designs despite assertions to the contrary. As might be expected, some of the strongest hints of continental influence occur in the early *coloniae* and in the south-east, though the mechanisms by which the designs were imported remains uncertain. All this raises questions about the overall range of provision at individual sites, their relative levels of prosperity and aspiration measured in terms of continental models, and their degree of urban 'success' compared to western counterparts. Much also remains to be learnt about the way in which individual building complexes were incorporated into the overall design and the extent to which any architectural 'master plan' was at work. In this respect the ritual and ideological dimension of urban planning deserves much closer attention.

Particularly critical to our understanding of urban morphology is a comparative study of the province's minor towns, roadside settlements, and military *vici*. Development among these sites is often seen as organic, rather than imposed, with streets developing away from the principal frontages only as need arose. This model has never been tested, however, despite its obvious attraction, yet it raises important issues about the planning agencies concerned and the extent to which the overall process was controlled. Certainly, at sites like Baldock and Dragonby, clear signs of continuity in the layout from the later Iron Age into the Roman period suggest a parallel continuity in landholding and social organisation. By contrast, the recent assertion that many roadside settlements like Chelmsford and Towcester originated as deliberate foundations, as part of the wider infrastructure of government, only serves to emphasise how little we actually know about their early layout and respective functions. Every opportunity should be taken, therefore, to examine the earliest levels, not least the initial layout and metrology of the associated plots, which should provide some useful comparisons with the practice at major towns.

Comparative work is also needed on the nature, size, and location of the basic domestic and workshop units, since therein lie clues to wider issues concerned with social identity and function. Recent years have seen considerable advances in our understanding of typology, as a result of excavations at a variety of sites. Yet many questions remain about the extent to which native forms of construction survived, the sources of inspiration for new building types, the pace of transition to more Romanised architecture at different sites, the changing density of the different types, and the nature and location of those properties associated with the decurions.

Ultimately, the study of internal morphology is not an end in itself. Much can obviously be learnt about the changing character of internal land-use, the distribution of different building types within the plan, and the nature of inter-site variation, but these are little more than basic building blocks to be used in conjunction with the artefacts and the environmental data in the analysis of broader issues concerned with function, social structure, and population, as well as problems of continuity and change, acculturation, and Romanisation. Herein lies the integrative challenge of future research.

Artefacts and urban research

Artefact studies provide an important, if frequently neglected, avenue of investigation into questions such as the nature and extent of social differentiation in urban settlements, the incidence of long-distance trade between major centres, and the interdependence of urban and rural settlements. One of the central features of the late Iron Age in most of southern Britain is the massive increase in artefact deposition which occurs from the late 1st century BC onward. This trend is most evident at the new nucleated settlements like Braughing-Puckeridge and Canterbury, at palace complexes (*oppida*) such as Colchester and Verulamium, and at religious shrines and sanctuaries like Harlow and Hayling Island, but it also affects smaller rural settlements like Gussage All Saints or Odell. Across this range of sites casual loss, refuse disposal, and deliberate deposition – as offerings, hoarding, and also in burials – all increase sharply. Previously rare artefact types like brooches become relatively common alongside new categories like coinage and toilet implements, while pottery and iron implements are abundant nearly everywhere.

This explosion in the quantities of material deposited continues after the conquest and is evidently symptomatic of changing attitudes to the disposal of rubbish and to the use of material culture, driven at least in part by ideas and innovations from the expanding Roman world. Imported brass, for example, with its potential for display, was rapidly adopted both for the manufacture of a range of new brooch types, themselves based on continental models, and also for traditional military equipment and trappings previously made in bronze. At one level, the increase in material deposited is a consequence of

increased availability brought about by changes in the scale and organisation of production; in other respects, however, it does seem to indicate fundamental changes in the nature of society, reflected in connected developments such as the appearance of formal cemeteries and religious sites.

The study of artefacts and environmental remains from urban settlements requires a change in attitude to the data collection process. At present this is too passive. Research is still geared to sites *per se* and to settlement archaeology, rather than to the society which generated these remains. This is true both of excavation strategies, which are primarily concerned with the recovery of structural evidence rather than with recording artefacts and their contextual relationships, and of modern excavation reports. To facilitate more rapid presentation of the basic structural evidence from excavation – itself a laudable aim – artefact studies are now frequently relegated almost to a post-publication exercise, with only summaries and lists appearing in the actual reports. This practice, and the attitude it betokens, must be reversed if we are to realise the potential of artefact analysis for yielding insights into questions such as increasing social complexity, acculturation, the development of market exchange, or the impact of long-distance trade as this affected different types of sites and regions. The King Harry Lane cemetery at Verulamium offers a good example of what can be achieved by this approach. Careful analysis of the spatial and chronological structure of the burials and the associated grave goods implied a breakdown of existing social networks and the emergence of an increasingly socially disembedded element in the population – presumably migrants who were drawn to the expanding settlement during the earlier 1st century AD, initially British, and after the conquest, both British and continental.

Changes are required in four main areas of research design and practice. Firstly, more consistent and explicit recovery procedures for artefacts and environmental remains need to be adopted for urban excavations. Comparable recovery procedures are required, and should be discussed, agreed, and made explicit in reporting. At present some excavators scan their occupation floors with metal detectors, for example, whilst others do not. Several published studies have shown how faunal assemblages appear to be dominated by different species according to whether sieving was or was not used. Similar biases are likely to affect artefact recovery. Whilst a sample-based approach is inevitable, there may be instances where the total recovery of artefact evidence is justified in excavation strategy – for example in seeking to identify areas where particular activities were performed, or to detect functional differences in similar-looking structures.

Secondly, we need to develop more standardised ways of presenting artefact evidence and the accompanying contextual information in the final excavation reports, so that different sites can be systematically compared. Full quantification is essential, especially for pottery, so that the proportions of different elements can be assessed, and a profile constructed of regional production, distribution, and consumption.

Thirdly, we need to establish standard methodologies for analysing the artefact evidence from particular sites, as has already been done, for example, for Roman coinage. It is well established that on its own the assemblage from a particular site can say only so much and is often misleading. The amount of coinage in circulation varied over time, for example, so a dramatic increase in coinage at a particular point in time at a given site may simply reflect the overall circulation pattern, rather than a change in the intensity of occupation. Or again, the presence of 2nd century AD samian on many native settlements in northern Britain appears to reflect the maximum distribution of the pottery, rather than the period of peak occupation of the sites themselves. As with coinage, we need to construct profiles of the losses which are normal for a given region for artefact categories like brooches and samian, against which the finds from a particular site can be compared to see whether they conform to the norm, or depart from it in ways which may be significant. Intra-site patterns can be treated similarly, by comparing, for example, the artefact profile from a suspected cult area or place of exchange with those normal to residential areas, although care is needed to avoid circular reasoning.

Fourthly, the depositional patterning and different site associations of particular categories of artefact demands greater attention. For the late Iron Age, this information is at the very least essential for building up a more detailed absolute chronology than we currently possess. More generally, sites encapsulate information about all kinds of past behaviour patterns, albeit severely scrambled by depositional and post-depositional processes. If we wish to investigate the principles articulating and structuring the social relationships of past urban populations, much of this information will have to be sought in the matrix of artefactual and contextual relationships which comprise the archaeological record of successive activities at that site. We need therefore to consider how future research agendas should be structured to meet this objective. We might even contemplate excavating some sites primarily for their artefact record, for example to learn more about the developing nature of coin use and exchange on different types of site in the pre-Roman period. We also require much more detailed information about how the artefact profiles associated with particular activities carried out in an urban context differ from rural settlements, and between different areas of Britain.

In the end, making the most of artefact data will entail developing regional research strategies on a scale more commensurate with the phenomenon of urbanisation, in which site, structural, contextual, artefactual, and environmental data are all fully integrated. We must also ensure a sufficient level of communication between archaeologists concerned with these problems, so that data are collected and analysed along comparable lines in respect of the questions which have been agreed.

Summing-up

The principal themes discussed in this report can be briefly summarised as follows:

- The precise date of many key developments in the period under review remains uncertain. Attention must be given to improving our overall chronological framework.
- Although this report concerns urban development in Britain between c 100 BC and AD 200, we must be prepared where appropriate to adopt a wider chronological and geographical perspective. The value of comparing insular developments with those in other provinces is a theme which emerges strongly throughout.
- Work in other European countries has highlighted the importance of adopting a regional rather than a site-specific approach, and of studying entire settlement networks. Our ability to work at this level has been greatly enhanced by the increasing availability of GIS and other technological advances.
- Research strategies need to take more account of the regional and cultural diversity of Britain before the conquest. This is essential if the Iron Age contribution to subsequent developments is to be properly assessed.
- The role of the Roman army in promoting or retarding the urban process also requires reappraisal. In this context, those towns which developed directly out of Iron Age sites without a military presence and those areas where urbanism never gained hold both deserve particular attention.
- Beyond the individual sites, research needs to focus on the impact of the different types of larger Iron Age and Roman settlements on the surrounding landscape and their assumed role as market centres.
- At a more general level, how the production, distribution and consumption of different categories of goods relate to particular classes of settlement has yet to be examined at the necessary level of detail.
- In addition to clarifying the economic dimensions of evolving settlement networks and hierarchies, the sociopolitical and religious roles of the different classes of site require more detailed investigation and comparison.
- Future research should be directed at elucidating the size and identity of urban populations. Such questions need to be built into excavation strategies and in some cases will require new methods of investigation to be adopted.
- Fruitful avenues for research include the shape and density of the urban housing stock at different times and places, and variations in the material

seen to exhibit complex regional and local variability between and within its constituent *civitates*, so there is reason to believe that the military presence – or better, community – was also structurally and socially highly complex and varied;

- the boundary between the military and the civil spheres was nowhere near as simple or as sharp as is widely assumed. Above all, it did not simply lie between the provincial army as an institution, and the rest of provincial life.

It seems to me that many received ideas about Roman Britain are often less sound interpretations firmly based on a century of archaeological investigation, rather than the products of particular, selective, 19th- and 20th-century readings of the very limited documentary record for the province, and of the wider history of the empire and its military. The power of these readings – shaped by modern assumptions, projected onto the ancient evidence – is seen in their tenacious persistence, even when there is, and always has been, plenty of testimony to contradict them.

The Roman army was a human organisation, not a machine

The idea that 'the Roman army' can be conceptualised as a monolithic machine, its soldiers brutally disciplined and murderously efficient automata, is a modern construct bearing no relation to the ways in which Romans thought and wrote about their own armed forces.

In thinking and writing about armies, our tradition has been to see them from the top downwards, as a single organisation subdivided into divisions, brigades, regiments, battalions, companies, platoons, sections, and men; soldiers are implicitly perceived (however unrealistically) as cogs in the machine, who can be expected to obey orders as the components of a tank respond to electrical and mechanical instructions. Ultimately this conceptualisation finds its roots in the political constitution of early modern Britain, where people were subjects rather than citizens, in a world where social inferiors like Wellington's 'scum'-soldiery in the Peninsular War were simply expected to do as they were told. These men were trained to behave like, and implicitly regarded as, parts of the machines they served, machines which have increasingly dominated the battlefield ever since, from flintlock muskets to multiple-launch rocket systems. Hence the 'mechanical analogy' applied to armies in general, and projected back onto the 'Roman war machine' in particular (eg Peddie 1994).

It is completely anachronistic to apply this conception to Rome. Romans – including those who served in the military, and the aristocrats and emperors who commanded them – conceived their military organisation in a manner precisely the opposite of our own tradition, ie from the bottom upwards. They thought of their military structure as consisting basically of the body of *milites* – 'the soldiers' – in the imperial period long-service professionals whose oath of loyalty was to the person of the emperor. The *milites* were organised into permanent regiments (legions, *auxilia*, fleets, and guards units). These units were almost entirely distributed in frontier provinces, where they came under the command of provincial governors directly responsible to the emperor for matters both civil and military. At least until the late empire, there was no specifically military hierarchy or organisation at all above the provincial level, no Ministry of War or General Staff. Indeed, the Romans had no established term equivalent to 'the Roman Army' at all. When used, the Latin word for 'army', *exercitus*, was employed of the body of *milites* in a province or on a particular frontier (eg the *exercitus Syriatica* in the Euphrates provinces (Whittaker 1994, 68)), or of composite campaign forces. It does not seem to have been applied in the singular to the Roman armed forces as a whole – perhaps not surprisingly given the principles of military organisation just outlined – although there are references to 'the armies', plural (*exercitūs*: eg Tacitus *Annals*, 1,3; 4,5). Where we write of 'the Roman army' (often implying a monolithic, centrally controlled entity, usually described in 'mechanistic' language), the Romans generally wrote of 'the soldiers' or 'the legions', emphasising multiplicity; they thought in terms of a *class of men* rather than an institution. *There was no such thing as 'The Roman Army' because there was no such concept.* (See now Haynes 1999a for a similar analysis.)

In my view, Romans held this image of their soldiers because the imperial legionaries in provinces like Britain were, institutionally and often literally, the direct descendants of republican legionaries, originally the wealthier free Roman citizenry under arms. While the military maintained its notoriously draconian disciplinary code, nonetheless the tradition that soldiers could make their feelings known to their superiors – often very forcefully – was maintained by the professional soldiery of the emperors. To read Roman accounts of the activities of their armies is to be struck by the effort required to lead, cajole, win over, persuade the soldiers to their duty, as much as to compel them to discipline by ferocity. This is illustrated by the routine and expected practice of emperors and generals to represent themselves as *commilitones*, 'fellow-soldiers' or 'comrades' of the men in the ranks. On campaign, commanders ostentatiously shared their burdens, concerns, and even fashions (Campbell 1984; James 1999). There was no question of conceptualising and treating *milites* as obedient automata, or cogs in a machine. Soldiers may have been rough and uncouth, but they were free, self-aware men, and potentially dangerous to their leaders.

Major disciplinary troubles are specifically recorded in Britain. The invasion force itself mutinied before departure (Dio 60.19.1–3), while the bizarre behaviour of Caligula on the Channel coast a few years earlier may have been triggered by a similar incident (Dio 59.25.1–3; Suetonius *Gaius* 46.1). From Clodius Albinus to Constantine III, there was a long series of military rebellions involving the soldiers of Britain, in which commanders incited their own men. But long before these, there is good evidence that the soldiers were sometimes out of control, either because their commanders were powerless as a result of political circumstances or because officers gave the troops license for their own reasons (eg the men of the procurator Decianus Catus before the Boudiccan revolt: Tacitus *Annals* 14.31–2; or the behaviour of the legionary legate Roscius Coelius during the dynastic uncertainties of AD 68–9: Tacitus, *Histories* 1.60). Perhaps the most startling case of British soldiers being incited to mutinous behaviour by their officers was the 'deputation' of 1500 men who carried their grievances to Commodus at Rome (Dio 72.9.2–3). Even with these perfectly well-known examples, the myth of the iron (*sic*) discipline of the Roman 'military machine' remains so strong that such cases are filtered out, ignored, or explained away as atypical aberrations. The evidence from Britain and the rest of the empire surely suggests these cases were simply the tips of a permanent iceberg of potential or actual soldierly unrest. In this, Roman soldiers and armies were remarkably *unlike* modern western armies (or at least, expectations of them) in terms of disciplined behaviour; Roman forces were far more unruly, and not only in times of civil war and dynastic uncertainty when things simply worsened.

The concept of the 'Roman military machine' and all it entails is more than an inappropriate model: it is actively pernicious, because it diverts attention from what was certainly a vastly complex interaction of institutions (eg the imperial regime, provincial commands, and regiments), powerful trans-provincial interest- and identity-groups (senatorial and equestrian officers, the centurionate, the community of *milites*: see below) and more local entities (individual regimental bodies of *milites*, and their dependants).

The community of soldiers, and the state's military institutions

Elsewhere, I have proposed that we should consider the soldiers of provincial garrisons the way other Romans saw them, and as the soldiers saw themselves: as constituent members of a huge, unique, empire-wide self-aware identity group, that of the *milites* (James 1999). The body of 'the soldiers' was intimately related to the political and military institutions of the state (provincial administrative, fiscal and command organisations, and regiments), but was distinct, and partly autonomous, from them. The official structures applied strong centripetal and normative pressures, as through indoctrination,

training, and discipline they sought to instil and maintain the soldiers' identification with the imperial power and loyalty to the regime. The awareness of common interests and identity which this encouraged among the soldiers developed into a powerful sense of an 'imagined community' of *commilitones* ('fellow-soldiers') stretching right across the empire (Anderson 1991; Campbell 1984; James 1999; for a rather different view of the 'army as a community' see Goldsworthy and Haynes 1999, especially Haynes 1999a; 1999b). This soldierly identity was itself normative, and closely linked with ideological ties to the imperial house, but was of course rooted in the frontier provinces of the empire as much as in relation to an imagined 'Rome' or usually unseen emperor (see below). The soldiers of Britain, therefore, were an important and active part of a distinctive provincial experience of 'becoming Roman', which in my view was fundamentally different from that seen in demilitarised 'civil' communities (Woolf 1998; James forthcoming).

Regimental communities I: the *milites* themselves

There were further levels of complexity in the military at more local scales. Soldiers' lives were conducted primarily at the level of their regiments; below the level of the centurionate, it was relatively unusual for men to change units, and they commonly would spend most or all of their adult life as part of the same, stable, slowly evolving local community of *commilitones*. These regiments – especially the auxiliary formations which made up such a large proportion of the British provincial army – had highly diverse ethnic origins. By the 2nd century many had long, continuous individual histories, constituting living communities which, even if continued recruitment from original homelands was the exception rather than the rule (Dobson and Mann 1973, 201–5; Mann 1985, 204), apparently maintained regimental traditions quite as distinctive and jealously guarded as those which in recent centuries have characterised the British army in particular (Haynes 1999a, 10). The circumstances of the middle empire, when many units settled in the same place for generations, at some distance from their neighbours, would have helped foster the rise of such unique characteristics within the overall collective traditions of the armies.

For the soldiers of a provincial garrison like that of Britain, then, the shape of their lives, the nature of their identities, and the cultural choices they made, were the result and expression not just of the maintenance of an armed force at the behest of the imperial elite; it was also the outcome of complex interplays between various groupings and forces. These included convergent pressures to conform, and the more divergent special traditions of the unit, to which we must add other, enormously significant but hitherto largely ignored local interactions with non-soldiers (see below) and the cultural impact of recruits of differing ethnic origin.

Regimental communities II: non-combatants, soldiers' dependants, and soldiers 'off duty'

Because of the notorious ban on soldiers being married attributed to Augustus (Allason-Jones 1999, 45), it is still widely assumed that early imperial regiments were quasi-monastic institutions, at least in barracks. Apart from some commanders bringing their families along on their relatively short tours of duty, the only other serving soldiers permitted to marry were centurions. Outside the walls were enterprising tradespeople and 'service providers' including prostitutes and performers. While they provide local colour, apart from traders or contractors, there has been a tendency to ignore such groups as peripheral, parasitic flies or carrion birds following the military herd, kept at arms' length by the officers.

It is now clear that such a view is simply wrong. Non-combatants were intimately integrated into the life of soldiers and regiments, in a variety of capacities. While not on the roster with the *milites* proper, servants could be *de facto* part of the regiment, notably cavalrymen's personal grooms, quasi-soldiers themselves who often appear on tombstones (Speidel 1992). Most, if not all, cavalrymen apparently had a groom; these men alone amounted to substantial numbers of non-soldiers formally attached to regiments with mounted components – ie most formations.

There were several other categories. In addition to independent sutlers and cavalry grooms, there is no doubt that foot-soldiers also maintained or owned private servants or slaves, male and female, although the numbers involved are unclear. There were various categories comprising a substantial 'support train', some of which were probably commercial opportunists, while others were quite clearly paramilitary (terms used include *calones*, *galearii*, *lixae*, and others (Roth 1999, 91–110; Speidel 1992; von Petrikovits 1980)). It is also beyond doubt that many serving soldiers were married, even if not 'officially': the wording of military diplomas directly recognises such *de facto* unions (Allason-Jones 1999, 49). Soldiers – especially older men and veterans – who had accumulated significant property made good marriage prospects. Younger soldiers might also be men of means, if they had inherited property from deceased parents (a high demographic probability: Saller 1987). However, at any one time many, perhaps most men, were probably still single (especially younger soldiers).

Nevertheless, a high proportion of troops will have had other dependants, such as a widowed mother, minor siblings or unmarried female relatives (Maxfield 1995; Wells 1997). Such dependants may often have been set up close to their source of financial support; examples are attested in Britain (Allason-Jones 1999, 48). The Vindolanda tablets suggest that this was already the case in the first century AD (eg *Tab. Vindol.* II, 310). Men without such economic burdens may have been those who acquired slave-concubines who often later became wives (Varon 1994).

There is, then, every reason to think that Roman regiments usually formed the armature for fully-fledged social communities, albeit of a special kind, in which soldiers and other citizens and provincials, freedmen and freedwomen, slaves, males and females, children, adults, and the elderly, were all active participants. And if many of these groups were regarded by the military authorities as dependants, we should recognise that they (not least women and older children) will have provided a considerable part, if not the bulk, of the labour/production capacity of the community, and were not mere hungry mouths (Harris 1988, 271). Further, I would argue that this was true right from the start of the province, for our evidence is consistent with the idea that the units of the provincial army arrived with, and were always accompanied by, substantial non-combatant 'tails'. Some at least of these non-soldierly groupings achieved a level of formal corporate identity (eg the *vicani* of Vindolanda (Birley 1979, 108)).

If military communities usually represent such complex social mixtures, then we must consider them not only in terms of the 'military–civilian' dimension of identity and action. Other dimensions will have been equally significant, and probably far more important, in many aspects of life, in different fields of activity, and at various times in the person's day. For the reconstruction of military communities outlined above suggests that their internal daily life was structured around issues of gender, class, and ethnicity, as well as around the vocational and political distinctiveness of groups of professional soldiers of a colonial power (Hill, this volume). Many soldiers, for example, evidently spent much time in domestic environments with non-soldiers. These non-soldiers – *and soldiers in such contexts* – might be expected to display cultural traits and practices outside the scope of the institutional life of the army and regiment, or even outside the 'on-duty' identity of *milites*. I have in mind soldiers acting as heads of families, husbands and fathers, as owners of slaves, as clients and as patrons of freedmen and women. Here class and age identities come to the fore. Of course gender is another major consideration: soldierly identity as a particular masculinity is yet to be fully analysed (Alston 1998; James 1999), while there is evidently an enormous amount of work yet to be done on the role of women and the nature of gender relations in military communities (Hill, this volume; Allason-Jones 1999). In private, personal contexts, the ethnic identity of individual soldiers and their families (from near or distant regions and provinces) might also come to the fore, in preserved routine domestic habits or as conscious expressions of origin.

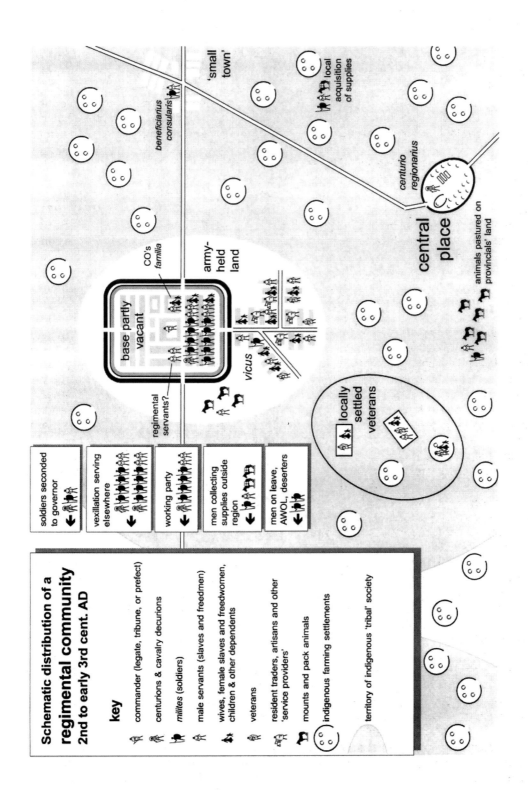

Schematic distribution of a regimental community 2nd to early 3rd cent. AD

key

- commander (legate, tribune, or prefect)
- centurions & cavalry decurions
- *milites* (soldiers)
- male servants (slaves and freedmen)
- wives, female slaves and freedwomen, children & other dependents
- veterans
- resident traders, artisans and other 'service providers'
- mounts and pack animals
- indigenous farming settlements
- territory of indigenous 'tribal' society

soldiers seconded to governor

vexillation serving elsewhere

working party

men collecting supplies outside region

men on leave, AWOL, deserters

CO's *familia*

base partly vacant

regimental servants?

army-held land

vicus

beneficiarius consularis

'small town'

local acquisition of supplies

centurio regionarius

central place

animals pastured on provincials' land

locally settled veterans

Figure 22   Schematic representation of the distribution of a Roman regimental community during the middle imperial period. Soldiers were usually much more scattered, and more mixed with the civilian population, than is usually realised

The need for context: military communities in their social and landscape settings

We remain woefully ignorant of the interactions between such military communities and their neighbours in the surrounding districts. The extent of the imbalance in our knowledge can be seen, for example, in the new edition of a book on north-west England largely about this very issue (Shotter 1999). While Shotter is able to present more than 50 pages on the evidence for the Roman military conquest, consolidation, and creation of the frontier, he can assemble just six pages (84–9) on Roman-period rural settlements, where he notes the lack of excavation effort on such sites. He is obliged to base the discussion of the relationship between forts, *vici* and the rural population, and the Romanisation of the latter, almost entirely on evidence from elsewhere (eg the Cotswolds), and speculation (Shotter 1999, 60, 84–9). This lacuna is not limited to the Roman period (Taylor, this volume); the Iron Age is equally unexplored in areas such as north-west England (Armit *et al* 2000, section E2). Clearly we need to know very much more about rural settlement and population in military-dominated areas.

Soldiers at large in the province

Much 'military–civilian interaction' will have taken place beyond these local contexts, for if military bases became fixed, soldiers did not (Fig 22). Bases apparently designed for whole units mask a reality of extensive outposting of detachments, such as the bodies of legionaries at Carlisle and Corbridge (McCarthy 1999, 170).

Significant numbers of soldiers were also usually on the move, if not stationed, in the 'civil zone' or even beyond the province. Beyond the well-known secondment of soldiers to the governor (Rankov 1999) or provincial procurator, evidence for common practice in other provinces, consistent with data from Britain itself, suggests that, even as the total garrison size seems to have declined markedly (James 1984), there was probably a notable and growing soldierly presence across the civil province. This was not necessarily large but more socially and politically significant than usually realised. In addition to parties of soldiers in transit, on specific errands connected with supply and conveying messages and individuals on leave for personal, business, or health reasons (eg at Bath), documentary information from the Vindolanda tablets (Bowman 1994; Bowman and Thomas 1994; 1996) and elsewhere in the empire reveals that many soldiers were frequently away from their home bases, for a wide variety of official, informal, or illicit reasons, including straggling or desertion.

Soldiers were essential to the control and suppression of dissent within provinces, through the threat of violence, and were not simply sentinels on the frontier; they performed local policing and surveillance tasks, in the absence of, or alongside, civil administration. Our clearest evidence is from the rich documentary record of early imperial Egypt, where *centuriones regionarii*, 'district centurions', were key policing officials in all unurbanised regions (Alston 1995, 86–96). *Centuriones regionarii* are known elsewhere, in Britain at Carlisle and Bath (*Tab Vindol* II, 310; RIB I 152). It seems likely that there was originally an extensive network of these officials across the early province, which presumably shrank as the *civitates* developed. However, the middle empire saw a great expansion of the deployment by governors of soldiers on surveillance/policing tasks even within civil zones, mostly *beneficiarii consularis*, often attested at *stationes* at strategic road junctions (Rankov 1999, 27–32). A number are attested epigraphically in Britain:

Dorchester, Oxon.	RIB I 235
Greta Bridge	RIB I 745
Housesteads	RIB I 1599
Lancaster	RIB I 602
Lanchester	RIB I 1085
Nr Risingham	RIB I 1225
Thornborough-on-Swale (2)	RIB I 725 & 726
Winchester	RIB I 88

In the provinces during the early and middle empire, soldiers, if relatively few in number, were increasingly prominent in civilian society, in everything from tax/supply collection to private business and simple extortion, as the quite detailed testimony, not only from Egypt (Alston 1995) but also from Judaea/Palestine and Syria makes clear (Isaac 1992; Speidel 1998, 170). It is hardly plausible that such a heavily militarised province as Britain – which apparently had several times as many soldiers per head of population as Egypt – should have been less affected.

Finding and defining 'the military' in archaeology

Archaeologically, how do we find and identify 'the military' against the 'civil' background, to allow us to address questions of interaction, and to test the reconstruction suggested above, so that it does not just become an alternative 'text-driven' or 'text-given' structure into which archaeology is forced?

Some aspects depend on the archaeological recovery of more texts, since people like *centuriones regionarii* can only (so far as we know) be detected through documentary evidence. It is hard to plan for this, but we can maximise the chances of recovery of such evidence. While new inscriptions will always be rare finds, we can be more alert to the possibility of texts on waterlogged organic materials as at Vindolanda. Examples have now also been recovered at Carlisle (Tomlin 1998) and Caerleon (Hassall and Tomlin 1986, 450–1).

However, it may be possible to identify direct archaeological traces of the presence of other officials, such as *beneficiarii*, who possessed highly characteristic badges of office in the form of symbolic lances, motifs also reflected in military uniform fittings (Rankov 1999, 31–2). For example, the device is worked into a fine baldric-plate of 3rd-century type from Silchester (Boon 1974, 68, fig 8, 4). Yet other 'military equipment', of types known to have been used by regular Roman soldiers – including weapons – need not denote the presence of such men at all. For under the *pax Romana*, non-soldiers could legitimately possess arms. The *Lex Julia de Vi Publica* (the 'Julian Law on Unlawful Public Violence') was essentially concerned with outlawing the bearing of arms in public contexts, or the maintenance of armed private retainers. Private ownership of weapons, for example for hunting and self-defence, was permitted and widespread (*Digest of Justinian*, XXXXVIII, vi; Mommsen *et al* 1985, 816–7; Hopwood 1989, 177). The maintenance of armed forces by client kings, and even city-state militias must also be born in mind: Tacitus seems to refer to British provincial levies at *Mons Graupius* (*Agricola* 29). And of course laws are broken; armed brigandage was endemic in many parts of the empire, including Italy (Hopwood 1989).

Deciding that military items represent soldiers *per se* depends on context. So, for example, the single, complete set of personal equipment in a grave at Lyon (Wuilleumier 1950), and the *combinations* of items interred with the Canterbury murder victims (Bennett *et al* 1982, 44–61, 85–90, figs 10, 99, 100, pls XII–XIII) are strong evidence that all three deceased were soldiers present in those cities. Conversely the horse-harness fittings of familiar Roman 'military' type, found at Folly Lane, Verulamium, Herts, were minor elements in an elaborate indigenous burial of the late 50s AD (Niblett 1999, 143–5, nos 8 and 9, figs 55–6). In isolation they might be taken as evidence for Roman soldiers, whereas they apparently represent the militaristic but culturally-fashionable taste of a British noble. These examples re-emphasise that, even for 'Roman' arms, ascription of cultural meaning is always dependent on context. Isolated items were always prone to appropriation, reuse and redefinition, as they are today, when 'real' combat jackets, some retaining rank and unit markings, are worn by civilians.

There was also, of course, much more to the life of soldiers than the bearing of personal equipment. Can we identify their presence through other traces? The most hopeful approach would appear to be to look at the nature of assemblages on known military sites, in an attempt to define specific patterns of association, practice, and disposal which can be characterised as military by contrast with those identified by parallel analysis on sites deemed to be 'purely civil' (eg southern villas and towns). Any such 'military' profiles can then be watched out for elsewhere (see also Allason-Jones, this volume). Identifying 'pure military assemblages' on this basis may appear straightforward, because it is commonly assumed that walls of Roman military bases marked a near-perfect boundary between the private world of the army, and everything else; with a few exceptions (such as the commander's personal household, and some centurion's wives), all 'civilians' would have lived outside the gates of military bases in the legionary *canabae*, or auxiliary *vici*. This is specifically stated by Salway (1967, 23), and taken for granted by Sommer who asserts that soldiers' families certainly, and slaves and freedmen probably, would not have been allowed to live inside forts (Sommer 1984, 4, 30–1). Digging inside the walls should therefore give us our 'military' reference profiles; in contrast, the archaeological remains in the extramural settlements are assumed to be either 'civilian' or mixed.

However, was there really such a neat spatial division between the soldiers and their regiment's non-soldierly 'tail'? Leaving aside the question of how grooms and personal servants could conduct their duties if they were not at least allowed into the forts in daylight (and so may have contributed to the intramural archaeological record, thereby 'contaminating' its militariness), there is the further consideration that not all forts reveal signs of attached 'civil' settlements (Sommer 1984, 24); while many have surely simply escaped detection so far, it seems probable that numerous forts, especially earlier ones, did lack them. Where, then, in the absence of *vici*, did all the people of the (in my view, ubiquitous and indispensable) non-combatant 'tail' live and sleep? The answer has to be, 'inside the walls'. The notion that non-soldiers were strictly excluded must be wrong.

In fact, the widely-held notion that military regulations banned civilians inside the ramparts is supported by no actual evidence known to me; neither Salway nor Sommer provides any evidence for their assertions. Rather, the supposed ban is another assumption, another projection backwards of military practice in some modern armies – significantly, those of Britain and Germany, countries dominant in shaping Roman military studies (for the continuing ban of this kind in British military barracks – and the reality that it is routinely flouted anyway – see Beevor 1991, 38). Recent work by van Driel-Murray on the archaeological evidence from Vindolanda highlights the rooting of the idea of civilian-free fort interiors in anachronistic back-projection of specific modern practices. It presents a very different potential modern parallel from Dutch colonial experience and, most importantly, details compelling evidence from a study of footwear for the presence of women and children in auxiliary barracks at the end of the 1st century AD (van Driel-Murray 1995). The late 1st-century fort apparently had no extramural settlement, yet has produced both archaeological and documentary evidence for a host of non-combatants attached to its garrison units

(Bowman 1994; Bowman and Thomas 1994; 1996). Modern objections citing lack of space and hygiene risks are misplaced, given abundant evidence for frequent overcrowding, squalor, and lack of privacy in civil and military contexts in Roman and much more recent times.

To conclude, the evidence suggests that that all assemblages from sites with a military component, even the interiors of military bases, represent mixed activities of soldiers and non-combatants whose status is a matter of opinion and definition. Soldiers were hardly ever unaccompanied by at least some non-combatants, even if these were confined to grooms and muleteers. I would argue that our default assumption should be that 'military assemblages' usually represent the activities of mixed communities of soldiers, servants, families, and hangers-on. If this conclusion is accepted, we must either broaden the definition of 'military' to mean 'military communities, including non-combatants and dependants', or recognise that we are *always* dealing with a 'soldier–civilian' mix. Either way, we must be careful to define explicitly the terms we use.

However, we must of course seek to test this conclusion. Allason-Jones has pointed out that in the late 3rd- and 4th-century phases of Housesteads Barrack 13, although apparently feminine artefacts were recovered from the centurion's quarters, none were identified in the separate 'chalets', even though by that stage military marriages were unrestricted (Allason-Jones 1999, 45). Does this observation support the 'traditional' segregated model, or is the apparent conflict with the Vindolanda evidence to be explained in terms of variation according to time, region, regimental tradition, or just different property-curation or cleanliness regimes? Was Barrack 13 simply a block reserved for unmarried soldiers? This highlights the limited extent of our knowledge, and the urgent need for more research.

What do we want to know about 'military–civilian interaction' in Roman Britain, and how can we find out more?

Taking the study of Roman Britain in the broadest, interdisciplinary sense, it seems to me that there is no greater priority than to push through a reappraisal of the documentary basis of the categories and binary oppositions applied to the archaeology, not the least of which is 'military–civilian'. However, field archaeology at large cannot, and need not, wait for this process to be worked through.

Much of the rest of this volume demonstrates how far our understanding of the 'civilian' half of the equation has progressed in scale, depth, and sophistication, for example in terms of awareness – if not yet comprehension – of the degree of regional and local complexity and variability. Yet proper deconstruction and reconceptualisation of the military side of the equation, so dependent as it is for its conceptual structure on texts, has hardly yet begun, at least in archaeology (although there has been some interesting and important work on areas like military equipment (Bishop and Coulston 1993)). However, a number of ancient historians have recently made ground-breaking contributions (eg Alston 1995; Goldsworthy 1996; Isaac 1992; Rich and Shipley 1993, etc). The number of military-related papers at the 1999 Theoretical Roman Archaeology Conference (Fincham *et al* 2000), and a full session on the army at TRAC2000, show an encouraging degree of renewed interest among younger archaeologists.

Archaeology can and should make its own contribution to the process of broadening our conceptualisation and deepening our understanding of the military aspects of the empire as a whole. In the case of the relatively document-poor, yet material-rich and well-explored province of Roman Britain, it should be leading, making its own fundamental contributions where it illuminates the many vast areas of life beyond the reach of any text. Where it impinges on documented areas, it must be used to test and challenge hypotheses arising from the best historical analyses.

Of the many potential avenues of investigation, some specific areas may be suggested to develop themes discussed above. A priority is to establish in much more detail the nature of assemblages from military sites, in the hope of identifying characteristically military 'signatures' which might be sought elsewhere, as a means of demonstrating a military presence on sites where other criteria of 'military' nature – epigraphic evidence, or characteristic site morphology – are lacking.

This demands comparison of assemblages across our known or presumed 'military' and 'civil' site-type categories. Beyond a tendency to have more of certain types of metalwork, are there demonstrable differences in recovered assemblages between evidently military sites – eg fort/vicus complexes – and securely 'civilian' centres – eg southern towns, villas, and rural settlements (Allason-Jones, this volume)? We only have an inkling so far of what these comparisons are likely to reveal of the relationship between, for example, communities in forts and towns (Millett, this volume).

Such inter-site comparison has been carried out, or is underway, for several particular categories of material. Reece, for example, has compared coin finds from 140 sites; he does not recognise specifically military patterns of coin loss clearly distinguishable from, for instance, urban patterns (Reece 1995). Others in the present volume look at the potential of studying particular categories of material, such as ceramic (Evans), archaeozoological (Dobney), and other data. Allason-Jones has raised this issue for 'small-finds', and reflects a growing awareness, seen elsewhere in this volume, that a more integrated approach, comparing across finds-category boundaries to look at entire assemblages, and comparison of these between sites, has great potential. At York,

Hilary Cool has been developing methodologies to attempt studies of assemblages across multiple categories of finds, in their archaeological contexts (Cool *et al* 1995). This work has looked at 'small-finds' and glass, with reference to the ceramic data, contextualised against structural evidence; however, on a limited scale so far, the samples (especially from within the legionary fortress walls) are not yet large enough really to address issues such as the intramural presence of women (on the difficulties of identifying gender-specific archaeological correlates see Allason-Jones, this volume). Work in progress on 4th-century Roman military identity by Andrew Gardiner is also multi-dimensional in much this way (Gardiner 1999).

As such work develops, it is likely to reveal that the varied institutions and identities comprising military communities were differentially manifested through the components of material culture, some more emphasised through the construction and use of space, others more through the manipulation of portable objects. Consequently, their material traces today are to be sought in different aspects of the archaeological record. It may be, then, that the only detectable and distinguishable archaeological correlates of the military as an institution were the settings and activities of assembled armies on campaign (elusive, fleeting across most of the province, and not our main concern here), and soldiers acting under direct orders, in formal contexts, eg laying out, building and epigraphically commemorating military installations, and especially engaging in formal activities in formal military spaces. Examples of the activities 'presencing' the institutions of emperor, state ('Rome') and regiment include men on duty at the gates and in the *principia* (notably the 24-hour 'colour guard' at the shrine of the standards), and formal ceremonial assemblies, such as those at festivals and sacrifices (imperial birthdays, pay parades, regimental vows). (For the 'presencing of Rome' in public spaces and through formal performances in civil fora in Britain see Revell 1999; see also Häussler 1999). Of course, most of these activities would leave no direct archaeological trace, but the dedicated spaces constructed for ceremonial, and for the surveillance and control of the soldiers, themselves constitute 'platial artefacts' attesting them (Schiffer and Miller 1999). These are sometimes supplemented by archaeologically-recovered documents (eg inscribed altars). An important component of bone assemblages may be the archaeological remains of the many official sacrifices and feasts of the military year attested in the Dura calendar (Nock 1952).

While the institutional identity of Roman regiments is manifested especially in the layout of forts, in the policing of their boundaries and spaces, in the rituals of the military day, and especially in the cults of the emperor and the standards, the 'on-duty' identity of the soldiers as part of the wider imagined community of *milites* was expressed much more through what was immediately personal to, yet shared by them all, ie their bodily appearance. This comprises grooming, dress, and personal equipment (with all the special practical and symbolic properties of these (James 1999)), extending to armour and some other specifically- or primarily military artefacts (eg tents, entrenching tools, and horse-harness). Materially, then, soldierly identity *per se* may have been very narrowly expressed, through a limited but highly characteristic repertoire of personal and activity/situational artefacts (Schiffer and Miller 1999), which formed only a limited element of the material culture of a military base. Apart from these, military tombstones may provide the only other field of direct expression of soldierly identity which survives archaeologically.

It is argued then that built space, at least inside forts, was evidently controlled by, and expressed, the military institution rather than its members; and that individual soldierliness was expressed primarily through items more personal to the *milites*. It may be that neither aspect of 'militariness' was perceived to be especially expressed through other aspects of action, practice, or materiality: so, for example, many routine domestic aspects of life may have been 'below the horizon' of both institutional military, and collective soldierly culture, expressing other dimensions of identity entirely. The domestic side of soldiers' lives, and perhaps almost the entire life experience of their dependants, was probably about the same cares, routines, and practices, articulated through effectively the same material culture, as that of people on equivalent 'civil' sites like small towns. For example, soldiers and many free male civilians probably shared various material correlates of gender and status (eg in tunic colours, or wearing of finger-rings (James 1999, 18–21)).

For the soldier 'off duty' in the context of his *familia*, then, activities and practices were probably dominated by the expression of gender, class, age, ethnic and other relations – dimensions of identity shared with the wider 'civil matrix' – rather than 'military–civilian' identity distinctions. The material expression of these facets may have been responsible for generating the bulk of 'military' finds assemblages (eg most of the ceramic record), which in these respects may therefore prove not to be particularly distinguishable as 'military' at all (as Reece has found for coinage of forts and towns (Reece 1995)).

The information potential of the complexities to be discerned within the data can be illustrated by considering the example of habits and traditions of eating and drinking (also known by the ugly Americanism, 'foodways') at military site complexes. Here the focus is not just on what was eaten but on how and why; eating and drinking constitute a field of cultural expression as well as simple sustenance (Meadows 1995, 1997). The several levels or components proposed above may be identified: expression of 'Rome' and the institutional, through official blood-sacrifices and feasting; collective maintenance and expression of cultural/ethnic identity of groups of soldiers (especially provincial auxiliaries) through their regimental consumption habits; and the traces of more private consumption practices of smaller groups of soldiers and dependants.

Much meat will have been consumed by soldiers in 'on duty' contexts (eg regular official sacrificial feasts mentioned above), and so its selection and preparation are likely to have been regarded as part of army culture. Other, regimentally specific consumption patterns preserved those of the ethnic groups from which units were drawn, are seen for example in the preference for beer of the soldiers from the Low Countries stationed at Vindolanda (Bowman and Thomas 1996, 323–5). Meat consumption patterns among northern European garrisons provide a striking general illustration (see also Dobney, this volume). Work on osteological evidence from the western empire has demonstrated the existence of broad military patterns of meat consumption which derive from northern provincial rather than Italian traditions, yet with distinctive characteristics, and differences between legionary and auxiliary sites (King 1984; 1999a). King suggests that, given the provincial origin of this military pattern, we should conceptualise it in the context of Britain more as 'Gallicisation' or Germanisation' rather than 'Romanisation' (King forthcoming).

Here we see maintenance of ethnic traits at the level of the soldiers; but more than this, through the material evidence we are also detecting cultural exchanges between the institutional and soldierly domains identified above. While it is clearly not 'Italianisation', I would argue that is it is precisely a material correlate, indeed an active part, of the creation of a cultural identity which (contra King) overtly saw itself as Roman; the culture of the soldiers. It forms a striking parallel to a process I have outlined elsewhere, the simultaneous 'de-Italianisation' or 'provincialisation' of the key area of military dress and equipment (James 1999). In such material evidence of meat-eating practices and evolving personal appearance we see no simple acculturation in either direction, but elements of the active creation of a new Roman identity by the multi-ethnic soldiery themselves, through selective adoption of some Italian ways (especially acceptance of the institutional ideology of Rome and the emperor), and the redeployment and relabelling as 'Roman' (military) of many aspects of their own, and each other's, provincial or 'barbarian' culture (diet, dress). These are examples of Terrenato's process of 'cultural bricolage' (Terrenato 1998). Here we also see the value of comparison across categories of archaeological evidence in revealing wider patterns and cultural trends.

At a more local scale, the design, manufacture and mode of use on particular sites of certain ceramics, for example, may reflect ethnically- and/or gender-related domestic and dietary traditions of individual soldiers or their dependants (eg immigrant wives, working children, or slaves). The Frisian pottery of Housesteads is a well-known example of this (Jobey 1979, Crow 1995, 72–3); there is epigraphic evidence

for many German soldiers, and also German women and children, in the military zone (Birley 1979, 110–1). Here we may see the personal ethnicity of individual soldiers and their immediate dependants coming through more directly, exhibited in domains of activity and cultural behaviour 'below the horizon' of martial identity, where people were not obliged to follow normalising 'Roman military' ways.

Another important area where we may seek evidence for complex interactions between such domains and identities is in funerary archaeology, where Roman and provincial traditions, beliefs, and practices so often come together in creative interaction. Yet, despite some valuable funerary epigraphy, our knowledge of the cemeteries of military communities, with all their potential for examining demographic and social structure, and the cultural testimony of burial rites remains as yet woefully thin (Allason-Jones, this volume).

Turning from fields of material expression of domains and identity categories to spatial issues, above I have challenged the widespread assumption that the walls of bases marked the boundary, par excellence, between the 'pure' military world, and a civilian world outside, with the mixed liminal zone of the vicus between. Do fort-vicus complexes represent two spatially- and socially-distinct communities (as still widely assumed) or, as argued here, only partly differentiated components of one complex community? What actually are the differences either side of fort perimeters? If non-soldiers really were as routinely present living inside the walls as I believe, then we might expect the variations in spatial patterning of finds deposition to be less marked across the base perimeter, than between (say) the extramural zones and some or all of the barrack blocks on the one hand, and the key administrative structures such as the principia on the other. Even if we do find strong distinctions across the perimeter, can this therefore be taken as archaeological evidence for a 'purely military' intramural community of soldiers, and non-soldierly extra-mural communities? (And should we call the latter, military-associated groups, 'civilian'?)

Spatial variation of deposition inside forts has been commented on, eg within the bone assemblage at South Shields (Huntley 1999, 62), and the small-finds from the Housesteads barracks (Allason-Jones 1999, 45). But answering this question fully demands much more work on the extramural components of military base complexes (annexes, vici, and so on). Our knowledge of vici is not vastly better now than 20 years ago (Sommer 1984). We do not know even the major military installations as well as is often assumed, as the recent Birdoswald geophysical survey has shown (Biggins and Taylor 1999; Biggins et al 1999; see Fig 23). We need much more work of this kind, supplemented where possible by excavation, especially around the better-explored forts, to investigate spatial patterning of occupation and activities. The potential is at least hinted at by the recent Newstead project, where variations in the

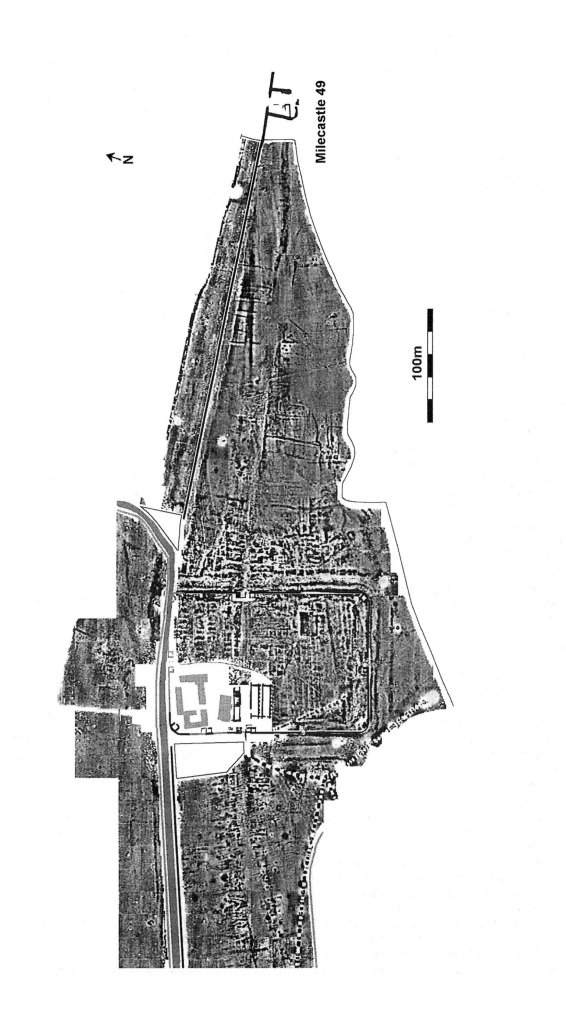

Milecastle 49

100m

Figure 23   Geophysical survey of Birdoswald fort. Reproduced by kind permission of J A Biggins and D Taylor

patterns of recovery within and between areas of the site, particularly between the fort and the various annexes has been analysed (S Clarke 1995). This study has indeed revealed interesting and important intra-site patterning; however, it seems to have been conducted against the background of a somewhat sketchy conceptualisation of the constitution of Roman presence, and we await full publication.

To comprehend the nature and meaning of military assemblages and their connection with 'civil' archaeology, we also need to consider the nature and degree of variation between military assemblages, to see how profiles might vary between forts, types of forts, and indeed between provincial armies (Allason-Jones, this volume); we then need to compare any variability with that which is now a focus of study in 'civil' archaeology (eg Millett and Taylor, this volume). For example, animal and plant data suggest dietary differences between forts such as Carlisle and Birdoswald (Huntley 1999, 58, 60). How extensive are such differences, and how far were they governed by local constraints of sources and routes of supply, as opposed to cultural factors of regimental tradition and ethnic origins of soldiers and their dependants, and convergence with, or deliberate distancing from, the indigenous cultural traditions of each base's immediate hinterland?

This brings us onto the issue of military communities in the wider civil landscape. We need to know far more about the local and regional contexts of military communities, both the major legionary bases, and the many smaller auxiliary garrisons. The relatively short-lived Newstead military community was certainly engaging directly with its locale for matters such as supply, but it remained a largely encapsulated presence within an indigenous social landscape which resolutely continued its traditional ways (Clarke 1999). In this and other local or regional contexts, soldiers may have largely occupied the 'niche' taken in the south by those prominent 'Romanising' natives who are thought to have been instrumental in the creation of provincial (especially urban) culture in the 'civil zone' (Millett, this volume; James forthcoming). The alienation from the local population which this seems to imply may well reflect cultural resistance, and perhaps endemic conflict: it certainly reflects trajectories very different from those of the 'peacefully Romanising' southern polities. However, detailed case studies like Newstead remain exceptional. In the northern military zone, it is clear that we need to put more effort into digging indigenous sites, to gain a fuller picture of regional cultural patterns within which military communities were planted, to see what evidence there may be for contacts and interaction or (equally important) continued divergence. The pioneering work of Jobey (Miket and Burgess 1984) has hardly been followed up properly, not least because such sites seem unrewarding, usually being short of finds and hard to date. However, answering present research questions demands more interventions, not fewer.

We need to explore the environs of a number of long-lived military bases in much greater detail than has generally been achieved so far, to characterise and date their evolving features, and then to relate these to the more detailed picture from military sites. Aerial reconnaissance by Tim Gates in the Northumberland National Park, for example, has revealed the enormous extent of unrecognised settlement and land-use evidence, much of which probably belongs to the Roman period, even within sight of Hadrian's Wall (Gates 1999a; 1999b; Woodside and Crow 1999).

How might progress regarding apparently 'low-yield' indigenous sites and landscapes be achieved? Even if cultural material is sparse on rural sites, the potential for a valuable contribution from environmental archaeology is great. Buried soils on settlement sites, and small bogs in particular, promise quite detailed insight into the nature and development of local environments (Huntley 1999, 49). While such evidence relies on a chronology relatively coarse by comparison with the exceptionally fine dating possible in many forts, it is no worse than for most 1st-millennium archaeology, BC or AD (Huntley 1999, 50–1); we can certainly ask of it questions about regional patterns and larger-scale chronological changes, which are highly relevant to the impact of the military. We already have a fair picture of the complexity and regional variation of the pre-Wall landscape (Huntley 1999, 52, 54). It is not unrealistic to aim for fairly full impressions of 'before, during, and after' the military episode, by region, across and beyond the military zone.

Was the kind of 'cultural encapsulation' of military communities identified at Newstead, and implied elsewhere, actually a widespread pattern? Clearly circumstances varied enormously between sites, as the differing trajectories of other centres such as York or Carlisle/Stanwix make plain. What were the varied contributions to particular cases of the size and ethnic composition of a unit (eg a newly-raised regiment of Dacians compared with a long-established legion), and of the varied cultural composition of indigenous populations around their bases, and of topographic and ecological conditions, and communications? Particular targets for projects investigating such issues could usefully build on existing investments of research effort, eg around Vindolanda/Housesteads and Birdoswald (Wilmott 1998, 1999; Biggins and Taylor 1999; Biggins et al 1999). In the hinterland, Binchester seems a promising case (Ferris and Jones 1999), while beyond the Hadrian's Wall zone, the results of the work on Newstead and its context are awaited with keen anticipation.

Organising and funding research

How might such work actually be carried out? Significant parts of what could be turned into a broader strategy are already underway in, for example, a substantial programme of geophysical prospection of *vici*, at least along Hadrian's Wall (Julia Robertson, pers comm). However, we need a major effort to integrate work being done piecemeal, in the field, in laboratories, and on archives. Huntley has called for more integrated teamworking among environmental specialists (Huntley 1999, 56); there is every reason for extending this to archaeology as a whole, in the form of projects conceptualised from the start as multi-disciplinary team efforts.

The larger-scale interdisciplinary research projects advocated here, such as comparative site assemblage analyses, and regional survey and excavation programmes, are likely to demand substantial special funding, and may best be addressed as 'multi-name' team projects more reminiscent of the sciences, involving university research fellowships and independent or unit-based finds specialists, rather than the 'single-name'-led projects with a list of subordinate contributors more typical of archaeological tradition. Here is an obvious role for English Heritage, to encourage cross-disciplinary links (its sponsorship of the RAC 'Romano-British agendas' session constitutes an example), to help articulate more effective co-ordination and deployment of existing resources and efforts, and also to provide some of the funding. In particular, provision of resources and structures to ensure maintenance of specialist expertise in material culture studies, highlighted elsewhere in this volume, is crucial to such work. Such projects also seem ideally suited to the Heritage Lottery Fund, which states as one of its main areas of support: 'Syntheses of the results of past fieldwork or research exercises in a discrete geographical area' (HLF Archaeological guidance notes, Sept 1998, 3, section 1.4). Other headings under which HLF or other funding might be sought include public/community archaeology. Wherever possible, archaeological projects must have a public presentation component as a primary concern, and Roman military archaeology in particular remains a supremely 'sexy' subject; this is manifest from public interest in everything from Hadrian's Wall to displays by re-enactment groups. If imaginative public archaeology projects cannot be successful in and around Roman fort sites, they are hardly practicable anywhere.

The attractiveness of such projects can be enhanced by emphasising that much of this work is equally relevant to other research agendas, within and beyond Romano-British archaeology, and therefore offers the potential of multiple benefits arising from even broader interdisciplinary cooperation: eg military base/*vicus* complexes should be treated as another type of nucleated settlement, perhaps as part of the phenomenon of towns, which so many sites closely resemble in morphology (Millett, this volume; Jeremy Taylor, pers comm), while work on their environs will contribute towards fundamental concerns in current landscape research shared by Romano-British and Iron Age scholars (Taylor this volume; Armit *et al* 2000) and medievalists.

Clearly much of the research advocated requires customised research projects. However, major

contributions can be made by developer-funded PPG 16 interventions. For example, many evaluation exercises, in the military zone in particular, are of direct, indeed crucial relevance in helping us cumulatively to build up our picture of conditions, cultural patterns, and changes across the regions sustaining, and willy-nilly directly interacting with, the Roman military presence. For this to reach fruition, information recovered must be made more accessible, as other have discussed.

Conclusion

In my view, our data are generally not currently adequate in coverage for the kind of synthesis English Heritage has proposed, but ways can be identified through which we can quite quickly move to remedy the situation. Paradoxically, we will best understand the Roman army of Britain by 'decentring' it, and considering it as part of a wider picture; and we will better understand military–civilian relations by deconstructing and replacing obsolete assumptions about what that provincial army was. Yet while demolishing the unduly narrow boundaries of 'Roman frontier studies' (*Limesforschung*) we should build on its undoubted strengths. Traditionally conservative areas retain major potential for addressing new questions, eg studies based on inscriptions and diplomas (Allason-Jones 1999; Maxfield 1995; Roxan 1997). We must seek better readings of the documentary evidence, which, particularly for the military, is too rich to be ignored as emphasised dramatically at Vindolanda. Most notably, we can learn from the traditional emphasis on comparative studies. We must be more active in looking at the rest of the empire, and other scholarly traditions working on it, for both comparative evidence and new ideas.

There is, then, ample reason to consider the military in Britain in terms beyond the institutional, in terms of identities, and transitions in identity, and to look at it not only or simply as a monolithic instrument of imperial power, but also as another Roman provincial community, or perhaps as a group of specially related communities, within the wider matrix of societies in Britain.

Acknowledgements

I would like to thanks Julia Robinson, Tim Gates, Jacqui Huntley, and Iain Hedley for information, David Taylor and Alan Biggins for permission to reproduce the Birdoswald geophysical survey plot, Lindsay Allason-Jones for comments, and Margaret Snape, Jeremy Taylor, and Martin Millett for criticism of earlier drafts.

10 The Roman to medieval transition

by Simon Esmonde Cleary

Introduction

There are huge differences in almost all areas of archaeological evidence between *c* AD 350 on the one hand and *c* AD 650 on the other. Because of this, a title such as 'The Roman to medieval transition' poses serious conceptual problems, since it implies a single, uniform movement from a defined start-point to a defined end-point. 'Empire to kingdom' suffers from the same problems and in addition sets out a definition that by stressing political formations is ultimately text-driven. Moreover, I would characterise each of these formulations as a topic rather than an agenda. In this paper I shall try to maintain a focus on the archaeology and to make the differences in the formation, recovery, and interpretation of the archaeological record a central concern. I shall try to identify themes which may bring coherence to the analysis of the data-sets, and integrate these within a unified frame of reference.

As well as being academically valid, this volume and the agendas proposed within it also need to be responsive to the concerns of those at the 'sharp end'. Curators, contractors, and consultants have to argue the case for archaeology, sometimes expensive, to funders, and to do this they need a justification which will cut ice with other professions who may regard archaeology as a costly inconvenience. The familiar historical framework for this period does have the benefit from this point-of-view of being part of the general historical consciousness of modern England – part of its origin myth, part of its lumber room of half-perceived memory. It is, after all, the time which saw the end of the Roman period (a civilisation which still fascinates the public), the arrival of the ancestors of the English, and the spread of Christianity, episodes still central to the modern identity of England. Rather different agenda currently seem to be taking shape in Wales and, especially, Scotland, where the search for a 'Celtic' identity risks 'writing out' the Roman period as a transient episode of foreign, colonial domination. Nonetheless, for these two countries also the period under consideration here is the one in which their historical identity has its ethnic, cultural, and religious roots. So the historical framework can still be of use in setting the context of archaeological work, but further and better particulars are also needed if we are to argue for specific projects. Whilst this paper will not be couched in terms with the immediate public recognition factor and appeal of the age of Arthur, the life and times of St Ninian, or the social shortcomings of Hengist and Horsa or Vortigern, I hope it will nonetheless help curators and contractors to show to other professions why this profession thinks work on this period is important and worth the effort and expense.

I shall also use a fairly wide definition of 'research', to encompass not just the library- and desk-based lucubrations of academics, but also how research agenda can be translated into areas such as fieldwork and publication. This may be of more immediate concern to some of those mentioned above and to organisations such as Cadw, English Heritage, and Historic Scotland. This will also, it is intended, maintain the link between research (seen as something done in universities) and fieldwork (seen as something done in units), the disjunction of which is a source of frequent lamentation.

The archaeology of the mid-1st millennium AD has huge problems. It is lacunose, and because of this, certain well-defined aspects are highly visible and attract the lion's share of attention whereas other aspects are near-invisible and thus hard to approach. There are huge disparities in the evidence types; for instance, settlements at some times, cemeteries at others. We have often tried to rescue ourselves by assimilating the archaeology to a historical 'narrative', enabling us to gloss over the inconsistencies. In other fields and periods archaeology has been emancipated from being the handmaid of history, and I see no reason why that should not be the case here. In what follows I propose to ignore the written sources and focus on the archaeology, though in places the interaction of the archaeology with historical models and narratives should become clear.

It is a truism that in Britain at this time there are at least three archaeological groups conventionally defined in terms of different cultural/ethnic categories: Romano-British, Anglo-Saxon, and British. Though originally deriving from textual sources, I have no problem with using these as broad descriptors, since they relate both to major observable differences in the archaeological record, and they make the point that each is the insular manifestation of a wider *Kulturkreis* – Roman, Germanic, Britonic (to avoid 'Celtic') – and thus is not fully comprehensible in isolation from its wider context. This gives me my starting point, that culturally determined processes of site formation are central to many of our problems, but also hold out the possibility of creating new ways of approaching the period. Each 'facies' may be briefly characterised:

Romano-British

(a) Elite culture: forts, towns, villas, burial, artefact-rich. A highly visible archaeology, also durable by virtue of stone buildings, pottery, metalwork, etc.

(b) Non-elite culture: 'native' settlements, some artefacts, few burials. An archaeology in timber, less durable, less visible, under-represented.

Both are archaeologies dominated by the settlement record, with less prominence given to, for example, burial, artefacts (other than for dating), landscape.

Anglo-Saxon
Traditionally dominated by the burial record. Cemeteries, graves, skeletal remains, artefacts. A premium on artefact studies. Settlement and landscape archaeology now more prominent, but again an archaeology in timber.

Britonic
The most shadowy of the three. By the mid-5th century it is an artefact-poor archaeology of flimsy timber buildings and few burials. Things improve towards the end of the century and a timber settlement archaeology and sporadic burial record, both with some artefacts (especially imports) emerge in the west.

One point which comes out clearly from this is the effects of archaeological visibility on our perception of this part of the past. Certain aspects such as Romano-British elite culture or Anglo-Saxon funerary practice have dominated the record simply because they leave behind easily recognised and distinctive remains. This must put a premium on trying to correct this imbalance, which involves thinking of ways to contact and explore the less visible types of archaeology.

Another point is that it shows clearly why there is no dominant narrative or discourse, such as 'Romanisation' has been for the earlier Roman period. The archaeological record and the specialisms it has engendered have been simply too fragmented and disparate to have sustained such over-arching schemes. There is no equivalent to the 'Romanisation' of the earlier period, and terms such as 'de-Romanisation', 'Germanisation' or 'Celticisation' make little headway because they all treat only a part of the evidence and that in a culture-historical fashion. There is, though, I believe, an intellectual discourse that does have the potential to integrate or re-integrate the diverse types of evidence and the varying types of inquiry, one to which I will return below after considering lines of enquiry arising out of the nature and problems of the evidence.

Axes of enquiry

One way of trying to break out of the current impasse would be to attempt to ignore conventional chronological and cultural boundaries and to propose that the focus of inquiry and analysis should be the evidence-type. This approach would examine, for example, burial or coinage or trade through the period, regarding each as a single process which can be addressed in a variety of ways. It would certainly be a thought-provoking break with tradition and would throw up interesting, occasionally worthwhile, new ideas. I think such approaches should be given a go as an academic exercise. But all empirical and theoretical perspectives insist that such phenomena are ultimately culturally-conditioned (and culturally-conditioning) so that we would end up confusing what should be separate categories in ways which would hinder understanding and might well invalidate the exercise as a means of structuring our understanding of the period as a whole.

Indeed, it is difference, and the explanation of difference, which must be factored into generalising approaches. The three archaeological groups outlined above seem at first sight to be so different as to be irreconcilable, and that is how they have usually been treated. But those very differences can in themselves be opportunities, for they offer a number of axes of inquiry. The three which would seem both obvious and useful are:

• the scale and structure of society,
• the ideology of society,
• regional and temporal variability.

These three not only respond to our experience of the archaeological record as it has come down to us, but also hold out the opportunity of understanding why that archaeological record is the way it is, thus closing the loop (without, I hope, arguing in a circle).

The scale of a society comprises both the geographical extent and the number of people within the society. As used here it relates to socio-political units rather than cultural formations – for instance, early Anglo-Saxon societies appear to be socio-politically small-scale even if they form part of a larger cultural consciousness. Processualism may be passé, but the categorisations it dealt in do have relevance. By-and-large, smaller-scale societies have access to and control over fewer resources than larger-scale, and contain fewer people, they are thus less prone to invest in durable expressions of their culture. This is not just a reflection of 'passive' resources such as metals or muscle-power, it is also a reflection of the 'active' role of the relative scale of information flow. The scale of a society is something that archaeologists are well-used to analysing through a variety of mediums such as settlement and burial evidence, central and monumental sites, evidence for access to and control of prestige-giving resources. But it is also a consideration which strongly conditions the formation of the archaeological record: one reason (but only one) why Roman Britain looks different from early Anglo-Saxon England is that in the Roman period there was a larger-scale, integrated society and it had command over more resources.

It is not just size, that matters, it is also the structure of the society – though in fact the two are so closely linked as to be reflexive. Societies operating over a larger area and containing larger numbers of people tend to be more hierarchical and specialised than do smaller-scale ones. Again, the comparison between Romano-British and post-Roman social organisations is a good example (cf Esmonde Cleary 1993). Hierarchy and specialisation are also ways of developing and structuring information flow, giving rise to new techniques of organisation and manipulation of the natural and human resource. Such societies tend to leave a more substantial mark in the archaeological record, partly because of increased control over resources, but also because of the wish of different groups within the society to mark themselves off in different ways. Of course, hierarchy and specialisation are not the only important criteria. Gender and age are equally, if not more, central to emic (internally generated) and etic (externally imposed) perceptions of the individual and thus likely to be manifest in the archaeological record. The structure of society is also a means of expressing power, and we need to be aware of the possible variations in the nature of power and their archaeological correlates, for examples:

Scale: national, regional, local, familial
Nature: institutional/personal, heritable/individual, secular/spiritual, male/female
Holders: rulers, officials, kin-leaders, family heads

All these aspects have, of course, been the subject of extensive recent theoretical considerations. This was initially from a processualist perspective on different forms of social organisation; more recently it has been from post-processualist perspectives and critiques, which lay more emphasis on the role of the individual agent and on social structures as a reflection of ideological structures.

The ideology of society is, of course, not readily separable from scale and structure, and they are often reflexive. Ideology is a concept which includes many different expressions. One which has received a great deal of attention over the last decade and which is crucially relevant to the period under consideration is cultural identity, especially the question of ethnicity. It is clear from the archaeological record that different statements are being made about identity and the geographical links of those identities. As noted above, the Romano-British, Anglo-Saxon, and Britonic identities are distinctive and parts of larger entities. But to a greater extent these cultural identities either co-existed or succeeded each other, so choices were being made about which identity to adopt. Clearly the intense recent theoretical interest in cultural identity, how it is manifested in the archaeology and how it changes has more to tell us. Much of the recent debate has focused on 'Romanisation' (eg Webster and Cooper 1996; Mattingly 1997; Laurence and Berry 1998; Woolf 1998 – all with references to more general theoretical literature), now perhaps it needs to address this later period (for an attempt at such an approach for this period see Halsall 1995). There are other elements of ideology which may be helpful in addressing the archaeological record. How did societies perceive themselves, both in the ideal and in reality? Was a society, for instance, perceived as egalitarian in essence even if hierarchical in operation? Was land 'owned' in common, or was it alienable and heritable? How were gender relations visualised? Were there free and unfree? Was a premium placed on the martial ethos? Ideology can mean religion. This can work at the level of the conventional distinction between Christian and 'pagan', or through trying to identify particular cults or activities attested in the literature. But perhaps more fruitful from an archaeological standpoint are concepts such as cosmology, relating to perceptions of how the divine, the human, and the natural worlds were ordered and how they interacted, or how the past conditioned the present. These perceptions could be written on and can be read off archaeological evidence at levels from the burial (cf Parker Pearson 1999) to the building (eg Parker Pearson and Richards 1994; Wallace-Hadrill 1994), or the ordering of the landscape (eg Tilley 1994).

The changes which characterise this period vary significantly in space and time, hence the importance of regionality and chronology. In a way this is a statement of the obvious, but even so chronology remains one of the key weaknesses in structuring the evidence for this period, yet it is crucial for calibrating what exactly is happening where and when. Pursuing a chronological axis also allows consideration of the notion of transition (or, better, transitions) and the use of theoretical models of and approaches to 'collapse'. This temporal weakness is more evident in some areas and at some times than in others, one aspect of regional variation. Other aspects are well-known, such as the gross differences between the Anglo-Saxon areas of the south and east in the 5th and 6th centuries as against the British regions of the north and west at the same time. But even within the former of these, what of the differences between East Anglia and Kent, where the earliest Anglo-Saxon material consistently occurs in clear stratigraphic and spatial relationships with what I would term 'ultimate Romano-British' (eg Mackreth 1996, 85–91, 205–15, 237–9), and other areas where these relationships do not occur. It means that we must be prepared to write a whole series of local or regional sequences, which may be incompatible with each other, rather than attempt to bend and stretch them all into a Procrustean narrative. It is another way of acknowledging that the study of difference and of differentiation is central to our approach to this period.

The three broad axes of enquiry I have proposed, the scale and structure of society, the ideology of society, and regional and temporal variability, all have clear uses in analysing the available archaeological data. They are also axes which can play down the primacy traditionally accorded the question of historically-attested ethnicity. Most of the approaches outlined above can be viewed in the context of any of the conventional cultural groups, or they can be approached across them. Thus the importance both to the people at the time and to modern scholarship of considerations of ethnicity is not denied, but we need not allow it to act as a strait-jacket on our thinking. But to my mind equally importantly, these axes relate to the whole subject, currently only very partially explored, of why the archaeological record is the way it is. It forces us to consider questions and processes of site formation and of taphonomy. In doing so it also forces us to confront the twin problems of over-concentration on the more visible aspects of the archaeological record and under-emphasis of those aspects which are poorly represented or absent altogether. This is where this approach ceases to be purely 'academic' and feeds back into the agenda of field research.

Field Research

It is all too easy to produce a wish-list for this, or any other, period which can be quarried to justify almost any field project which someone wishes to undertake. What will be proposed here is a short series of topics and approaches which are designed to correct what appear to be the great weaknesses for the period, especially the under-representation of key elements. Until serious steps are taken to try to re-balance our knowledge and perceptions it is unlikely that we shall make much progress in our understanding of the period as a whole. This is not to say that we know all we need to know about other aspects, even the 'well-known' (or at least well-represented) ones, we patently do not. But it is to say that we need to prioritise.

The obvious 'black hole' in our knowledge and understanding is the post-Roman, non-Anglo-Saxon population of Britain through the 5th century. Little escapes the 'event horizon' resulting from the implosion of Romano-British material culture. But this group is crucial to our understanding of the processes of change between AD 350 and AD 650 because geographically, spatially, demographically, and culturally, these are the people who mediate between the structures of late Roman Britain and those of the emergent polities of 7th-century England and western Britain. Yet the archaeological record for this group is woefully deficient, a result, naturally, of the formation and ideology of the society which created it.

It is instructive to take one of the few extensively excavated settlement sites of this period, Poundbury, Dorset, as an example (Sparey Green 1988). The structural remains consist of shallow beam-slots and gullies, some sunken-featured buildings, pits (some possibly 'grain-driers') and postholes (Sparey Green 1988, 71–92). The artefact assemblage consists of a maximum of 31 objects, including 2 sherds of 5th-/6th-century pottery and 11 pieces of bone comb of generic late to post-Roman type (Fig 24). These are the items which are at all datable to the period of occupation. Otherwise there are items, for example of iron, which may be of this period but typologically could be earlier, and there are items which are certainly earlier such as early Roman brooches and prehistoric flints (Sparey Green 1988, 95–113, 128). The point is that our present methods of survey would find it almost impossible to identify such a site so that it could be targeted for excavation. To the aerial camera, such a site would appear at best as a series of indistinct and undiagnostic features. To the field survey, the site might not appear at all, depending on the survival rate of the pottery and bone, or if it did appear it might well be mis-dated. Geophysical and geochemical techniques would fare no better (or worse). Archaeology is adapted to recognise the visible, it really struggles with the (near-)invisible.

But given the difficulties of identifying and targeting suitable sites, how are we to proceed? I would suggest that an important contribution to research on this period will be the end result of fieldwork and research: publication – the appearance in print of many of the large-scale excavations on areas of landscape undertaken in the 1970s and 1980s in areas such as the Upper Thames, the Severn and Avon basins, and Yorkshire. There, the stripping of many acres, often of river gravels, revealed long, datable sequences of features running through the Roman period. Often the datable sequence resumes in the 5th or 6th century with the appearance of Anglo-Saxon pottery and artefacts. What may be the case is that stratigraphically and spatially 'between' the ends of the datable sequences lie the features and possibly the artefacts which characterise the 5th to 6th century. If that is so, then not only shall we be able to discuss this material and its relation to the Romano-British and Anglo-Saxon, but it will also give us an idea of what the settlement and artefact evidence for this period looks like. We will thus know better what to look for in future survey and excavation projects. This is, of course, an optimistic view.

There seems to me to be an inevitable corollary of this when devising excavation projects. It is that in small-scale excavations it is very difficult to impossible to identify and make sense of features of this period. Area stripping is needed for features and their relationships to be understood and to maximise the potential to recover artefacts and evidence which can be used in scientific analyses, for example, for dating. This has been forcefully stated for urban sites by Barker as a result of his work on the Wroxeter baths-basilica (Barker *et al* 1997). It is also true of non-urban sites. If we look across the Channel to areas of northern France where recent excavations in advance of TGV lines and *autoroutes* have involved *grand décapage* of many hectares at a time, it has been in such operations that the archaeological evidence for the 5th century and its various inhabitants and their activities have appeared (van Ossel and Ouzoulias forthcoming) . It may be that the British analogue to this activity, the Channel Tunnel Rail Link, will prove to have similar outcomes, especially since it runs through a county with the nearest thing to a complete 5th-century artefactual sequence in England. Advocating the excavation of hectares-

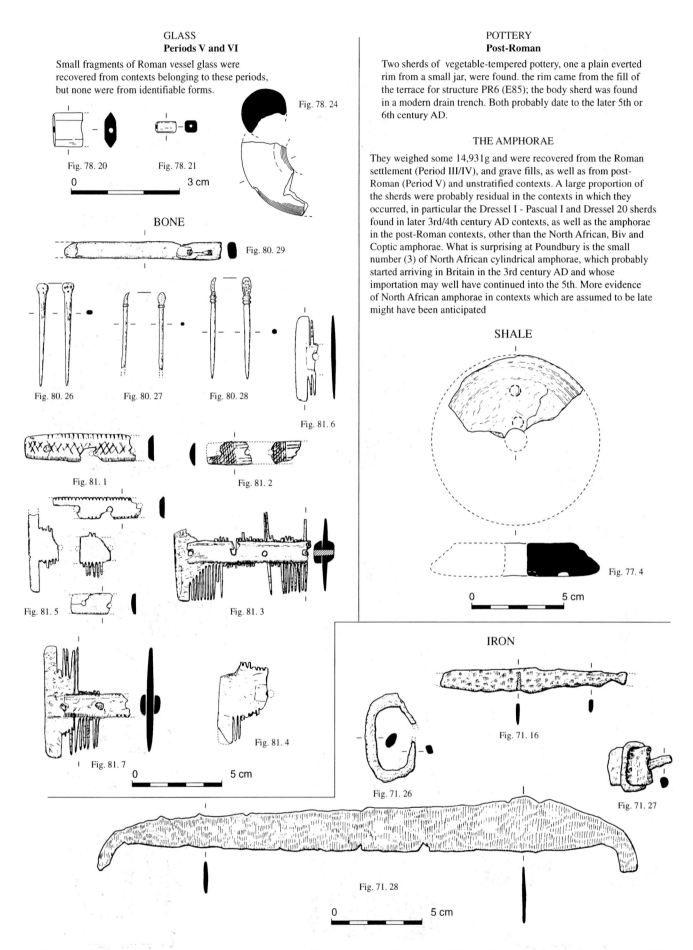

GLASS
Periods V and VI

Small fragments of Roman vessel glass were recovered from contexts belonging to these periods, but none were from identifiable forms.

Fig. 78. 24

Fig. 78. 20   Fig. 78. 21

0   3 cm

BONE

Fig. 80. 29

Fig. 80. 26   Fig. 80. 27   Fig. 80. 28

Fig. 81. 6

Fig. 81. 1   Fig. 81. 2

Fig. 81. 5   Fig. 81. 3

Fig. 81. 4

Fig. 81. 7   0   5 cm

POTTERY
Post-Roman

Two sherds of vegetable-tempered pottery, one a plain everted rim from a small jar, were found. the rim came from the fill of the terrace for structure PR6 (E85); the body sherd was found in a modern drain trench. Both probably date to the later 5th or 6th century AD.

THE AMPHORAE

They weighed some 14,931g and were recovered from the Roman settlement (Period III/IV), and grave fills, as well as from post-Roman (Period V) and unstratified contexts. A large proportion of the sherds were probably residual in the contexts in which they occurred, in particular the Dressel I - Pascual I and Dressel 20 sherds found in later 3rd/4th century AD contexts, as well as the amphorae in the post-Roman contexts, other than the North African, Biv and Coptic amphorae. What is surprising at Poundbury is the small number (3) of North African cylindrical amphorae, which probably started arriving in Britain in the 3rd century AD and whose importation may well have continued into the 5th. More evidence of North African amphorae in contexts which are assumed to be late might have been anticipated

SHALE

Fig. 77. 4

0   5 cm

IRON

Fig. 71. 16

Fig. 71. 26

Fig. 71. 27

Fig. 71. 28

0   5 cm

Figure 24   Material culture associated with the 5th-century settlement at Poundbury (from Sparey-Green 1988)

BRONZE

STONE

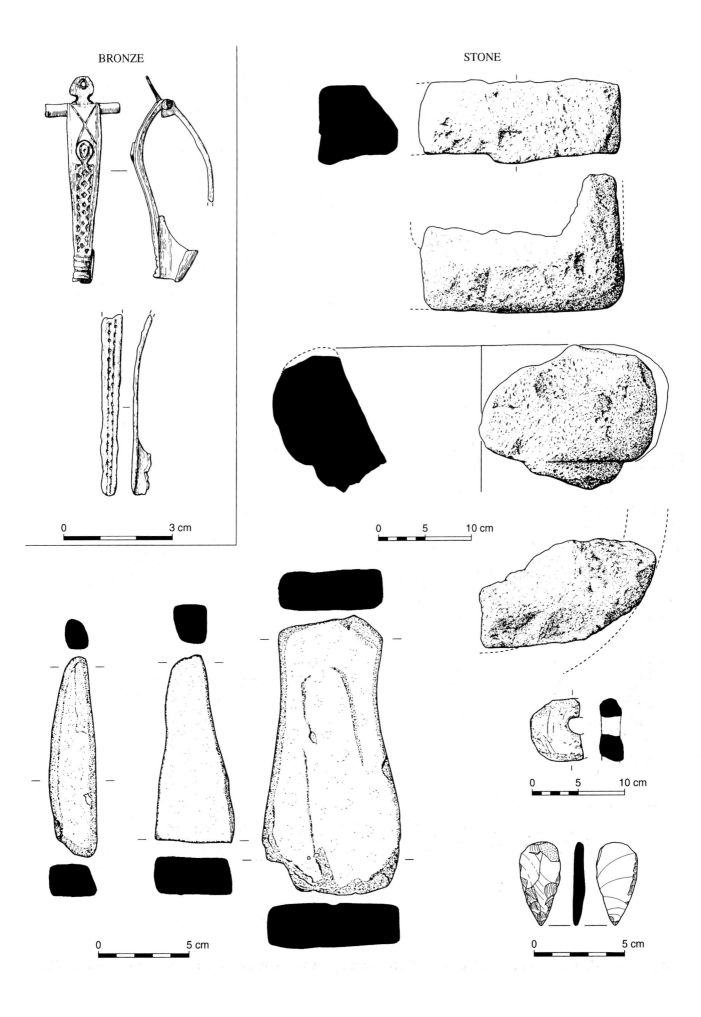

0   3 cm

0   5   10 cm

0   5   10 cm

0   5 cm

0   5 cm

worth of the landscape, together with the consequent post-excavation programme is hardly likely to be music to the ears of those who would have to fund such projects, nor indeed to the curators who will have to recommend such works. But it does seem to be the inevitable consequence of the problems posed by the diffuse nature of the archaeological record.

The approaches developed as a result of interest in landscape archaeology may well be particularly relevant for the analysis of this period. This is in part because of the opportunity to extract meaning from the positioning of sites and activities in the landscape, especially in relation to pre-existing features of the landscape – an application of some of the concepts of the phenomenology of landscape (Tilley 1994), and of how perceptions change between societies. Work on the nature of monuments and monumentality (eg Bradley 1993) and on how succeeding peoples relate to existing monumental landscapes will also have its relevance (for the Roman to Anglo-Saxon periods cf Williams 1997; 1998). Landscape approaches are also important because differing contemporary groups (eg British, Anglo-Saxon) were present in the same landscape, so the influence of each on the other may be detectable.

Because of the fugitive nature of much of the archaeology, above all for the 5th century, as much information as possible will have to be extracted from what remains there are, which will necessarily include the application of scientific approaches. Scientific techniques of dating will be particularly critical, since over much of the country for much of the period there is no good artefactual dating material. [14]C, AMS, dendrochronology, and other techniques are all expensive, but for this period indispensable, and will need to be factored in at the start of projects. Scientific techniques of analysis will also be central to exploring the relations between populations. Structured programmes of mitochondrial DNA (mtDNA) analysis need to be put in place in order to examine genetic relationships (or lack of) between the different culturally-defined populations of Britain in this period. These will of course depend on finding human bone of the right date, and burial is another area where the post-Roman population has been notoriously deficient, though a horizon of burial sites for this period is now becoming visible. Artefact studies will also be central, not just for the traditional purposes of dating and ethnic ascription (for what that is worth), but much more to profit from current concern with the social significance and the symbolism of material culture. Enquiries along these lines are increasingly being undertaken on later Romano-British and on Anglo-Saxon material (eg Richards 1992).

There is another, related approach, which may commend itself even less to those who seek to justify expenditure. It is to recognise that many significant sites, particularly of the 5th century, have been found entirely by chance whilst looking for something else – the Poundbury settlement is an excellent example of this. This approach would not specifically target 5th-century sites (other than the identifiably Anglo-Saxon), but would require us to be alive to the possibility of their appearing as part of the sequence in excavations (particularly large-scale ones) targeted on other periods. It would mean resources would have to be made available, particularly perhaps for post-excavation. If a characterisation of this approach is wanted it would be 'rigorous serendipity'.

I would also advocate that there is another group whose activities we need to know and understand better: the non-elite population of late Roman Britain. The problem of the relatively low visibility and consequent lack of understanding of this section of society in the north and west has been a source of concern for some time now (cf Hingley 1989, chs 9, 10). It is also appreciated that probably a majority of the population of the south and east, though less invisible, also operated in ways less affected by conventional Roman culture than their villa-dwelling neighbours. But as we increasingly realise that the ending of Roman Britain in archaeological terms affected principally a small, influential, and highly-visible section of the population (the army, the elite, and the urban), the question of the effect on the rest of the population and how they transmuted into the post-Roman population becomes critical. This was an agrarian population living in timber structures with an apparently low level of material prosperity, one to which masonry buildings, pottery, coins, and burial, though available, were not central concerns. Given that the environmental evidence shows that by and large the countryside remained open and exploited in the 5th century, this must be the population whose descendants we know so little about. Given that the settlements, field-systems, and so on, of this sector of the population are again much better understood through extensive excavation, the emphasis placed above on large-scale excavation would also be appropriate for them and for attempting to capture the relationship between what happened either side of AD 400.

That chronological horizon either side of AD 400 is the third main area which needs further work. The settlement sequences have increasingly been explored, most of them terminating c AD 400, a famous few running on later. But here I would advocate more work on the artefacts. It still seems to me that the really odd thing about the collapse of Roman Britain is not so much the disappearance of elite culture, but the apparently total loss of all levels of material culture, including relatively simple technologies such as pottery-making. The precise sequence of this demise needs to be described and calibrated, both at the level of particular ceramic industries, but also at the level of individual sites. Was the decline steady and smooth, or precipitous? Was it a decline in quantity, variety of forms and decoration, or technical quality? Similar questions can be asked of other categories of material. Theoretical work on the collapse of complex societies (eg Tainter 1988; Yoffee and Cowgill 1988) offers useful insights into the causes and processes of such collapses. But even so it generally finds that there is a reversion to a lower but still visible level of material culture, reflecting the collapse in social and cultural complexity. The virtually complete collapse in 5th-century Britain may well be more fruitfully approached through consideration of collapse of social ideology rather than of social structure.

As well as artefact studies, sources of evidence for environmental conditions (cf Dark 1999), for the development of the landscape, and for the agrarian regime need to continue to be pursued. The subsistence base was of equal concern to all the groups who inhabited Roman and post-Roman Britain, and change or the lack of it may have a lot to tell us both about what went on at the end of the Roman period and on how post-Roman societies evolved and interacted. This may yet have much to tell us about the circumstances of the arrival and settlement of the Anglo-Saxons within the existing agricultural and social landscapes.

As stated above, the premium placed on these groups, on excavation and other techniques for locating them, and on maximising the evidence yield for them is a consequence of the imbalance in the archaeological record. It is an exercise in redressing the balance. It is not to be taken to imply that work on other aspects such as elite Romano-British culture, or the Anglo-Saxons, or urban excavations is supererogatory; it most certainly is not, and much more remains and needs to be done.

A new discourse?

In the preceding two sections I have not only tried to identify axes of enquiry at an 'academic' research level, but have also tried to show how these can feed back into problematising past, current, and future field research (including post-excavation analyses), thus, as I put it, closing the loop. But in the Introduction it was also noted that a major problem with research into, and understanding of, this period was fragmentation and the consequent lack of any integrative framework. I would like to conclude by proposing that there is such a framework, that it can both integrate distinctive approaches and supply a structure which gives shape and dynamic to the debates. I would propose that this is Late Antiquity.

Late Antiquity covers the right chronological span, starting with the 4th century and coming down to at least the beginning of the 7th century. It therefore surmounts the chronological particularism of many traditional approaches. It allows for chronological variation; not everywhere has to proceed at the same pace along the same path. It is a discourse of the longer term, within which are subsumed particular events such as the collapse of the western empire. It is an approach that is essentially integrative whilst allowing for difference, it therefore surmounts the ethnic and cultural particularism of many traditional approaches. It embraces a wide geographical area, on the premise that there are common major trends, whilst expecting local differences – Spain is not the same as Syria but is subject to comparable trends. It recognises that the origins of the medieval world lie within and cannot be understood without reference to the late Roman world. It has as one of its central dynamics the transformation of the pagan into the Christian world. But it is not simply all things to all people. It is a period which is distinct from the preceding classical world and the succeeding medieval world, and mediates between the two. It also has its own internal coherence and dynamic, and a problematic and agenda of its own.

The applicability of Late Antiquity to Britain is clear. It almost exactly coincides with the period under consideration here. It is perhaps more relevant to study of the area of the late Roman diocese than it is to what had lain beyond, a feature which recurs also on the continent. But aspects of Late Antiquity such as Christianisation, the development of the successor kingdoms, and of ethnic/cultural/legal identities are equally valid for the former *externae gentes*. But the greatest merits of the idea of Late Antiquity are twofold. The first is that it is an integrative discourse; there may be many different aspects to social structure, ideology, material culture, and textual record, but they are subsumed within a greater whole. Like a cloisonné enamel, there may be separate cells of different colours, but seen together they reveal pattern or image. This should help us dismantle the walls (often jealously guarded) that have grown up between different evidence types and different specialisms, and which actively hinder our understanding of the period. The second great merit of Late Antiquity is that it covers a huge area, thus it re-integrates Britain with what is going on in the continent. The 5th- and 6th-century lapse of England into the Germano-Scandinavian Iron Age and the clustering of the west and north around the Celtic pond have added to the modern British attitude of 'Fog in Channel, Continent isolated' to produce very insular approaches to this period (a comment on general perceptions, not on the work of individual scholars). But looked at from the other side of the Channel in Frankish domains, Britain starts to fit into a wider culture province with similar archaeological manifestations of similar processes and transitions from the Roman to the medieval. Much in British 5th- and 6th-century archaeology makes so much more sense when seen in its wider context rather than in splendid isolation. Indeed, as we approach the end of the period we are considering here, we come to the second and far more successful Roman invasion of Britain, the Augustinian rather than the Claudian, which brings England back into the Christian, literate, urban late-antique world.

So if a simple, short title and agenda are needed for this period, let us go for the one that integrates all the various evidence types and analytical disciplines for the period in Britain, and which puts Britain back in its wider European context. Let us have research agenda for Late Antiquity.

Bibliography

Ancient Sources

Ammianus Marcellinus, *Roman History*
Caesar, *The Alexandrian War*
Columella, *De re rustica*
Dio Cassius, *Roman History*
Josephus, *Jewish Antiquities*
Justinian, *Digest of Roman Law* (trans. Mommsen *et al* 1985)
Livy, *History of Rome*
Martial, *Epigrams*
Pausanias, *Description of Greece*
Pliny the Elder, *Natural History*
Polybius, *Histories*
Sallust, *The Jugurthine War*
Suetonius, *Twelve Caesars: Augustus*
Suetonius, *Twelve Caesars: Divus Julius*
Suetonius, *Twelve Caesars: Gaius*
Tacitus, *Agricola*
Tacitus, *Annals*
Tacitus, *Histories*
Varro, *De Lingua Latina*
Velleius Paterculus

Abbreviations

RIB *The Roman Inscriptions of Britain*
Tab. Vindol. II = Bowman & Thomas 1994.

Modern sources

Aitchison, K, 1999 Monumental architecture and becoming Roman in first centuries BC and AD, in Baker *et al TRAC 98: Proceedings of the eighth annual Theoretical Roman Archaeology Conference, Leicester 1998*. Oxbow Monographs, 26–35

Albarella, U, 1997 The Roman mammal and bird bones excavated in 1994 from Great Holts Farm, Boreham, Essex. Ancient Monuments Laboratory Report 9/97

Albarella, U, in prep Midlands regional review of environmental archaeology: Vertebrates

Alcock, S (ed), 1997 *The early Roman empire in the East*. Oxbow Monographs

Aldhouse-Green, M (ed), 1995 *The Celtic world*. Routledge

Allason-Jones, L, 1986 An eagle mount from Carlisle, *Saalburg Jahrbuch* 42, 68–9

Allason-Jones, L, 1988 Small finds from turrets on Hadrian's Wall, in Coulston 1988, 197–233

Allason-Jones, L, 1989 *Women in Roman Britain*. British Museum Publications

Allason-Jones, L, 1995 'Sexing' small finds, in Rush 1995, 22–32

Allason-Jones, L, 1999 'Women and the Roman army in Britain', in Goldsworthy & Haynes 1999, 41–51

Alston, R, 1995 *Soldier and society in Roman Egypt: A social history*. Routledge

Alston, R, 1998 Arms and the man: Soldiers, masculinity and power in republican and imperial Rome, in Foxhall & Salmon 1998, 205–23

Anderson, B, 1991 *Imagined Communities; Reflections on the origins and spread of nationalism* (revised edn). Verso

Applebaum, S, 1972 Roman Britain, in Finberg 1972, 3–277

Armit, I, Champion, T C, Creighton, J, Gwilt, A, Haselgrove, C C, Hill, J D, Hunter, F, & Woodward, A, 2000 *Understanding the British Iron Age; an agenda for action*. Cambridge University Press

Armitage, P L, West, B, & Steedman, K, 1984 New evidence of the black rat in Roman London, *London Archaeol* 4, 375–83

Arnold, B, & Gibson, D B (eds), 1995 *Celtic chiefdom, Celtic state*

Ashbee, P, 1996 Halangy Down, St Marys, Isles of Scilly, Excavations 1964–1977, *Cornish Archaeol* 35.

Audouze, F, & Buchsenschutz, O, 1991 *Towns, villages and countryside of Celtic Europe*. Batsford

Ayres, P, 1997 *Classical culture and the idea of Rome in eighteenth-century England*. Cambridge University Press

Bailey, J (ed), 1998 *Science in archaeology: An agenda for the future*. English Heritage

Baker, P, Forcey, C, Jundi, S, & Witcher, R (eds), 1999 *TRAC 98: Proceedings of the eighth annual Theoretical Roman Archaeology Conference, Leicester 1998*. Oxbow Monographs

Barker, P, White, R, Pretty, K, Bird, H, & Corbishley, M, 1997 *The baths basilica, Wroxeter, excavations 1966–90*. English Heritage Archaeological Report 8

Barrett, J C, 1994 *Fragments from Antiquity: An archaeology of social life in Britain 2900–1200 BC*. Blackwell

Barrett, J C, 1997a Romanization: A critical comment, in Mattingly 1997, 51–66

Barrett, J C, 1997b Theorising Roman Archaeology, in Meadows *et al* 1997, 1–7

Barrett, J C, Fitzpatrick, A P, & Macinnes, L (eds), 1989 *Barbarians and Romans in north-west Europe: from the later Republic to late Antiquity*, BAR Int Ser 471

Bateman, N, & Locker, A, 1982 The sauce of the Thames. *London Archaeologist* 4(8), 204–7

Bates, W, 1983 A spatial analysis of Roman Silchester, *Scott Archaeol Rev*, 2(2), 134–44

Bayley, J (ed), 1998 *Science in Archaeology: An agenda for the future*. English Heritage

Beard, M (ed), 1991 *Literacy in the Roman world*. Journal of Roman Archaeology Supplementary Ser 3.

Beevor, A, 1991 *Inside the British army* (updated edn). Corgi

Bénard, J, Mangin, M, Goguey, R, & Roussel, L (eds), 1994 *Les Agglomérations Antiques de Côte-d'Or,* Annales Litteraires de l'Université de Besançon, 522, Série archéologique 39

Bennett, P, Frere, S S, & Stow, S, 1982 *Excavations at Canterbury Castle* Vol 1. Kent Archaeological Society

Berry, J, & Taylor, D J A, 1999 Halton Chesters – *Onnum*, in Bidwell 1999, 105–9

Bevan, B, 1997 Bounding the landscape: Place and identity during the Yorkshire Wolds Iron Age, in Gwilt & Haselgrove 1997, 181–91

Bevan, B (ed), 1999 *Northern exposure: Interpretative devolution and the Iron Ages in Britain.* Leicester Archaeol Monogr Ser 4. School of Archaeological Studies, University of Leicester

Bewley, R H, 1994 *Prehistoric and Romano-British settlement in the Solway Plain, Cumbria.* Oxbow

Bewley, R H, (ed) 1998a *Lincolnshire's Archaeology from the Air.* Occasional Papers in Lincolnshire History and Archaeology 11, Lincoln: Society for Lincolnshire History and Archaeology

Bewley, R H, 1998b England's National Mapping Programme: a Lincolnshire perspective, in Bewley 1998a, pp 9–17

Bewley, R H, 1999 Aerial Photography – Editorial, *Antiquity* **73**, 5–10

Bewley, R H, & Fulford, M G, 1996 Aerial photography and the plan of Silchester (*Calleva Atrebatum*), *Britannia* 27, 387–8

Bidwell, P (ed), 1999 *Hadrian's Wall 1989–1999.* Cumberland & Westmoreland Antiquarian and Archaeological Society/Society of Antiquaries of Newcastle Upon Tyne

Bidwell, P, & Speak, S (eds), 1994 *Excavations at South Shields Roman fort.* Soc Antiq Newcastle upon Tyne (with Tyne and Wear Museums) Monogr Ser 4

Biggins, J A, Robinson, J, & Taylor, D J A, 1999 Geophysical Survey [of Birdoswald], in Bidwell 1999, 157–61

Biggins, J A, & Taylor, D J A, 1999 A survey of the Roman fort and settlement at Birdoswald, Cumbria, *Britannia* 30, 91–110

Bird, J, Hassall, M W C, & Heighway, C (eds), 1995 *Interpreting Roman London: A collection of essays in memory of Hugh Chapman.* Oxbow

Birley, A, 1979 *The people of Roman Britain.* Batsford

Birley, R (ed), 1970 Excavations at Chesterholm-Vindolanda 1967–1969, *Arch Aeliana* 4th Ser, 48, 97–155

Bishop, M C, 1991 Soldiers and military equipment in the towns of Roman Britain, in Maxfield & Dobson 1991, 21–7.

Bishop, M C, & Coulston, J C N, 1993 *Roman military equipment.* Batsford

Bishop, M C, & Dore, J N, 1988 *Corbridge: Excavations of the Roman fort and town 1947–80.* English Heritage Archaeol Rep 8

Black, E W, 1995 *Cursus publicus: The infrastructure of government in Roman Britain*, BAR 241

Blagg, T F C, 1990 First-century Roman houses in Gaul and Britain, in Blagg and Millett 1990, 194–209

Blagg, T F C, & King, A C (eds), 1984 *Military and civilian in Roman Britain*, BAR Int Ser 136

Blagg, T F C, & Millett, M J (eds), 1990 *The early Roman empire in the west.* Oxbow Monographs

Boon, G C, 1974 *Silchester: The Roman town of Calleva* (revised edn). David & Charles

Booth, P, 1991 Inter-site comparisons between pottery assemblages in Roman Warwickshire; Ceramics indicators of site status, *J Roman Pottery Stud*, 4, 1–10

Booth, P, 1997 *Asthall, Oxfordshire: Excavations in a Roman 'small town'*, Thames Valley Landscape Monogr 9. OUCA

Booth, P, forthcoming *Excavations in the suburbs of Roman Alchester*, Thames Valley Landscape Monogr

Bowman, A K, 1991 Literacy in the Roman empire: Mass and mode, in Beard 1991, 119–32

Bowman, A K, 1994 *Life and letters on the Roman frontier.* British Museum Press

Bowman, A K, & Thomas, J D, 1994 *The Vindolanda writing-tablets (Tabulae Vindolandenses II).* British Museum Press

Bowman, A K, & Thomas, J D, 1996 New writing-tablets from Vindolanda, *Britannia* 27, 299–328

Bradley, R, 1993 *Altering the earth*, Soc Antiq Scotl Monogr Ser 8

Bradley, R, Entwhistle, R, & Raymond, F, 1994 *Prehistoric land divisions on Salisbury Plain.* English Heritage

Branigan, K, 1985 *The Catuvellauni.* Sutton

Branigan, K (ed), 1985b *The economies of Romano-British villas.* Department of Archaeology and Prehistory, University of Sheffield

Braund, D C, 1984 *Rome and the friendly king: The character of client kingship.* Croom Helm

Braund, D C (ed), 1987 *The administration of the Roman empire*

Braund, D C, 1996 *Ruling Roman Britain: Kings, queens, governors and emperors from Julius Caesar to Agricola.* Routledge

Brewer, R J, 1993 *Venta Silurum*: A civitas capital, in Greep 1993, 56–65

Brown, A E (ed), 1995 *Roman small towns in the east of England and beyond.* Oxbow Monographs 52

Bryant, S R, & Niblett, B R K, 1997 'The late Iron Age in Hertfordshire and the North Chilterns', in Gwilt & Haselgrove 1997, 270–281

Burleigh, G R, 1982 Excavations at Baldock 1980–81: an interim report, *Hertfordshire's Past*, 12, 3–18

Burleigh, G R, 1995 The plan of Romano-British Baldock, Hertfordshire, in Brown 1995, 177–82

Burnham, B C, 1986 The origins of Romano-British small towns, *Oxford J Archaeol*, 5(2), 185–203

Burnham, B C, 1988 The morphology of Romano-British 'small towns', *Archaeol J* 144 (1987), 156–90

Burnham, B C, 1989 A survey of building types in Romano-British 'small towns', *J British Archaeol Assn* 141 (1988), 35–59

Burnham, B C, 1995a Sites explored; 1 Wales, in *Britannia* 26, 326–31

Burnham, B C, 1995b Small towns: The British perspective, in Brown 1995, 7–18

Burnham, B C, & Johnson, H B (eds), 1979 *Invasion and response*, BAR 73

Burnham, B C, Keppie, L J F, & Esmonde Cleary, A S, 1998 Roman Britain in 1997: I sites explored, *Britannia* 29, 365–432

Burnham, B C, & Wacher, J S, 1990 *The 'small towns' of Roman Britain*. Batsford

Campbell, D B, 1984 *The emperor and the Roman army, 31 BC – AD 235*. Oxford University Press

Carreras-Montfort, C, 1994 *Una reconstrucción del comercio en céramicas: La red de transportes en Britannia; Aplicaciones de modelos de simulación en PASCAL y SPANS,* Cuadernos de Arquelogia 7

Carrott, J, Dobney, K M, Hall, A, Kenward, H, Jaques, D, Large, F, & Milles A, 1993 *An assessment of environmental samples from excavations in Crankleys Lane, on the Easingwold by-pass* (YAT/Yorkshire Museum site code 1993.5000). Reports from the Environmental Archaeology Unit, York 93(32)

Carrott, J, Dobney, K M, Hall, A, Issitt, M, Jaques, D, Johnstone, C, Large, F, & Milles, A, 1994 *Assessment of biological remains from excavations at Welton Road, Brough, North Humberside* (YAT/Yorkshire Museum site code: 1994.294). Reports from the Environmental Archaeology Unit, York 94(50)

Carrott, J, Dobney, K M, Hall, A, Issitt, M, Jaques, D, Johnstone, C, Kenward, H, Large, F, McKenna, B. & Milles, A, 1995 *Assessment of biological remains from excavations at Wellington Row, York* (YAT/Yorkshire Museum site code 1988–9.24). Reports from the Environmental Archaeology Unit, York 95(14)

Carver, M O H (ed), 1992 *The age of Sutton Hoo.* Boydell

Chadwick, A, 1999 Digging ditches but missing riches? Ways into the Iron Age and Romano-British cropmark landscapes of the north Midlands, in Bevan 1999, 149–72

Champion, T C, & Collis, J R (eds), 1996 *The Iron Age in Britain and Ireland. Recent trends*

Charlesworth, D, 1973 A re-evaluation of two turrets on Hadrian's Wall, in *Archaeol Aeliana* 5th Ser, 1, 97–109

Clarke, A, 1995 *A study of aerial photographic evidence in the area of Hayton, East Yorkshire.* Unpublished MA dissertation, University of Durham

Clarke, S, 1990 The social significance of villa architecture in Celtic north-west Europe, *Oxford J Archaeol*, 9, 337–53

Clarke, S, 1995 A quantitative analysis of the finds from the Roman fort of Newstead – some preliminary findings, in Cottam *et al* 1995, 72–82

Clarke, S, 1998 Social change and architectural diversity in Roman period Britain, in Forcey *et al* 1998, 28–41

Clarke, S, 1999 Contact, architectural symbolism and the negotiation of cultural identity in the military zone, in Baker *et al* 1999, 36–45

Clarke, S, & Robinson, D J, 1997 Roman' urban form and cultural difference, in Meadows *et al* 1997, 163–72

Collingwood, R G, & Myres, J N L, 1941 *Roman Britain and the English settlements.* Oxford University Press

Collingwood, R G, & Richmond, I A, 1969 *The archaeology of Roman Britain.* London: Methuen

Collis, J R, 1984 *Oppida: Earliest towns north of the Alps.* Dept of Prehistory and Archaeology, University of Sheffield

Collis, J R, 1995 The first towns, in Aldhouse-Green 1995, 159–75

Collis, J R (ed), forthcoming *Society and settlement in Iron Age Europe. L'habitat et l'occupation du sol en Europe*, Actes du 18e Colloque de l'AFEAF, Winchester – April 1994

Connell, B, & Davis, S J M, unpublished manuscript, Animal bones from Roman Carlisle, Cumbria; The Lanes (2) excavations, 1978–1982. Ancient Monuments Lab Rep New Series

Cool, H E M, 1995 *Finds from the fortress*, The Archaeology of York 17, Council for British Archaeology for York Archaeological Trust

Cool, H E M, & Baxter, M J, 1998 *Glass vessel assemblages in Roman Britain; Aspects of Romanization explored via correspondence analysis*, Research Report 12/98, Dept of Mathematics, Statistics and Operational Research, Nottingham Trent University

Cool, H E M, & Philo, C, 1998 *Roman Castleford. Excavations 1974–85. I. The small finds.* Yorkshire Archaeology 4. West Yorkshire Archaeological Service

Cool, H E M, Lloyd-Morgan, G, & Hooley, A D, 1995 *Finds from the fortress*, The Archaeology of York, The Small Finds, 17(10). Council for British Archaeology for York Archaeological Trust

Cornell, T J, & Lomas, K (eds), 1994 *Urban society in Roman Italy*, UCL Press

Cottam, S, Dungworth, D, Scott, S, & Taylor, J (eds), 1995 *TRAC 1994: Proceedings of the fourth Theoretical Roman Archaeology Conference, Durham*. Oxbow Monographs

Coulston, J C, 1981 A sculptured Dacian falx from Birdoswald, in *Archaeol Aeliana* 5th Ser, 9, 348–51

Coulston, J C (ed), 1988 *Military equipment and the identity of Roman soldiers; Proceedings of the fourth Roman military equipment conference*, BAR Int Ser 394

Cowell, R W, & Innes, J B, 1994 *The wetlands of Merseyside*. Lancaster University Archaeological Unit

Creighton, J, 1992 Interpreting villas, *Britannia*, 23, 349–51

Creighton, J, 1999 A la mode de Rome, *L'Archaéologue* 41, (April/May), 24–7

Creighton, J, 2000 *Coins and power in late Iron Age Britain*. Cambridge University Press

Creighton, J D, & Wilson, R J A (eds), 1999 *Roman Germany: Studies in cultural interaction*, J Roman Archaeol Supplementary Series 32

Croll, E, & Parkin, D (eds), 1992 *Bush base, Forest farm: Culture, environment and development*. Routledge

Crow, J, 1988 An excavation of the north curtain wall at Housesteads 1984, *Archaeol. Aeliana*, 16, 61–124

Crow, J, 1995 *Housesteads Roman fort*. London: Batsford

Cumberpatch, C G, & Blinkhorn, P W (eds), 1997 *Not so much a pot more a way of life*. Oxbow Monographs

Cunliffe, B W, 1971a *Excavations at Fishbourne 1961–1969, volume 1: The site*, Reports of the Research Committee of the Society of Antiquaries of London 26

Cunliffe, B W, 1971b *Excavations at Fishbourne 1961–1969, Volume 2: The Finds*, Rep Res Comm Soc Antiq London 26

Cunliffe, B (ed), 1984 *Danebury, an Iron Age hillfort in Hampshire*, CBA Res Rep 52

Cunliffe, B W, 1987 *Hengistbury Head, Dorset. Vol. 1: The prehistoric and Roman settlement, 3500 BC – AD 500*, OUCA Monograph 13

Cunliffe, B W, 1991 *Iron Age communities in Britain* (3rd edn). Routledge & Kegan Paul

Cunliffe, B W, 1998 *Fishbourne Roman palace* (revised edn). Tempus

Cunliffe, B W, Down, A, & Rudkin, D, 1995 *Excavations at Fishbourne 1969–1988*, Chichester Excavations 9. Chichester Excavations Committee

Cutting, C L, 1955 *Fish saving*. Hill

Dabrowa, E (ed), 1994 *The Roman and Byzantine army in the East*. Krakow

Dark, P, 1999 Pollen evidence for the environment of Roman Britain, *Britannia* 30, 247–72

Davies, J, & Gregory, A, 1991 Coinage from a *civitas*: A survey of the Roman coins found in Norfolk and their contribution to the archaeology of the *civitas Icenorum*. *Britannia*, 22, 65–101

Davies, J A, & Williamson, T (eds), *Land of the Iceni: The Iron Age in northern East Anglia*, Studies in East Anglian History 4

Davies, R W, 1971 The Roman military diet, *Britannia*, 2, 122–42

Deetz, J, 1977 *In small things forgotten: The archaeology of early American life*. Doubleday

Department of the Environment, 1990, *Planning Policy Guidance Note No 16. Archaeology and Planning (PPG16)* Novmber 1990. London: HMSO

Dimbleby, G, & Jones, M (eds), 1981 *The environment of man: The Iron Age to the Anglo-Saxon periods*, BAR 87

Dobinson, C, 1993 Studies in Romano-British urban structure. Unpubl PhD thesis, University of Cambridge

Dobney, K M, forthcoming *Northern regional review of environmental archaeology: Vertebrates*

Dobney, K M, Hall, A, & Kenward, H, 1999 It's all garbage… A review of bioarchaeology in the four English *colonia* towns, in Hurst 1999, 15–35

Dobney, K M, & Jaques, D, 1994 *The remains of a chicken from a Roman grave at Saltersford water treatment plant, near Grantham, Lincolnshire*, Reports from the Environmental Archaeology Unit, York 94/30

Dobney, K M, & Jaques, D, 1996 Animal bones, in Williams *et al* 1996

Dobney, K M, Jaques, D, & Irving, B, 1996a *Of butchers and breeds. Report on vertebrate remains from various sites in the City of Lincoln*, Lincoln Archaeol Stud 5

Dobney, K M, Jaques, D, Carrott, J, Hall, A, Issitt, M, & Large, F, 1996b *Biological remains from excavations at Carr Naze, Filey, North Yorkshire: Technical report*, Reports from the Environmental Archaeology Unit, York 96(26)

Dobney, K M, Kenward, H K, Ottaway, P, & Donel, L, 1998 Down, but not out: Biological evidence for complex economic organisation in Lincoln in the late fourth century, *Antiquity*, 72, 417–24

Dobson, B, & Mann, J C, 1973 The Roman Army in Britain, and Britons in the Roman Army, *Britannia*, 4, 191–205

Down, A, 1989 *Chichester excavations* 6. Chichester Civic Society Excavations Committee

Drinkwater, J, 1989 Patronage in Roman Gaul and the problem of the *Bagaudae*, in Wallace-Hadrill 1989, 189–203

Dungworth, D B, 1996 The production of copper alloys in Iron Age Britain, *Proc Prehist Soc*, 62, 399–421

Ellis, P, Hughes, G, Leach, P, Mould, C, & Sterenberg, J, 1996 *Excavations alongside Roman Ermine Street, Cambridgeshire*, BAR 276

English Heritage, 1991a *Exploring our Past: Strategies for the Archaeology of England*. London: English Heritage

English Heritage, 1991b *The management of archaeological projects* (2nd edn). English Heritage

English Heritage, 1998 *Exploring our past 1998* (draft version 2, 13 February 1998). English Heritage

Esmonde Cleary, A S, 1989 *The ending of Roman Britain*. Batsford

Esmonde Cleary, A S, 1993 Approaches to the differences between late Romano-British and early Anglo-Saxon archaeology, *Anglo-Saxon Stud Achaeol Hist*, 6, 57–63

Evans, J, 1987 Graffiti; Evidence of literacy and pottery use in Roman Britain, *Archaeol J*, 144, 191–204

Evans, J, 1993 Pottery function and finewares in the Roman north, *J Roman Pottery Stud*, 6, 95–118

Evans, J, 1995a Later Iron Age and 'native' pottery in the north-east, in Vyner1995, 46–68

Evans, J, 1995b Roman finds assemblages: Towards an integrated approach? in Rush 1995, 33–58

Evans, J, forthcoming (a) The A421 Iron Age, Roman and Saxon pottery, in Booth forthcoming

Evans, J, forthcoming (b) The Salford Priors Roman pottery, in Palmer forthcoming

Evans, J, forthcoming (c) The Pottery, in Millett, forthcoming

Fasham, P J, Kelly, R S, Masson, M A, & White, R B, 1998 *The Graenog Ridge: The evolution of a farming landscape and its settlements in north-west Wales*. Cambrian Archaeological Association.

Faulkner, N, 1994 Later Roman Colchester, *Oxford J Archaeol*, 13(1), 93–120

Faulkner, N, 1996 Verulamium: Interpreting decline, *Archaeol J*, 153, 79–103

Fenner, V E P, not dated *The Thames Valley Project: A report for the National Mapping Programme*. RCHME

Ferris, I, 1995 Shoppers' paradise: Consumers in Roman Britain, in Rush 1995, 132–40

Ferris, I, & Jones, R, 1999 Transforming an elite: Reinterpreting late Roman Binchester, in Wilmott & Wilson 1999, 1–11

Finberg, H P R (ed), 1972 *The agrarian history of England and Wales*. Cambridge

Fincham, G, forthcoming (a) Romanisation, status and the landscape: Extracting a discrepant perspective from survey data, in Fincham *et al* 2000

Fincham, G, forthcoming (b) Landscapes of imperialism: Roman and native interaction in the Fenland. Unpubl PhD thesis, University of Leicester

Fincham, G, Harrison, G, Holland, R, & Revell, L (eds), 2000 *TRAC 1999: Proceedings of the ninth Theoretical Roman Archaeological Conference*. Oxbow

Finley, M, 1983 The ancient city: From Fustel de Coulanges to Max Weber and beyond, in Finley, M, *Economy and society in ancient Greece* (originally published in *Comparative Studies in Society and History* 19 (1977), 305–27)

Fitzpatrick, A, 1989 Cross-channel relations in the British later Iron Age: With particular reference to the British archaeological evidence. Unpubl PhD thesis, University of Durham

Flower, B, & Rosenbaum, E, 1958 *The Roman cookery book: A critical translation of the art of cooking by Apicius*. Harrap

Forcey, C, 1997 Beyond 'Romanization': Technologies of power in Roman Britain, in Meadows *et al* 1997, 15–21

Forcey, C, 1998 Whatever happened to the heroes? Ancestral cults and the enigma of Romano-Celtic temples, in Forcey *et al* 1998, 87–98

Forcey, C, Hawthorne, J, & Witcher, R (eds), 1998 *TRAC 97: Proceedings of the seventh annual Theoretical Roman Archaeology Conference, Nottingham 1997*. Oxbow Monographs

Forster, E S, & Heffner, E H (trans), 1945 *Columella: De re rustica*. Volume 2. Heinemann

Foster, J, 1986 *The Lexden Tumulus: A re-appraisal of an Iron Age burial from Colchester, Essex*, BAR 156

Foster, R H, & Knowles, W H (eds), 1911 Corstopitum: Report on the excavations in 1910, *Archaeologia Aeliana* 3rd Ser, 7, 143–268

Foster, S, 1989 Analysis of spatial patterns in buildings (gamma analysis) as an insight into social structure; Examples from the Scottish Atlantic Iron Age, *Antiquity*, 63, 40–50

Foxhall, L, & Salmon, J (eds), 1998 *When men were men: Masculinity, power and identity in classical Antiquity*. Routledge

Freeman, P W M, 1991 The study of the Roman period in Britain; A comment on Hingley, *Scott Archaeol Rev*, 8, 102–4.

Freeman, P W M, 1993 'Romanisation' and Roman material culture. Review of M Millett, The Romanisation of Britain, *Journal of Roman Archaeology*, 6, 438–45

Freeman, P W M, 1996 British imperialism and the Roman empire, in Webster & Cooper 1996, 19–34

Freeman, P W M, 1997a Mommsen through to Haverfield: The origins of Romanization studies in late 19th-century Britain, in Mattingly 1997, 27–50

Freeman, P W M, 1997b 'Romanization' – 'imperialism': What are we talking about? in Meadows *et al* 1997, 8–14

Frere, S S, 1987 *Britannia: A history of Roman Britain*. Routledge.

Fulford, M G, 1984 *Silchester; Excavations on the defences, 1974–80*. Society for the Promotion of Roman Studies

Fulford, M G, 1987 *Calleva Atrebatum*: an interim report on the excavation of the *oppidum*, 1980–1986, *Proc Prehist Soc*, 53, 271–9

Fulford, M G, 1993 Silchester: The early development of a *civitas* capital, in Greep 1993, 16–33

Fulford, M G, & Clarke, A, 1999 Silchester and the end of Roman towns, *Current Archaeol*, 161, 176–80

Fulford, M G, & Nichols E (eds), 1992 *Developing landscapes of lowland Britain: The archaeology of the British gravels, a review*. Society of Antiquaries of London

Fulford, M G, & Timby, J, 2000 *Silchester: Excavations on the site of the forum-basilica, 1977, 1980–86*, Britannia Monogr 15

Gaffney, V, & Tingle, M, 1989 *The Maddle Farm project: An integrated survey of prehistoric and Roman landscapes on the Berkshire Downs*. BAR Brit Ser 200

Gardiner, A, 1999 Military identities in Roman Britain, *Oxford J Archaeol*, 18(4), 403–18

Gates, T, 1999a Hadrian's Wall amid fields of corn, *British Archaeology*, 49, 6–7

Gates, T, 1999b *The Hadrian's Wall landscape from Chesters to Greenhead: An air photographic survey: Final project report*. Northumberland National Park

Geary, P, 1983 Ethnic identity as a situational construct in the early Middle Ages. *Mitteilungen der Anthropologischen Gesellschaft in Wien*, 113, 15–26

Giddens, A, 1979 *Central problems in social theory: Action, structure and contradiction in social analysis*. Macmillan

Giddens, A, 1984 *The constitution of society; Outline of the theory of structuration*. Polity

Gidney, L J, 1998 *Creyke Beck, Cottingham, nr Hull: CBC97. Animal bone assessment*. Durham Environmental Archaeology Report 22(98)

Gidney, L J, & Rackham, D J, unpublished manuscript *The animal bones from Piercebridge Roman fort*

Going, C J, 1987 *The mansio and other sites in the south-eastern sector of Caesaromagus: The Roman pottery*, CBA Res Rep 62

Goldsworthy, A K, 1996 *The Roman army at war 100 BC – AD 200*. Oxford University Press

Goldsworthy, A K, & Haynes, I (eds), 1999 *The Roman army as a community*, J Roman Archaeol Supplementary Ser 34

Grahame, M, 1997 Towards a theory of Roman urbanism: Beyond economics and ideal-types, in Meadows *et al* 1997, 151–62

Grahame, M, 1998 Redefining Romanization: Material culture and the question of social continuity in Roman Britain, in Forcey *et al* 1998, 1–10

Grant, A, 1984 Animal husbandry, in Cunliffe 1984, 496–548.

Grant, A, 1989 Animals in Roman Britain, in Todd 1989a, 135–46

Greep, S (ed), 1993 *Roman towns: The Wheeler inheritance. A review of 50 years' research*, CBA Res Rep 93

Grigson, C, & Clutton-Brock, J (eds), 1984 *Animals and archaeology 4. Husbandry in Europe*, BAR Int Ser 227.

Grimes W F (ed), 1951 *Aspects of archaeology in Britain and beyond*

Groenman-van Waateringe, W, van Beek, B L, Willems, W J H, & Wynia, S L (eds), 1997 *Roman frontier studies 1995: Proceedings of the 16th International Congress of Roman Frontier Studies*, Oxbow Monograph 91

Grove, R, 1988 The bone report, in Crow 1988, 100–110

Guichard, V, Otte, M, & Sievers, S (eds), forthcoming *Les processus d'urbanisation à l'age du fer*. Glux-en-Glennes: Collections Bibracte

Gwilt, A, & Haselgrove, C C (eds), 1997 *Reconstructing Iron Age societies*, Oxbow Monographs 71

Haigh, D and Savage, M J D, 1984 Sewingshields *Archaeologia Aeliana* 5th series, Vol. 12, 33–148

Halkon, P, & Millett, M (eds), 1999 *Rural settlement and industry: Studies in the Iron Age and Roman archaeology of lowland East Yorkshire*, Yorkshire Archaeological Report 4. Leeds

Hall, A R, & Kenward, H K (eds), 1995 *Urban-rural connections: Perspectives from environmental archaeology*

Hall, A R, Kenward, H K, & Williams, D, 1980 *Environmental evidence from Roman deposits in Skeldergate*, The Archaeology of York 14(3), 101–56. Council for British Archaeology for York Archaeological Trust

Halsall, G, 1995 *Settlement and social organisation: The Merovingian region of Metz*. Cambridge University Press

Hamshaw-Thomas, J, 2000 When in Britain do as the Britons: Dietary identity in early Roman Britain, in Rowley-Conwy 2000

Hancocks, A, Evans, J, & Woodward, A, 1996 The prehistoric and Roman pottery, in Ellis *et al* 1996, 34–78

Hanson, W S, 1987 Administration, urbanisation and acculturation in the Roman West, in Braund 1987, 53–68

Hanson, W S, 1994 Dealing with barbarians: The Romanization of Britain, in Vyner 1994, 149–63

Hanson, W S, 1997 Forces of change and methods of control, in Mattingly 1997, 67–80

Hanson, W S, & Keppie, L J F (eds), 1980 *Roman frontier studies XII*, BAR Int Ser 71

Harris, M, 1988 *Culture, people, nature*. Harper Collins

Harrison, G, 1999 Quoit brooches and the Roman–Medieval transition, in Baker *et al* 1999, 108–21

Haselgrove, C C, 1984 Romanisation before the conquest, in Blagg & King 1984, 5–63

Haselgrove, C C, 1989 The later Iron Age in southern Britain and beyond, in Todd 1989, 1–18.

Haselgrove, C C, 1995 Late Iron Age society in Britain and north-east Europe: Structural transformation or superficial change? in Arnold & Gibson 1995, 80–7

Haselgrove, C C, 1996 Roman impact on rural settlement and society in southern Picardy, in Roymans 1996, 127–85

Haselgrove, C C, 1997 Iron Age brooch deposition and chronology, in Gwilt & Haselgrove 1997, 51–72

Haselgrove, C C, forthcoming The character of *oppida* in Iron Age Britain, in Guichard *et al* forthcoming

Haselgrove, C C, & Millett, M J, 1997 Verlamium reconsidered, in Gwilt & Haselgrove 1997, 282–96

Hassall, M W C, & Tomlin, R S O, 1986 Roman Britain in 1985: II inscriptions, *Britannia*, 17, 428–54

Häussler, R, 1999 Architecture, performance and ritual: The role of state architecture in the Roman empire, in Baker *et al* 1999, 1–13

Haverfield, F, 1913 *Ancient town planning*. Clarendon Press

Haverfield, F, 1915 *The Romanization of Britain* (3rd edn). Oxford University Press

Hawkes, C F C, & Crummy, P, 1995 *Camulodunum 2: The Iron Age dykes*. Colchester Archaeological Report 11. Colchester Archaeological Trust

Hawkes, G, 1999 Beyond Romanisation: The creolisation of food. A framework for the study of faunal remains from Roman sites, *Papers from the Institute of Archaeology* 10, 89–96

Haynes, I, 1999a Introduction: The Roman army as a community, in Goldsworthy & Haynes 1999, 7–14

Haynes, I, 1999b Military service and cultural identity in the *auxilia*, in Goldsworthy & Haynes 1999, 165–74

Hermansen, G, 1981 *Ostia: Aspects of Roman city life*. Alberta University Press

Hill, J D, 1995 The pre-Roman Iron Age in Britain and Ireland: An overview, *J World Prehist*, 9, 47–98

Hill, J D, 1996 Hillforts and the Iron Age of Wessex, in Champion & Collis 1996, 95–116.

Hill, J D, 1997 The end of one kind of body and the beginning of another kind of body? Toilet instruments and 'Romanization' in southern England during the first century AD, in Gwilt & Haselgrove 1997, 96–107

Hill, J D, 1999 Settlement, landscape and regionality: Norfolk and Suffolk in the pre-Roman Iron Age of Britain and beyond, in Davies & Williamson 1999, 185–207

Hind, J G F, 1989 The invasion of Britain in AD 43 – an alternative strategy for Aulus Plautius, *Britannia*, 20, 1–22

Hines, J (ed), 1997 *The Anglo-Saxons from the Migration period to the eighth century: An ethnographic perspective*. Boydell Press

Hingley, R, 1989 *Rural settlement in Roman Britain*. Seaby

Hingley, R, 1990 Public and private space: Domestic organisation and gender relations among Iron Age and Romano-British households, in Samson 1990b, 125–49

Hingley, R, 1991 Past, present and future: The study of the Roman period in Britain. *Scottish Archaeological Review*, 8, 90–101.

Hingley, R, 1992 Society in Scotland from 700 BC to AD 200. *Proc Soc Antiq Scotl*, 122, 7–53.

Hingley, R, 1993 Attitudes to Roman imperialism, in Scott 1993, 23–7

Hingley, R, 1995 Britannia, origin myths and the British empire, in Cottam *et al* 1995, 11–23

Hingley, R, 1996 The legacy of Rome: The rise, decline and fall of the theory of Romanization, in Webster & Cooper 1996, 35–48

Hingley, R. 1997 Resistance and domination: Social change in Roman Britain, in Mattingly 1997, 81–101

Hingley, R. 2000 *Roman Offices and English Gentlemen*. Routledge

Hodgson, G W I, 1970 Report on the animal remains from the Diocletianic south gate, in Birley 1970, 150–3

Hodgson, G W I, 1976 *The animals of Vindolanda*. Barcombe

Hodgson, G W I, 1977 *The animal remains from excavations at Vindolanda 1970–1975*. Vindolanda II. Vindolanda Trust

Holder, P A, 1982 *The Roman army in Britain*. Batsford

Hopwood, K, 1989 Bandits, elites and rural order, in Wallace-Hadrill 1989, 171–87

Horn, H G, & Rüger, C B (eds), 1979 *Die Numider*. Theinland-Verlag

Hull, M R, 1958 *Roman Colchester*. Society of Antiquaries

Hunn, J R 1992 The Verulamium *oppidum* and its landscape in the late Iron Age, *Archaeol J*, 149, 39–68

Huntley, J P, 1999 Environmental evidence for Hadrian's Wall, in Bidwell 1999, 48–64

Huntley, J P, & Stallibrass, S, 1996 *Plant and vertebrate remains from archaeological sites in northern England: Data reviews and future directions*, Architecture and Archaeology Society of Durham and Northumberland Research Report 4

Hurst, H R (ed), 1999 *The* Coloniae *of Roman Britain: New studies and a review*, J Roman Archaeol Supplementary Ser 36

Ingold, T, 1992 Culture and the perception of the environment, in Croll & Parkin 1992, 39–56

Ingold, T, 1993 The temporality of the landscape, *World Archaeol*, 25, 152–74

Ingold, T, 1995 Building, dwelling, living, in Strathearn 1995, 57–80

Isaac, B, 1992 *The limits of empire: The Roman army in the East* (2nd edn). Oxford University Press

Izard, K, 1998 The animal bones, in Wilmot 1998, 363–400

James, S T, 1984 Britain and the late Roman Army, in Blagg & King 1984, 161–86

James, S T, 1999 The community of the soldiers: A major identity and centre of power in the Roman empire, in Baker *et al* 1999, 14–25

James, S T, forthcoming 'Romanization' and the peoples of Britain, in Keay & Terrenato forthcoming

Jaques, S D, 2000 *Technical report: Vertebrate remains from Garforth, West Yorkshire* (site code B1530A). Reports from the Environmental Archaeology Unit, York 2000(10)

Jobey, I, 1979 Housesteads ware – a Frisian tradition on Hadrian's Wall, *Arch Aeliana* 5th Ser, 7, 127–43.

Johnson, M, 1999 *Archaeological theory: An introduction*. Blackwell

Jones, A K G, 1988 Fish bones from excavations in the cemetery of St Mary Bishophill Junior, in O'Connor 1988, 126–31

Jones, A K G, 1996 Fishes, in May 1996, 163

Jones, M K, 1981 The development of crop husbandry, in Dimbleby & Jones 1981, 95–128

Jones, M K, 1989 Agriculture in Roman Britain: The dynamics of change, in Todd 1989a, 127–34

Jones, M K, & Miles, D, 1979 Celt and Roman in the Thames Valley: Approaches to culture change, in Burnham & Johnson 1979, 315–26

Jones, R F J, 1991 The urbanization of Roman Britain, in R F J Jones (ed) *Roman Britain: Recent trends*. Collis, 53–65

Jones, S, 1997 *The archaeology of ethnicity: Constructing identities in the past and the present*. Routledge

Jundi, S, & Hill, J D, 1998 Brooches and identities in first century AD Britain: More than meets the eye? in Forcey *et al* 1998, 125–37

Keay, S, & Terrenato, N (eds), forthcoming *Italy and the West: Comparative issues in Romanization*

Kennedy, D L (ed), 1998 *The twin towns of Zeugma on the Euphrates: Rescue work and historical studies*, JRA Supplementary Ser 27

Kent, S (ed), 1990 *Domestic architecture and the use of space*. Cambridge University Press

King, A C, 1978 A comparative survey of bone assemblages from Roman sites in Britain, *Bulletin of the Institute of Archaeology*, 15, 207–32

King, A C, 1984 Animal bones and the dietary identity of military and civilian groups in Roman Britain, Gaul and Germany, in Blagg & King 1984, 187–217

King, A C, 1999a Animals and the Roman army: The evidence of animal bones, in Goldsworthy & Haynes 1999, 139–49

King, A C, 1999b Diet in the Roman world: A regional inter-site comparison of the mammal bones, *J Roman Archaeol*, 12, 168–202

King, A C, forthcoming, The Romanization of diet in the western empire, in Keay & Terrenato forthcoming

King, A C, & Soffe, G, 1991 Hayling Island, in Jones 1991, 111–13

Kitson-Clark, M, 1935 *A gazetteer of Roman remains in East Yorkshire*. Roman Malton and District Research Report 5

Laurence, R, 1994 *Roman Pompeii: Space and society*. Routledge

Laurence, R, 1999a *Roads of Roman Italy: Mobility and cultural change*. Routledge

Laurence, R, 1999b Theoretical Roman Archaeology, *Britannia* 30, 387–90

Laurence, R, & Berry, J, (eds), 1998 *Cultural identity in the Roman empire*. Routledge

Lauwerier, R C G M, 1983 A meal for the dead: Animal bone finds in Roman graves, *Palaeohistoria*, 25, 183–93

Lauwerier, R C G M, 1988 *Animals in Roman times in the Dutch Eastern River Area*. Nederlandse Oudheden 12/ Project Oostelijk Rivierengebied 1. Amersfoort

Lauwerier, R C G M, 1994 Bird remains in Roman graves, *Archaeofauna*, 2, 75–82

Laver, P G, 1927 The excavation of a tumulus at Lexden, Colchester, *Archaeologia*, 76, 241–54

Leah, M D, Wells, C E, Stamper, P, Huckerby, E, & Welch, C, 1998 *The wetlands of Shropshire and Staffordshire*. Lancaster University Archaeological Unit

Legge, A J, 1991 The animal bones, in Stead 1991, 140–7

Levitan, B, 1989 The vertebrate remains from Chichester cattle market, in Down 1989, 242–76

Lewis, M J T, 1966, *Temples in Roman Britain*. Cambridge University Press

Locock, M (ed), 1994 *Meaningful architecture*, Avebury

Longacre, W A, 1970 *Archaeology as anthropology; A case study*, Anthropological papers of the University of Arizona 17. University of Arizona

Longley, D, Johnstone, N, & Evans, J, 1998 Excavations on two farms of the Romano-British period at Bryn Eryr and Bush Farm, Gwynedd, *Britannia*, 29, 185–246

Lowther, P, Ebbatson, L, Ellison, M, & Millett, M, 1993 The city of Durham: An archaeological survey, *Durham Archaeol J*, 9, 27–119

Lucy, S J, 1998 *The Anglo-Saxon cemeteries of East Yorkshire*. British Archaeological Reports Brit Ser 272

Macauley, S, & Reynolds, T, 1993 *Excavations and site management at Cambridgeshire Car Dyke, Waterbeach (TL 495 645)*, Fenland Research 8

Macauley, S, & Reynolds, T, 1994 *Car Dyke: A Roman canal at Waterbeach*, Archaeological Field Unit, Cambridgeshire County Council Report 98

106

Mackreth, D F, 1995 Durobrivae, Chesterton, Cambridgeshire, in Brown 1995, 147–56

Mackreth, D F, 1996 *Orton Hall Farm: A Roman and early Anglo-Saxon farmstead*, East Anglian Archaeology 76

Maltby, M, 1984 Animal bones and the Romano-British economy, in Grigson & Clutton-Brock 1984, 125–38

Maltby, M, 1989 Urban–rural variations in the butchering of cattle in Romano-British Hampshire, in Serjeantson & Waldron 1989, 75–106

Maltby, M, 1995 The meat supply in Roman Dorchester and Winchester, in Hall & Kenward 1995, 85–102

Mangin, M, Jacqhuet, B, & Jacob, J-P, 1986 *Les agglomérations secondaires en Franche Comté romaine*, Annales Litteraires de l'Université de Besançon, Paris

Mann, J C, 1985 Epigraphic consciousness, *J Roman Stud*, 75, 254–6

Martin-Kilcher, S, 1976 Das römische Gräberfeld von Courroux im Berner Jura, *Basler Beiträge zur Ur- und Frühgeschichte*, 2

Matthews K J, 1997 Immaterial culture: Invisible peasants and consumer subcultures in northwest Britannia, in Meadows *et al* 1997, 120–32

Mattingly, D J (ed), 1997 *Dialogues in Roman imperialism: Power, discourse and discrepant experience in the Roman empire*, Journal of Roman Archaeology Supplementary Series 23

Maxfield, V A, 1986, Pre-Flavian forts and their garrisons, *Britannia*, 18, 59–72

Maxfield, V A, 1995 *Soldier and civilian: Life beyond the ramparts*, Eighth Annual Caerleon Lecture. National Museum of Wales

Maxfield, V A, & Dobson B (eds), 1991 *Roman frontier studies 1989 : Proceedings of the 15th International Congress of Roman Frontier Studies*. University of Exeter Press

May, J, 1996 *Dragonby: Report on excavations at an Iron Age and Romano-British settlement in North Lincolnshire*, Oxbow Monograph 61

McCarthy, M R, 1990 *A Roman, Anglian and medieval site at Blackfriars Street, Carlisle*, Cumberland and Westmoreland Antiquarian and Archaeological Society Research Report 4

McCarthy, M R, 1991 *Roman waterlogged remains at Castle Street, Carlisle*, Cumberland and Westmorland Antiquarian and Archaeological Society Research Report 5

McCarthy, M R, 1999 Carlisle – Luguvalium, in Bidwell 1999, 168–77

Meadows, I, 1996 Wollaston, *Current Archaeology*, 150, 212–15

Meadows, K I, 1995 You are what you eat: Diet, identity and Romanization, in Cottam *et al* 1995, 133–40

Meadows, K I, 1997 Much to do about nothing: The social context of eating and drinking in early Roman Britain, in Cumberpatch & Blinkhorn 1997, 21–36

Meadows, K I, Lemke, C, & Heron, J (eds), 1997 *TRAC 96: Proceedings of the sixth annual Theoretical Roman Archaeology Conference, Sheffield 1996*. Oxbow Monographs

Meddens, B, 1990 Animal bones from Catterick Bridge (CEU 240), a Roman town (North Yorkshire) excavated in 1983. Ancient Monuments Laboratory Report 31/90

Meek, A, & Gray, R A H, 1911 Animal remains, in Foster & Knowles 1911, 220–67

Meheux, K L, 1996 *Space and Time in Roman Britain: A Case Study of the Severn Valley / Welsh Marches Region*, Unpublished University of London PhD Thesis

Metzler, J, Millett, M J, Roymans, N, & Slofstra, J, 1995 *Integration in the early Roman West: The role of culture and ideology*. Luxembourg

Miket, R, & Burgess, C (eds), 1984 *Between and beyond the Walls: Essays on the prehistory and history of North Britain in honour of George Jobey*. Edinburgh

Miles, D, 1989 The Romano-British countryside, in Todd 1989, 115–26

Millett, M J, 1979 An approach to the functional interpretation of pottery, in Millett, M J (ed) *Pottery and the archaeologist*. Institute of Archaeology Occasional Publications 4, 35–47

Millett, M J, 1983 A comparative study of some contemporaneous pottery assemblages. Unpubl PhD thesis, University of Oxford

Millett, M J, 1987 Boudicca, the first Colchester potters' shop and the dating of Neronian samian, *Britannia*, 18, 93–123

Millett, M J, 1990a *The Romanization of Britain: An essay in archaeological interpretation*. Cambridge University Press

Millett, M J, 1990b Romanization: Historical issues and archaeological interpretation, in Blagg and Millett 1990, 35–41

Millett, M J, 1993 A cemetery in an age of transition: King Harry Lane reconsidered, in Struck 1993, 255–82

Millett, M J, 1995 Strategies for Roman small towns, in Brown 1995, 29–38

Millett, M J, 1999 *Coloniae* and Romano-British studies, in Hurst 1999, 191–6

Millett, M J, forthcoming *Shiptonthorpe, East Yorkshire: Archaeological studies of a Romano-British roadside settlement*, Yorks Archaeol Society Roman Antiquities Section monogr

Millett, M J, & Graham, D, 1986 *Excavations on the Romano-British small town at Neatham, Hants 1969–86*, Hampshire Field Club and Archaeological Society

Millett, M J, Roymans, N, & Slofstra, J, 1995 Integration, culture and ideology in the early Roman West, in Metzler *et al* 1995, 1–6

Mommsen, T, Krüger, P, & Watson, A (eds), 1985 *The digest of Justinian*. University of Pennsylvania

Neal, D S, Wardle, A, & Hunn, J, 1990 *Excavation of the Iron Age, Roman and medieval settlement at Gorhambury, St Albans*. English Heritage Archaeological Report 14

Newman, R (ed), 1996 *The archaeology of Lancashire: Present state and future priorities*. Lancaster University Archaeology Unit

Niblett, B R K, 1985 *Sheepen; an early Roman industrial site of Camulodunum*, CBA Research Report 57

Niblett, B R K, 1993 Verulamium since the Wheelers, in Greep 1993, 78–93

Niblett, B R K, 1999 *The excavation of a ceremonial site at Folly Lane, Verulamium*, Britannia Monogr Ser 14

Niblett, B R K, & Thompson, I, forthcoming *Alban's buried towns: An assessment of St Albans archaeology up to AD 1600*. English Heritage

Nicolet, C, 1988 *L'inventaire du monde: Géographie et politique aux origines de l'empire romain*. Paris: Fayard

Nock, A D, 1952 The Roman army and the Roman religious year, *Harvard Theological Review*, 45, 187–252

Noddle, B, 1979 Animal bones from Garton Slack. Ancient Monuments Laboratory Report 2754

O'Connor, T P, 1988 *Bones from the General Accident Site, Tanner Row*, The Archaeology of York 15(2). Council for British Archaeology for York Archaeological Trust, 61–136

Olivier, A C H, 1996, *Frameworks for Our Past: A Review of Research Frameworks, Strategies and Perceptions*, London: English Heritage

Olivier, A C H, 1997 Owmby-by-Spital, Lincolnshire: Conservation and management of a plough damaged site, *English Heritage Archaeology Review 1996–97*, 33–4

Orton, C R, & Tyers, P A, 1992 Counting broken objects: The statistics of ceramic assemblages, *Proceedings of the British Academy*, 77, 163–84

Oswald, A, 1997 A doorway on the past: Practical and mystic concerns in the orientation of roundhouse doorways, in Gwilt & Haselgrove 1997, 87–95

Ottaway, P, 1993 *Roman York*. Batsford

Palmer, S, forthcoming *Report on excavations on the Norton–Lenchwick bypass*

Parker Pearson, M, 1999 *The archaeology of death and burial*. Alan Sutton

Parker Pearson, M, & Richards, C (eds), 1994 *Architecture and order: Approaches to social space*. Routledge

Parkins, H (ed), 1997 *Roman urbanism: Beyond the consumer city*. Routledge

Partridge, C, 1981 *Skeleton Green: A late Iron Age and Romano-British site*, Britannia monogr 2. Society for the Promotion of Roman Studies

Pearce, J, 1999a Case studies in a contextual archaeology of burial practice in Roman Britain. Unpubl PhD thesis, University of Durham

Pearce, J, 1999b The dispersed dead: Preliminary observations on burial and settlement space in rural Roman Britain, in Baker *et al* 1999, 151–62

Pearce, J, Millett, M J, & Struck, M, (eds) forthcoming *Burial in the Roman world*. Oxbow

Peddie, J, 1994 *The Roman war machine*. Sutton

Perring, D, 1987 Domestic buildings in Romano-British towns, in Schofield & Leech 1987, 147–55

Perring, D, 1991 *Roman London*. Seaby

Petit, J-P, Mangin, M & Brunella, P (eds), 1994 *Les agglomérations secondaires; La Gaule Belgique, les Germanies et l'occident romain*. Paris : Errance

Philpott, R, 1991 *Burial practices in Roman Britain; a survey of grave treatment and furnishing AD 43–410*. BAR Brit Ser 219

Piggott, S, 1966 *Approach to archaeology* (Penguin edn). London

Pohl, W, 1997 Ethnic names and identities in the British Isles: A comparative perspective, in Hines 1997, 7–32

Powlesland, D, 1998 The West Heslerton assessment, *Internet Archaeology* 5

Purcell, N, 1994 The Roman villa and the landscape of production, in Cornell & Lomas 1994, 151–79

Quinnell, H, 1993 A source of identity; Distinctive Cornish stone artifacts in the Roman and post-Roman periods, *Cornish Archaeol*, 32, 29–46

Rackham, D J, 1979 *Rattus rattus*. The introduction of the black rat into Britain, *Antiquity*, 53 112–20

Rackham, D J, Stallibrass, S M, & Allison, E P, 1991 The animal and bird bones, in McCarthy 1991, 73–88

Rackham, H, 1940 (trans) *Pliny: Natural History*. Volume 3. Heinemann

Ramm, H, 1978 *The Parisi*. Gloucester: Sutton

Rankov, B, 1999 The governor's men: The *officium consularis* in provincial administration, in Goldsworthy and Haynes 1999, 15–34

Rapaport, A, 1990 Systems of activities and systems of settings, in Kent 1990, 9–20.

Raynaud, C (ed), forthcoming *Les campagnes de la Gaule à la fin de l'antiquité: Habitat et peuplement au IVe et Ve siècles*, Colloque AGER IV

Reece, R M, 1982 Review of P Salway, Roman Britain, *Archaeol J*, 139, 453–6

Reece, R M, 1988 *My Roman Britain*. Cotswold Studies

Reece, R M, 1989 Coins from villas, in Branigan & Miles 1989, 34–41

Reece, R M, 1991 *Roman Coins from 140 sites in Britain*. Cotswold Studies

Reece, R M, 1993 British sites and their Roman coins, *Antiquity*, 67, 863–9

Reece, R M, 1995 Site finds in Roman Britain, *Britannia*, 26, 179–206

Revell, L, 1999 Constructing Romanitas: Roman public architecture and the archaeology of practice, in Baker *et al* 1999, 52–8

Rich, J, & Shipley G (eds), 1993 *War and society in the Roman world*. Routledge

Rich, J, & Wallace-Hadrill, A (eds), 1991 *City and country in the ancient world*

Richards, J D, 1992 Anglo-Saxon symbolism, in Carver 1992, 131–47

Rippon, S, 1997 *The Severn estuary: Landscape evolution and wetland reclamation*. Leicester University Press

Robinson, M, 1992 Environmental archaeology of the river gravels: Past achievements and future directions, in Fulford & Nichols 1992, 47–62

Rodwell, W, & Rowley, T (eds), 1975 *The small towns of Roman Britain*, BAR 15

Roskams, S, 1999 The hinterlands of Roman York: Present patterns and future strategies, in Hurst 1999, 45–72

Roth, J P, 1999 *The logistics of the Roman army at war (264 BC–AD 235)*. Brill

Rowley-Conwy, P (ed), 2000 *Animal bones, human societies*. Oxbow

Roxan, M M, 1997 Settlement of veterans of the *auxilia* – a preliminary study, in Groenman-van Waateringe *et al* 1997, 483–91

Roymans, N (ed), 1996 *From the sword to the plough*. Amsterdam

Rush, P (ed), 1995 *Theoretical Roman archaeology: Second conference proceedings*. Avebury

Said, E W, 1993 *Culture and imperialism*. Chatto & Windus

Saller, R, 1987 Men's age at marriage and its consequences in the Roman family, *Classical Philology*, 82, 21–34

Salway, P, 1967 *The frontier people of Roman Britain*. Cambridge University Press

Samson, R, 1990a Comment on Eleanor Scott's 'Romano-British villas and the social construction of space', in Samson 1990b, 173–80

Samson, R (ed), 1990b *The social archaeology of houses*. Edinburgh University Press

Serjeantson D, & Waldron, T (eds), 1989 *Diets and crafts in towns*, BAR 199

Schiffer, M B, & Miller, A R, 1999 *The material life of human beings: Artifacts, behaviour, and communication*. Routledge

Schlüter, W, 1999 The battle of the Teutoburg Forest: Archaeological research at Kalkreise near Osnabrück, in Creighton & Wilson 1999, 125–59

Schofield, J, & Leech, R (eds), 1987 *Urban archaeology in Britain*, CBA Res Rep 61

Scott, E, 1990 Romano-British villas and the social construction of space, in Samson 1990b, 149–72

Scott, E (ed), 1993 *Theoretical Roman archaeology: First conference proceedings*. Avebury

Scott, E, 1995 Women and gender relations in the Roman empire, in Rush 1995, 174–89

Scott, E, 1998 Tales from a Romanist: A personal view of archaeology and 'equal opportunities', in Forcey *et al* 1998, 138–49

Scott, S, 1994 Patterns of movement: Architectural design and visual planning in the Romano-British villa, in Locock 1994, 86–99

Scott, S, 1995 Symbols of power and nature: The Orpheus mosaics of fourth century Britain and their architectural contexts, in Rush 1995, 105–23

Scott, S, 2000 *Art and society in fourth century Roman Britain*. Oxford University Committee for Archaeology Monogr

Sharples, N, 1991 *Maiden Castle: Excavations and field survey 1985–6*, English Heritage Archaeol Rep 19

Sharples, N, & Parker-Pearson, M, 1997 Why were brochs built? Recent studies in the Iron Age of Atlantic Scotland, in Gwilt and Haselgrove 1997, 254–65

Shotter, D, 1999 *Romans and Britons in north-west England* (2nd edn). University of Lancaster

Smith, J T, 1978 Villas as a key to social structure, in Todd 1978, 149–56

Smith, J T, 1987 The social structure of a Roman villa: Marshfield-Ironmongers Piece, *Oxford J Archaeol*, 6, 243–55

Smith, J T, 1997 *Roman villas: A study in social structure*. Routledge

Sommer, C S, 1984 *The military* vici *in Roman Britain: Aspects of their origins, their location and layout, administration, function and end*, BAR 129

Sparey Green, C, 1988 *Excavations at Poundbury Volume I: The settlements*, Dorset Natural History and Archaeol Soc Monogr 7

Speidel, M A, 1998 *Legio IIII Scythica*, its movements and men, in Kennedy 1998, 163–204

Speidel, M P, 1992 The soldiers' servants, in M P Speidel (ed) *Roman army studies II*, Mavors 8, 342–52 (originally published in *Ancient Society*, 20 (1989), 239–48)

Stallibrass, S, 1991 Animal bones from excavations at Annetwell Street, Carlisle, 1982–4 period 3: The earlier timber fort. Ancient Monuments Laboratory Report 132/91

Stallibrass, S, 1993a Animal bones from excavations at Old Grape Lane, trenches A and B, The Lanes, Carlisle, 1982. Ancient Monuments Laboratory Report 93/93

Stallibrass, S, 1993b Animal bones from excavations in the southern area of The Lanes, Carlisle, Cumbria, 1981–1982. Ancient Monuments Laboratory Report 96/93

Stallibrass, S, 1996 The Lanes, Carlisle, Cumbria: Lanes 2. An assessment of the Romano-British animal bones recovered from excavations in the northern part of The Lanes, 1978–1982. Durham Environmental Archaeology Report 7/96

Stallibrass, S, 1997 The animal bones from excavations at Thornbrough Farm, Catterick, North Yorkshire, within the locality of the Roman (Antonine) fort and small town: CAS sites 452 (1990) and 482 (1993). Ancient Monuments Laboratory Report 104/97

Stead, I, 1991 *Iron Age cemeteries in East Yorkshire*, English Heritage Archaeol Rep 22

Stead, I M, & Rigby, V, 1986 *Baldock; The excavation of a Roman and pre-Roman settlement 1968–1972*, Britannia Monogr 7

Stead, I M, & Rigby, V, 1989 *Verulamium: The King Harry Lane site*, English Heritage, Archaeol Rep 12

Stevens, C E, 1951 Britain between the invasions (BC 54–43 AD): A study in ancient diplomacy, in Grimes 1951, 332–44

Stevens, C E, 1966 The social and economic aspects of rural settlement, in Thomas 1966, 108–28

Stoertz, C, 1997 *Ancient landscapes of the Yorkshire Wolds: Aerial photographic transcription and analysis*. RCHME

Stokes, P R G, 2000 in Huntley, J and Stallibrass, S, (eds) 2000, *Taphonomy and Interpretation*, symposia of the Association of Environmental Archaeology, No 14. Oxbow, 65–70

Strathearn, M (ed), 1995 *Shifting contexts; Transformations in anthropological knowledge*. Routledge

Struck, M (ed), 1993 *Römerzeitliche Gräber als Quellen zu Religion, Bevölkerungsstruktur und Sozialgeschichte*, Archäologische Schriften des Instituts für Vor- und Frühgeschichte der Johannes Gutenberg-Universität Mainz 3

Tainter, J A, 1988 *The collapse of complex societies*. Cambridge University Press

Taylor, J, 1997 Space and place: Some thoughts on Iron Age and Romano-British landscapes, in Gwilt & Haselgrove 1997, 192–204

Taylor, J, 1999 Aerial photography and the Holme-on-Spalding Moor landscape, in Halkon & Millett 1999, 14–41

Taylor, J, 2000, Stonea in its Fenland context; moving beyond an imperial estate, *Journal of Roman Archaeology* 13, 647–658

Taylor, J, forthcoming (b) *Agrarian landscapes: The transformation of Iron Age and Roman social relations*. Leicester University Press

Taylor, J, in prep (a) Houses, tradition and social discourse: some thoughts on rural architecture in Roman Britain

Taylor, J, in prep (b) *Rural society in Roman Britain*

Terrenato, N, 1998 The Romanization of Italy: Global acculturation or cultural *bricolage*? in Forcey *et al* 1998, 20–7

Thomas, A C (ed), 1966 *Rural settlement in Roman Britain*, Council for British Archaeology Res Rep

Tilley, C, 1994 *The phenomenology of landscape: Places, paths and monuments*. Berg

Timby, J R, 1999 Pottery supply to Gloucester *colonia*, in Hurst 1999, 37–44

Tipping, R, 1997 Pollen analysis and the impact of Rome on native agriculture around Hadrian's Wall, in Gwilt and Haselgrove 1997, 239–47

Todd, M, (ed) 1978 *Studies in the Romano-British villa*. Leicester: Leicester University Press

Todd, M, 1981 *Roman Britain, 55 BC – AD 400*. Fontana History of England

Todd, M (ed), 1989a *Research on Roman Britain*, Britannia Monogr 11

Todd, M, 1989b The early cities, in M Todd (ed) *Research on Roman Britain 1960–89*, Britannia Monogr 11, 1–18.

Tomlin, R S O, 1998 Roman manuscripts from Carlisle: The ink-written tablets, *Britannia*, 29, 31–84

Trow, S D, 1991 By the northern shores of Ocean: Some observations on acculturation process at the edge of the Roman world, in Blagg & Millett 1991, 103–18

van de Noort, R & Ellis, S (eds), 1997 *Wetland heritage of the Humberhead Levels: An Archaeological Survey*. School of Geography & Earth Resources, University of Hull

van der Veen, M, 1989 Romans, natives and cereal consumption – food for thought, in Barrett 1989, 99–107

van der Veen, M, 1992 *Crop husbandry regimes: An archaeobotanical study of farming in northern England 1000 BC–AD 500*. Collis

van der Veen, M, & O'Connor, T, 1998 The expansion of agricultural production in late Iron Age and Roman Britain, in Bailey 1998, 127–44

van Driel-Murray, C, 1995 Gender in question, in Rush 1995, 3–21

van Driel-Murray, C, 1999 And did those feet in ancient time… Feet and shoes as a material projection of the self, in Baker *et al* 1999, 131–40

van Mensch, P J A, 1974 A Roman soup kitchen at Zwammerdam? *Berichten van de Rijksdienst voor het Oudheidkundig Bodemonderzoek*, 24, 159–65

van Neer, W, & Lentacker, A, 1994 New archaeozoological evidence for the consumption of locally-produced fish sauce in the northern provinces of the Roman empire, *Archaeofauna*, 3, 53–62

van Ossel, P, & Ouzoulias, P, forthcoming Dynamiques du peuplement dans l'Ile de France, in Raynaud forthcoming

Varon, P, 1994 *Emptio ancillae / mulieris* by Roman army soldiers, in Dabrowa 1994, 189–95

von Petrikovits, H, 1980 *Lixae*, in Hanson and Keppie 1980, 1027–35

Vyner, B (ed), 1994 *Building on the past: Papers celebrating 150 years of the Royal Archaeological Institute*. Royal Archaeological Institute

Vyner, B (ed), 1995 *Moorland monuments; Studies in the archaeology of north-east Yorkshire in honour of Raymond Hayes and Don Spratt*, CBA Res Rep 101

Wacher, J S (ed), 1966 *The* civitas *capitals of Roman Britain*. Leicester University Press

Wacher, J S, 1975 *The towns of Roman Britain*. Batsford

Wacher, J S, 1995 *The towns of Roman Britain* (2nd edn). Batsford

110

Wahl, J, & Kokabi, M, 1987 Osteologische Untersuchungen and den im Rosgartenmuseum aufbewahrten spät-römischen Skelettresten aus Konstanz, *Fundberichte aus Baden-Württemberg*, 12 456–61

Wahl, J, & Kokabi, M, 1988 *Das römische Gräberfeld von Stettfeld I: Osteologische Untersuchung der Knochenreste aus dem Gräberfeld*. Stuttgart

Waite, G, forthcoming *Report on excavations at Plas Coch, Wrexham*

Wallace-Hadrill, A, 1989 *Patronage in ancient society*. Routledge

Wallace-Hadrill, A, 1994 *Houses and society in Pompeii and Herculaneum*. Princeton University Press

Waurick, G, 1979 Die Schutzwaffen im Numidischen Grab von Es Soumâa, in Horn & Rüger 1979, 305–32

Webster, G, 1988 *Fortress into city: The consolidation of Roman Britain, first century AD*. Batsford

Webster, J, 1995a The just war: Roman text as colonial discourse, in Cottam *et al* 1995, 1–10

Webster, J, 1995b Interpretatio: Roman word power and the Celtic Gods, *Britannia*, 26, 153–61

Webster, J, 1996a Ethnographic barbarity: Colonial discourse and 'Celtic warrior societies', in Webster & Cooper 1996, 111–24

Webster, J, 1996b Roman imperialism and the 'post-imperial age', in Webster & Cooper 1996, 1–17

Webster, J, 1997 A negotiated syncretism; Readings on the development of Romano-Celtic religion, in Mattingly 1997, 165–84

Webster, J, 1999 At the end of the world: Druidic and other revitalization movements in post-conquest Gaul and Britain, *Britannia*, 30, 1–20

Webster, J, & Cooper N (eds), 1996 *Roman Imperialism; Post-colonial perspectives*, Leicester Archaeol Monogr 3

Wells, C M, 1997 'The daughters of the regiment': sisters and wives in the Roman army, in Groenman-van Waateringe *et al* 1997, 571–4.

Wenham, L P, & Heywood, B, 1997 *The 1968–70 excavations in the vicus at Malton, North Yorkshire*, Yorkshire Archaeological Report 3

Whimster, R, 1989 *The emerging past*. London: RCHME

White, K D, 1970 *Roman farming*. Thames & Hudson

White, R H & van Leusen 1997 Aspects of Romanization in the Wroxeter hinterland, in Meadows *et al* 1997, 133–43

White, R H & Barker, P, 1998 *Wroxeter: Life and death of a Roman city*. Tempus

Whittaker, C R, 1994 *Frontiers of the Roman empire; A social and economic study*. Johns Hopkins University Press

Wild, J P, 1970 Button-and-loop fasteners in the Roman provinces, *Britannia*, 1, 137–55

Williams, H M R, 1997 Ancient landscapes and the dead: the re-use of prehistoric and Roman monuments as early Anglo-Saxon burial sites, *Medieval Archaeol*, 41, 1–32

Williams, H M R, 1998 The ancient monument in Romano-British ritual practices, in Forcey *et al* 1998, 71–86

Williams, R J, Hart, P, & Williams, A T L, 1996 *Wavendon Gate. A late Iron Age and Roman site in Milton Keynes*, Buckinghamshire Archaeol Soc Monogr Ser 10

Williamson, T M, 1984 The Roman countryside: Settlement and agriculture in north-west Essex, *Britannia*, 15, 225–30

Willis, S, 1996 The Romanization of pottery assemblages in the east and north-east of England during the first century AD: A comparative analysis, *Britannia*, 27, 179–221

Willis, S, 1997 Samian; Beyond dating, in Meadows *et al* 1997, 38–54

Willis, S, 1998 Samian pottery in Britain; Exploring its distribution and archaeological potential, *Archaeol J*, 155, 82–133

Willis, S H forthcoming *The amphorae and Iron Age and Roman Pottery*, in C C Haselgrove and P C Lowther, L'habitat gaulois et Gallo-Romain de Beaurieux Les Grèves (Aisne)

Wilmott, T, 1998 *Birdoswald: Excavations of a Roman fort on Hadrian's Wall and its successor settlements: 1987–92*, English Heritage Archaeol Rep 14

Wilmott, T, & Wilson, P R (eds), 1999 *The late Roman North*, BAR 299

Wilmott, T, 1999 Birdoswald, in Bidwell 1999, 145–57

Wilson, D R, 1977 A first-century fort near Gosbecks, Essex, *Britannia*, 8, 185–7

Wilson, P R, 1999 Catterick, *Current Archaeol*, 166, 379–86

Wilson, P R, forthcoming *Roman Catterick (Cataractonium): A Roman town and its hinterland. Excavations and research 1958–97*. CBA Res Rep

Witcher, R, 1998 Roman roads; Phenomenological perspectives on roads in the landscape, in Forcey *et al* 1998, 60–70

Woodside, R, & Crow, J, 1999 *Hadrian's Wall: An historic landscape*. National Trust

Woolf, G, 1992 The unity and diversity of Romanization, *J Roman Archaeol*, 5, 349–52

Woolf, G, 1993 Rethinking the *oppida*, *Oxford J Archaeol*, 12(2), 223–34

Woolf, G, 1997a Beyond Romans and natives, *World Archaeol*, 28(3), 339–50

Woolf, G, 1997b The Roman urbanisation of the East, in Alcock 1997, 1–14

Woolf, G, 1998 *Becoming Roman: The origins of provincial civilization in Gaul*. Cambridge University Press

Wroxeter Hinterland Project: <http://www.bufau.bham.ac.uk/newsite/projects/WH/base.html>

Wuilleumier, P, 1950 Lyon – la bataille de 197, *Gallia*, 8 146–8

Yalden, D, 1999 *The history of British mammals*. T & A D Poyser. Academic Press

Yoffee, N, & Cowgill, G L (eds), 1988 *The collapse of ancient states and civilizations*. University of Arizona Press

Younger, D A, 1994 Report on bones, in Bidwell & Speak 1994, 243–68

Yule, B, 1989 Excavations at Winchester Palace, Southwark, *London Archaeol*, 6(2), 31–9

Yule, B, 1990 The dark earth and late Roman London, *Antiquity*, 64: 620–8

Index   *by Peter Gunn*

Illustrations are indicated by page numbers in *italics*. There may also be textual references on these pages.